Parables of a Prodigal Son

Joel Lehman

Trilogy Christian Publishers
A Wholly Owned Subsidiary of Trinity Broadcasting Network
2442 Michelle Drive
Tustin, CA 92780

For information, address Trilogy Christian Publishing
Rights Department, 2442 Michelle Drive, Tustin, Ca 92780.
Trilogy Christian Publishing/ TBN and colophon are trademarks of Trinity Broadcasting Network.

For information about special discounts for bulk purchases, please contact Trilogy Christian Publishing.

Manufactured in the United States of America

10 9 8 7 6 5 4 3 2 1

Library of Congress Cataloging-in-Publication Data is available.

ISBN 978-1-64773-508-1 (Print Book)
ISBN 978-1-64773-509-8 (ebook)

Contents

Introduction

We've just moved to the country in the Colorado mountains. I have been working for one of the ski resorts in the Summit County area for over six years, and until now, there were always people around and everything was close at hand. I've stayed at home sick today, and my wife has gone to work, so I am home by myself. I have been lying on the couch when I realized that the power has gone out, so I've started a fire in the wood-burning stove. It has just started snowing. We are expecting a big snowstorm, and it looks like it may be here earlier than expected. All the laptops are dead, and because we are on our own well and the pump is electric, I don't even have water. Nothing to do but sit and look out the window, watch it snow, and watch the fire eat up the logs I've just put in. I find myself with a pen and paper, reflecting back on the many things that seem to get lost in the business of everyday life. It is two weeks till Christmas 2019, and I have been so busy moving things and just trying to keep up with life that it hasn't even really hit me that it is almost 2020. I never thought I would even see 2020, and now I am right on its doorstep. As I think back to all the Christmases of the past, there are so many that stand out. There were certain ones as a kid growing up. There was the first Christmas with my wife and each of my children. But the one Christmas that probably most defined my life was the last Christmas with my mom, dad, and little brother thirty-three years ago. They were all killed in a car accident in February the following year. Had I realized I had less than two months to spend with them, I would have spent more time with them. I would have asked more questions and tried to learn more about how they managed to navigate this life so well.

At twenty-six, you are still learning that you don't know more than your parents and that one day you may need what they have learned. All kids go through this phase of life, but it seems like ever since the identity revolution of the sixties, disrespecting your elders and any authority is not only normal but seems as if it is encouraged as well. Instead of learning from our parents' mistakes and trying to expand on their wisdom, we seem to reject everything they have to offer because they were not perfect parents. News flash: there is no such thing as a perfect parent, and you will never be the first. Our generation blundered ahead, rejecting everything that our parents did and starting from scratch. All the time getting further and further away from the thoughts and principles that made their generation and this country so great. This is the most foolish thing our generation has done by far. We let so much of the wisdom of our parents and their parents slip away, gone forever. All that life experience gone, completely wasted. We see our country, our communities, and our families struggling because of this. We ignore the command "Honor your father and your mother," and we are missing out on the promise that was given with that command: "So that you may live long and it may go well with you in the land the Lord your God is giving you." Our children are paying a heavy price for our example, as are we.

After my parents died, before the funeral, my brothers were in my dad's office, looking for papers needed for settling their affairs, and came across some letters dad had written to us for Christmas. My older brother said that Dad had told him he had written one letter for each kid but couldn't think of what to write to Randy, so he would have to give them to us later. Since Randy died with mom and dad, each of us got a letter. Many things in that letter have guided me through this life, not only from what he said in the letter, but also because it encouraged me to look back on my parents' entire life. It changed my perspective. No longer was I resisting what they had to offer; instead, I was clinging to every word I could remember and trying to remember what they did as well, always hoping to learn a little more about what made them who they were.

At fifty, I decided that I wanted to pass on what my parents had taught me and the things I had learned, but I was afraid that they, like me, would probably not value what I had learned until I was gone. So I decided to write a letter for every year I had been alive, in hopes that someday, maybe some of the things I had learned would be of value to them and then handed down to my grandchildren. It is not that I am so wise, but it is my hope that the things I've learned in life and from my parents will help them navigate this world a little better. I gave the letters to them at fifty-one because at that time, I had outlived my mother and was getting close to the age my father was when they died. This year I updated the letters and gave them an updated version. This is the last Christmas before I turn sixty, and I'm not sure how many years I have left. Life is short. I believe our lives are measured by two things: what we did in our life to help others and what we leave behind. I have decided to share these letters with anyone willing to listen, not because what I have learned is so profound, but because if one person's life is affected in a positive way by them, it will all be worthwhile. We can only make our family, community, country, and world a better place if we are involved in other people's lives. I humbly offer these letters to you in that spirit. I hope they help you navigate this life as I hope they help my children and grandchildren in theirs.

The Letters

Parables of a Prodigal Son

This is a summation of some of the things learned or experienced by the second son of Samuel and Marilynn Lehman. You may ask why I would title this little adventure the way I have. All I can say is, my father's noticeable hair deficiency was probably due largely to me. It seemed no matter what I did or said, I came out wrong, or so it seemed. It many times felt like I was so different that I was on the outside looking in. But the important thing was, I knew I was loved and that I was looking. These parables of this prodigal son are evidence that you're never too far for love to reach and never too old to learn or to teach.

Passing the Torch

Having a clear understanding of history, not only the things that were done right but also the things that were done wrong, is vital to making wise decisions for the future. If you look at history, you can see what brought about the collapse of entire nations and societies and what caused them to thrive. When a society or nation begins to change history to make it more to their liking or ignore it entirely, it is usually the beginning of the end, because they only change it or ignore it when history tells them something they don't want to acknowledge. If history says what I am doing will lead to failure and I want to do it anyway, then I either have to ignore history or skew the perspective from which I view it. Because most people will acknowledge that doing the same thing over and over and expecting different results is insane and stupid.

As of late, I have seen and heard teachers and political people comparing our president to Adolf Hitler. Now, I don't know where they got their history, but there has never been a president in the history of the United States of America that can remotely be compared to Adolf Hitler and the evil associated with him. Yet educators and people with political agendas are making statements that are historically inaccurate in order to obtain a future that they want. To base a future on a lie means certain failure, as does omitting the beliefs and convictions of the nation's forefathers and discounting their importance in the building of this country. I believe the same is true of families! In order for children to learn from their parents and their parents' parents and so on, we must be diligent to pass on the things learned, whether it is what to do or what not to do. If we, as parents, fail to communicate things learned and history of our forefathers correctly, then our descendants are doomed to learning the same things over and over or losing it altogether.

My father was never very good at expressing himself to me, and I many times did not heed his advice as well as I should have. When Mom, Dad, and my little brother, Randy, were killed in a car wreck, my older brother pulled out these Christmas letters. One to each of the five kids remaining. Dad had not given them to us that Christmas and told my older brother that he hadn't been able to write one for Randy so he would have to give them to us later. Since Randy went to heaven with them, all of us received a letter from Dad. It was like a last bit of advice to us from our father after he was gone. This is his letter to me:

> Joey:
>
> Your childhood challenged all my expertise as a father, and yet with your own unique way, you could always steal my heart with your songs and dance around the record player.
>
> I never quite got control of your strong will. I have seen from your early childhood you were more competitive than any of my children. Determination under God's control is the most admira-

ble of qualities. Such are never known as quitters. My neglect has made you more determined to succeed. I am excited at the things you have done. Things I never knew you had ability in. I believe God has some very wonderful things for you as you follow Him. Don't neglect your artistic ability. Keeping your family high in your priorities has also encouraged me. I'm proud to call you my son, and I love you as an equal.

Christmas Blessings on You and Your Family

There have been many times when I am discouraged that I will pull out this letter and read it over and over. This letter represented my father's advice, wisdom, and love. The Bible is God's letter of love to us, and we need to pore over it much the same way I do this letter. "Oh, how I love your law! I meditate on it all day long. Your commandments are always with me and make me wiser than my enemies. I have more insight than all my teachers, for I meditate on your statutes. I have more understanding than the elders, for I obey your precepts. I have kept my feet from every evil path so that I might obey your word. I have kept my feet from every evil path so that I might obey your word. I have not departed from your laws, for you yourself have taught me. How sweet are your words to my taste, sweeter than honey to my mouth! I gain understanding from your precepts; therefore I hate every wrong path. Your word is a lamp to my feet and a light for my path" (Ps. 119:97–105 NIV). I also have found that my father is still teaching me long after he is gone. Not only him but also my mother, grandparents, aunts, and uncles are still sharing the history and life lessons, whether still here or in heaven. God is continually bringing things they have done or said to mind and revealing the wisdom in those things. But still, so much of the wisdom God imparted to those who have gone to be with Him went with them when they died. God's children are commanded to teach their children so it could be passed on from generation to generation. "Only be careful, and watch yourselves closely so that you do not forget the things your eyes have seen or let them fade from your heart as long as you live. Teach them to your children and to their children after them. Remember the day you stood before the Lord your God at Horeb, when he said to me, 'Assemble the people before me to hear my words so that they may learn to revere me as long as they live in the land and may teach them to their children'" (Deut. 4:9, 10 NIV). "Love the Lord your God with all your heart and with all your soul and with all your strength. These commandments that I give you today are to be upon your hearts. Impress them on your children. Talk about them when you sit at home and when you walk along the road, when you lie down and when you get up. Tie them as symbols on your hands and bind them on your foreheads. Write them on the doorframes of your houses and on your gates" (Deut. 6:5–9 NIV). We are to be historians, passing on from one generation to the next our history, our heart, and all the things God has revealed to us. It is our privilege, honor, and calling. The purpose of these letters is to share the things I have learned from those who went before me and the things God has taught me, with you, my children, and your children, and so on. "My people, hear my teaching; listen to the words of my mouth. I will open my mouth with a parable; I will utter hidden things, things from of old-things we have heard and known, things our ancestors have told us. We will not hide them from their descendants;

we will tell the next generation the praiseworthy deeds of the Lord, his power, and the wonders he has done. He decreed statutes for Jacob and established the law in Israel, which he commanded our ancestors to teach their children, so the next generation would know them, even the children yet to be born, and they in turn would tell their children" (Ps. 78:1–7 NIV).

Hopefully, you each will continue to add to this the things God has taught you. You may not hear much of what I say now, but I hope later these will mean as much to you as my father's letter means to me. If you are reading these and you are not related in some way to me, then God has, for some reason, seen fit to bring you into my little world. Be forewarned, I am not an educated man or an authority on anything. I am just a simple man trying to share the little I have with my family. So welcome to the fam! "This is what the Lord says: 'Stand at the crossroads and look; ask for the ancient paths, ask where the good way is, and walk in it, and you will find rest for your souls'" (Jeremiah 6:16 NIV).

Love,
Dad

The Boomerang

When I was ten or eleven years old, I went through this phase where I thought boomerangs were the coolest things ever made. I had a couple small plastic ones that I used to throw around a lot. (Never could get them to come back to me!) One day, when we were shopping in town, I spotted a big wooden boomerang in a sporting goods store, at least twice as big as the ones I had. I was sure that this boomerang would give me the edge I needed to be an expert at the boomerang, so I saved all my lawn mowing money for about a month to buy the boomerang. Just a few days before we left for Indiana to visit our grandparents and all the aunts and uncles living in the Fort Wayne area, I bought my boomerang, so naturally I had to take it with me. On the entire trip, every time we stopped at a park or were someplace with a little room, I had to try it out. Now, this boomerang went twice as far as the other ones I had; unfortunately, it also meant I had to chase it farther.

Finally came the time on the trip when we got to go to see Uncle Jim and Aunt Bonnie. They had bought the farm. (not that way!) Uncle Jim had purchased the farm they grew up on when Grandma Lehman moved to town, and we always loved to play in the barn, and more importantly, this trip there was lots of space to throw my boomerang. After all the greetings and hugs, the parents went inside and I and my brothers and cousins got out my boomerang and proceeded to see just exactly how far we could throw it. Now, the barn was about a hundred yards from the house, and we were hoping to get it to go that far. The first several throws from the house fell way short. Finally, I got a throw that seemed to just keep on going. It sailed close to the barn and curved off to the left just before it reached the barn and went right between the barn and a small shed then out into the cornfield. Now, even if it didn't come back, that was the mother of all flights, so I took off running as fast as I could to get it, following the same path it took. As I rounded the corner between the shed and the barn, I saw the pigs in the pen by the barn, but everything else looked okay, so I kept going as fast as I could. Suddenly, I was facedown in waist-deep pig crap. Apparently, the hole where the pigpen ran off into had crusted over, and dust had blown over that, making it look like all the rest of the ground around—that is, until I hit it at full speed.

It no longer looked like dirt or smelled like dirt. Of course, I was completely covered and no longer thinking about my boomerang. I began to head up to the house. My cousins and brothers, who had been following, stopped dead in their tracks, turned, and headed for the house to tell my folks. By the time I got to the house, my parents were waiting at the back door. Now, I stunk, I was embarrassed, and all I wanted to do was go in and shower. That wasn't going to happen, though. My mom stopped me and said I couldn't go into the house that way because I would smell up Jim and Bonnie's house. So she got out a hose and, from a safe distance, hosed me down. Then to add insult to injury, she sent the rest of the kids inside and told me to strip to my underwear to finish washing off. After she decided I was clean enough to walk to the shower, she gave me a towel to dry off and sent me to the shower while she took my clothes to the washing machine and washed them. In half an hour, the only evidence left to let anyone know that the whole thing had ever happened was the lingering smell in the grass where I was hosed off and the gaping hole in the crust on the pig pit by the shed. Now, I don't remember who found my boomerang or anything about it after that day, even though I know I did still play with it, but I remember my swim in the pig crap like it was yesterday.

Now, you wonder, What does this have to do with anything? Well, just like I had to be clean to go into my aunt and uncle's house so I wouldn't stink it up, we also have to be clean to enter God's house. The minute God allowed anything unclean or smelly in, then His house would stink. God can't tolerate the smell, so God gave us a way to get hosed off. "Therefore, just as sin entered the world through one man, and death through sin, and in this way death came to all people, because all sinned" (Rom. 5:12 NIV). "For the wages of sin is death, but the gift of God is eternal life in Christ Jesus our Lord" (Rom. 6:23 NIV). "But God demonstrates his own love for us in this: While we were still sinners, Christ died for us. Since we have now been justified by his blood, how much more shall we be saved from God's wrath through him!" (Rom. 5:8, 9 NIV). These list the problem and solution, but our response is a choice only we can make! If I had refused to wash off, I would have never been able to go into the house. I could have claimed it unfair or that my parents didn't love me. I could have learned to live with the smell, gotten used to, even thought it was normal or the way to smell, but it still wouldn't have gotten me in the house, and most everyone would agree that the adults that day were not being unreasonable. Unfortunately, we constantly hear how God is being unloving or mean because He won't let everyone in His house with no standards, but if He didn't have standards, He wouldn't be God. When talking of heaven, Revelations 21:27 says, "Nothing impure will ever enter it, nor will anyone who does what is shameful or deceitful, but only those whose names are written in the Lamb's book of life" (NIV). Now, we can't get in or clean ourselves up, so God, in love, made a way, as mentioned in the previous verses, and the only thing missing is us letting Him hose us off. "If we confess our sins, he is faithful and just to forgive us our sins, and to cleanse us from all unrighteousness" (1 John 1:9 KJV). To humble ourselves, strip off our pride, and let him clean us up is our only option.

Now, you would think with that done, I'm in the family, I'm clean, and that is true. But my mother wouldn't come too close to me when I was covered in pig crap. I was still her son, and I knew she loved me, but she kept a distance between herself and me until I was clean. If I had fallen in again, she would have kept her distance until I let her hose me off again. In the same way, once you're in God's family, you're in, but God can't keep a close relationship with you if you're covered in crap.

You kids might remember the refrigerator magnet that was on our refrigerator for years. It was a cow looking at its hoof with. Well, you know what stuck to it, and it said, "Some days you step in it and some days you don't." Well, I have to say, some weeks I step in it and some weeks I fall headlong into a whole pool of it, so I find myself having to echo the words of David in the Psalms. "Have mercy on me, O God, according to your unfailing love; according to your great compassion blot out my transgressions. Wash away all my iniquity and cleanse me from my sin. For I know my transgressions and my sin is always before me. Against you and you only, have I sinned and done what is evil in your sight; so you are right in your verdict and justified when you judge. Surely I was sinful at birth, sinful from the time my mother conceived me. Yet you desire faithfulness even in the womb; you taught me wisdom in the secret place. Cleanse me with hyssop, and I will be clean; wash me, and I will be whiter than snow. Let me hear joy and gladness; let the bones you have crushed rejoice. Hide your face from my sins and blot out all my iniquity. Create in me a pure heart, O God, and renew a steadfast spirit within me. Do not cast me from your presence or take your Holy Spirit from me. Restore to me the joy of your salvation and grant me a willing spirit, to sustain me" (Ps. 51:1–12 NIV). You will only be happy when you're clean, so try to stay out of the pits as you chase life, and if you occasionally fall in, don't waste time smelling it up—go get washed off.

Love,
Dad

Fertilizer

When we were young, our neighbors had a son that was probably ten years younger than I was. He was kind of spoiled, and his mother was way overprotective. He would come over almost daily, wind up getting mad or hurt for one reason or another, then run home to his mom, telling her that we were being mean to him, and she, like clockwork, would be over, telling our parents about us being mean to her son. Most generally, it was me she complained about. It didn't matter who had made him mad; I was the one that he said did it. Maybe my name was the easiest to remember. Anyway, it was usually my name that came up, not that I was always innocent—I did my share of teasing him. One day, I decided to be nice to him, and since he was sitting on our swing set, I asked him if he wanted to swing. He said yes, so I was pushing him on the swing, being careful not to push him too high. All of a sudden, he jumped out of the swing without letting it come to a stop, started crying, said I pushed him off the swing, and said that he was going to tell his mom. Then ran home to tell his mom. I went inside the house and just waited, knowing his mother would be over before long. A few minutes later, she was pounding on the door. My mom answered the door, and unfortunately, my dad was also right there. She immediately began telling my parents how awful I was and how I deliberately pushed her son out of the swing while he was just sitting there, then proceeded to tell them I had told him to stay off our swings. I tried to tell my parents what had really happened, but then she just started hollering at me, and my parents told me to be quiet. I had to sit and listen to her elaborate even more on how I had hurt her son. None of which was true. After she left, I was lectured on how I should be ashamed of myself for picking on little kids and was sent to my room. (I don't think Mom or Dad fully believed her, or they probably would have spanked me.)

From that day on, I didn't go near him. If he came around, I left. Then one day, right before the Fourth of July, my younger brothers were playing, driving the mower around, with the wagon tied to the back. One was driving, one was sitting in the wagon, throwing firecrackers, and the boy next door was riding his tricycle in his driveway. Every time my brothers went by, I would hear him tell them he was going to tell his mom if they didn't stop throwing firecrackers, so my brothers just threw more. The more he whined, the madder I got, so I got my brothers and said if he was gonna whine, I'd give him something to whine about. "Let me show you how it's done." I got in the wagon, and when we were right across from him, I lit a whole pack of ladyfingers and threw them behind the tricycle. When they started going off, he flipped clear over the handlebars and went running into the house. We hadn't even made the next turn when his mom was beating me over the head and hitting me in the back. She then grabbed me by the hair and pulled me out of the wagon and pulled my bother off the mower while it was still running. He was able to pull it out of gear before she pulled him off, so it just rolled to a stop. She took us to our dad and was telling him what I had done, and I remember thinking at least this time when I got in trouble, I actually did something to deserve it. When I was banned from shooting fireworks, I remember thinking it was worth it—nothing that she or my dad did to me bothered me at all. All I could think about was the time I tried to be nice and got in trouble for it, and to see him flipped over his handlebars and scare him that good meant I earned my punishment, and it was actually somewhat satisfying.

At school, I had been getting made fun of and ridiculed for trying to do what was right, so I had very few friends at school, yet at home and at church, I was perceived as a troublemaker, the naughty kid, the black sheep. So one Sunday that year, when a missionary from Africa had come to our church who had become a close friend of the family, he called me aside by ourselves to talk. I thought he was just going to tell me more stories of Africa. I loved to listen to the stories he told. Only this time he proceeded to tell me that my parents were very concerned about me and that I couldn't serve God if I was walking the fence and that I had to choose. Now, I agreed wholeheartedly and thanked him and left the room confused. The more I thought about it, the madder I got. What had I been doing? I had very few friends, I was the butt of everyone's jokes all because I was trying to live a life honoring God, and yet every one of the Christians in my life seemed to think I had sold my soul to the devil. A bit melodramatic, I know, but at fourteen, I guess everything seems bigger than it really is. But from that day forward, I began to systematically and slowly move to the other side of the fence. Much the same as I had done with the neighbor boy, I determined, if I was going to be punished and looked down on for something I didn't do, then I was at least going to get the satisfaction of doing it. I did all the things you shouldn't do as a Christian, and now I know why you shouldn't do them. I hurt my parents, God, myself, and most of all, years later, those things hurt my wife and children. (Yeah, you guys.) Looking back, I wish I had an attitude more like Joseph, who, after being sold into slavery by his brothers for telling them what God had told him, who was imprisoned for doing what was right with his master and having men he had helped forget their promises to him, was still able to say to his brothers in Genesis 50:19–20, "Don't be afraid. Am I in the place of God? You intended to harm me, but God intended it for good to accomplish what is now being done, the saving of many lives" (NIV). I heard a speaker say that the greatest miracle of God is the fact that He is able to orchestrate and use our wrong choices and evil to accomplish His perfect will, much like He did with Christ's life and death and with Joseph in Egypt. But I have to take it one step further as I look at my life and all the stupid things I've done and how God was able to teach me and has used those things to help others.

I've come to believe God's greatest miracle of life is that He turns crap into fertilizer. Think about it. We can take dead things, used up, smelly, disgusting waste, and unusable by products, put them in the ground and mix it with the soil, and it makes our gardens grow bigger, better food. That which was unfit to sustain life is used to grow things that are sweet, smell good, and give and sustain life. This is God's design, His creation. Our lives outside of Christ are crap. We stink it up. We destroy ourselves and those around us. Paul said in Philippians 3:7–9, "But whatever were gains to me I now consider loss for the sake of Christ. What is more, I consider everything a loss because of the surpassing worth of knowing Christ Jesus my Lord, for whose sake I have lost all things. I consider them garbage [the King James version says *dung*], that I may gain Christ and be found in him, not having a righteousness of my own that comes from the law, but that which is through faith in Christ—the righteousness that comes from God on the basis of faith" (NIV). We are not capable of doing anything truly worthy on our own. Paul recognized that what he did was crap.

What is amazing about our God is, He takes all those bad things if we let Him, and He uses them to grow a life that is sweet and productive. He'll use it to grow new attitudes, new hearts, to change the course of someone else's life. So some may say God takes the old and makes it new, but I myself, like Paul, have to say he takes my life and all its crap and He turns it into fertilizer. So remember, not only does God use the things others around you have meant for evil for good and, like Joseph, moves you to a position to save others, but God also turns our own crap into fertilizer. Even more so if we invite him to.

Love,
Dad

Forgiveness

The summer after I turned sixteen, my dad took me to a state auction where they sold the Roads Departments old cars. I bought my first car there, an old AMC Matador that I drove all over the place through my high school years. I many times would be going five to ten miles over the speed limit when the state patrol or a police car would pass, and usually, they never gave me a second look. If they did stop me, it was just a verbal warning. Then shortly after I graduated, I bought a '69 fastback Mach 1 Mustang and painted it black with flames. Suddenly, if I was traveling five miles over the speed limit, I got a ticket. If I even looked like I was doing something wrong, officers would stop me and ask me all kinds of questions. A year later, I parked the Mustang and bought a '77 Datsun 280Z. It was a fast little sports car, and so right away I got another ticket. I decided, if I was going to keep my license and thus keep driving, I was going to have to drive the speed limit, or at least close to it. Now, at that time none of the cars I drove had cruise control, so you were constantly watching your speed, but it was also very easy to lose track, especially in traffic. Several times I would be cruising behind a station wagon or any number of family vehicles going the exact same speed, and sure enough, the lights would come on and I would get a ticket. So I started driving the speed limit exactly, and cars would be passing me right and left, and still I would get pulled over. They would say I was speeding, then only give me a warning and say they couldn't tell me how fast I was going or they would have to give me a ticket. Now, my hair was also getting long, so they would ask me questions like where my guitar was. "Those are pretty big speakers for this car, aren't they?" "Have you been doing drugs" or "Are you in a band?" As if playing a guitar had anything to do with driving. It was like they automatically assumed that if I drove a sports car and had long hair, I also played the guitar, was in a rock band, and did drugs. Now, I had sped many times before, and I had done drugs. I also loved rock and roll, but in these cases, I was not doing any of those things. I remember riding with friends who were high as kite and speeding in an old car, and they had short hair, and if they were stopped, the officer would smile, joke with them like they were old friends, tell them to watch their speed, and walk off. I began to resent and view the police as macho jerks who used the law to make themselves feel important and to pick on people they didn't approve of.

My attitude toward them got even worse after my parents and brother were killed, because the accident report filled out by the police at the scene of the accident was so vague that it left the possibility that the guy who hit them could have come after us. In fact, if my uncle had not taken us to a lawyer and the lawyer hadn't gotten an expert to come in and go over the crime scene, it might have very well happened. The man had been drinking and on drugs. The police had written three paragraphs and a little diagram. The expert came two days later, looked at both vehicles and the scene, and had a sixteen-page report. Later, we were told the man had been called in for erratic driving and stopped half an hour before the accident, only to be released because he wasn't yet over the legal limit. I thought I needed to forgive the man, because that's what God asks us to do, but I didn't realize how much anger I was carrying toward the police until I was pulling into work one night and a patrol car pulled up and turned on the lights. He came over and said he had been following me and that I had crossed the white line on the side of the road and not used my turn signal to turn into work, then asked if I had been drinking. I got really rude and angry and made a comment about them not really stopping the people who needed to be stopped, and even if they did, they would just let them go anyway. He just gave me a warning and left, and I went in and went to work. But I was so angry I was shaking for a good two hours. As the night wore on, God really began to convict me about it. I could forgive the man who killed them, but I couldn't forgive the police for their mistakes, and I assumed that every officer was bad and had bad intentions because a few had made mistakes.

It still is a struggle to maintain a forgiving heart toward law enforcement, but I had to because the bitterness had begun to rule my life, not Christ. I had begun to store up the hurts every time someone wronged me. I talked forgiveness but couldn't let those unfair, unjust things go. Life wasn't fair. I was getting the short end of the stick, and I was fighting back. Things my wife had said or done that seemed unfair to me, I was unable to let go of, and I became abusive. People who had known me for years began to notice I was angry and unhappy. Even though I knew what needed to be done, it somehow escaped me. Then shortly after we moved to Colorado, I was looking for a full-time job, and my wife's employer suggested that I go see a man that he went to church with who had a business delivering batteries. So, I went to talk to the man. I sat down across the desk from him. He smiled, but I had seen the look before. He started off with, "Ken thinks very highly of you, and you have a very good résumé, but if you were going to ever work for me, you would first have to cut your hair. My customers need to see someone who looks trustworthy, and they might be offended and not trust someone who looks like you. My first thought was, *These are service stations, mechanics who deal with the public,* but all I did was smile, thank him, and leave. But as I was leaving, I noticed the men working for him; they all had short hair, but they were also all white. My wife being Hispanic, I have heard different people talk about how you can't trust this race or that race, and I have seen the hurt in her when she feels that prejudice.

Now, all of a sudden, I was realizing I could change my appearance, change the car I drove to avoid certain prejudice, but my wife and people stereotyped by the color of their skin could not. Suddenly, my focus was on the injustice done to others, not myself, and I felt sorry for them and that man, for he was missing out on the blessings and enjoyment of some amazing people because of his prejudice. Like I said earlier, God does take our crap and makes it fertilizer, which is comforting if we're talking about our own mistakes. Not so easy to swallow when it's what someone else is doing to you. I was holding all sorts of grudges, and if someone did something that reminded me of what someone else had done, then they were guilty, too, and so it went until it was too heavy for me to handle. Jesus said in Matthew 16:24–26, Mark 8:34–37, and Luke 9:23–25, "Whoever wants to be my disciple must deny themselves and take up his cross and follow me. For whoever wants to save their life will lose it, but whoever loses their life for me will find it. What good will it be for someone to gain the whole world, yet forfeit their soul? Or what can anyone give in exchange for their soul?" (NIV). My focus had been wrong. I was looking at myself. Christ says, if I want to follow him, I have to deny myself.

Now I see Christians of all races who, because of past injustices, some committed before they even were alive, are living in unforgiveness, anger, and even downright hatred, and I have to ask myself, Whom are we thinking about, ourselves or others? "I urge you to live a life worthy of the calling you have received. Be completely humble and gentle; be patient, bearing with one another in love. Make every effort to keep the unity of the Spirit through the bond of peace" (Eph. 4:1–3 NIV). I continue to hear people say, when bad things happen, we need to forgive God as if he is to blame. That people who are not prejudiced should apologize to those who have been wronged in the past in one way or another. This is wrong! Who are we to forgive the Creator of the universe, and are we greater than Christ, who, while being crucified, said in Luke 23:34, "Father forgive them, for they do not know what they are doing"? (NIV). This is the same Christ who, in Matthew 6:12, taught us to pray, saying, "And forgive us our debts, as we also have forgiven our debtors" (NIV). Then after the prayer goes on in 6:14–15 and says, "For if you forgive other people when they sin against you, your heavenly Father will also forgive you. But if you do not forgive others their sins, your Father will not forgive your sins" (NIV). No wonder, we, the church, are not experiencing the full blessings of God. No wonder our marriages are falling apart at record rates. No wonder there are so many issues in our families. Joseph, so many years before Christ, got it right. Even in slavery and complete and total betrayal, he was able to see that God was bigger than the situation and that he could work it for good.

God does take crap and turn it into fertilizer, but crap by itself won't grow anything; it has to be mixed into soil, and

I believe the only soil God can mix our crap in to make things grow are the soils of true repentance and forgiveness. "Has not my hand made all these things, and so they came into being? declares the Lord. These are the ones I look on with favor; those who are humble and contrite in spirit, and who tremble at my word" (Isa. 66:2 NIV). We can never receive forgiveness until we swallow our pride, recognize our need for it, and accept what has been given us. So until we can humble ourselves and accept forgiveness, we cannot truly give forgiveness. "Bear with each other and forgive one another if any of you has a grievance against someone. Forgive as the Lord forgave you" (Col. 3:13 NIV). I know you kids have seen and felt firsthand what I am talking about, and I fear I have given you a heritage of unforgiveness. So I trust you can forgive me for what you endured and begin forgiving those around you who have hurt you. Unforgiveness is like cancer. If you leave any in your life no matter how small it is, it will grow and eventually it will destroy you.

Love,
Dad

Houdini

My dad always used little stories to illustrate his sermons. I don't remember many sermons, but I remember a lot of the stories and God continues to use those stories to show me things in my life. This is one such story.

The great Houdini was challenged to break out of a new jail with the newest, most sophisticated locks ever made at that time. He accepted gladly and was placed in an inner cell in a straitjacket. Then the door and a series of gates were locked, and he was left alone in an empty prison. He quickly freed himself of the straitjacket, and with tools of the trade he had hidden on himself, he began to pick the lock on the cell door. It quickly opened with a resounding click. Each gate he came to fell to his expert hands as the click echoed through the empty halls. He came to the final gate that separated him from his freedom and knelt to open the gate in the same manner as the other gates before, but no click. He began to work more feverishly on the lock. Still nothing. Anxiety set in, and sweat was dripping from his forehead as panic began to set in. Had he failed? Was he actually trapped? Finally, completely exhausted, he stumped against the gate, and to his surprise, it swung open. Realizing it had never been locked in the first place, he asked the guard in charge of locking the gates why he hadn't locked the last gate. He replied, "I figured if you had unlocked all the other gates, the only lock you wouldn't be able to pick was the one that was only locked in your mind."

Now, I never thought much about that story till a few years back. After my mom, dad, and little brother were killed in the car wreck, it just seemed like one bad thing after another was happening to me, or to the people around me that I loved. I began to feel like a caged animal. I wanted all that peace and joy that God had promised, but how could I when there was so much hurt and pain all around me? How could I be happy when life sucked so much? I desperately was looking for the key to my cell. I tried more prayer. I tried spending time with friends. The more I looked for the keys to happiness, peace, and joy, the angrier and more frustrated I became. And I began snapping at everyone who came close. I was angry all the time and beginning to think I was going crazy. Then one day in church, after a series of events in which it seemed like God was telling me to just let go, I went forward, knelt at the altar, and basically told God I couldn't live like this anymore but I couldn't get out of it. "Please help me," I implored Him. He brought this story from my dad's sermon so many years earlier to my mind, and I really felt like he was telling me that he unlocked the gates of everything that could hold me captive over two thousand years ago. All I had to do was walk into his freedom, because my happiness did not depend on my circumstances, only on how close I was to him.

He unlocked the gates, but He won't make us leave the cell. That is something we have to choose to do ourselves. Looking back, I realize God was waiting just outside my cell door. Waiting for me to ask for help. But the other thing I see now is that the door was only locked in my mind. When I finally threw myself at that door and God's mercy, the door swung wide open. I'm finding I have had a lot of cells, a lot of doors in my life that I lock in my mind, and when I come to one of those doors in my life, I always have a tendency to fret and pace and try to find the key. But I do realize now that they aren't really locked. Christ tells us to knock and it will be opened for us. "Ask and it will be given to you; seek and you will find; knock and the door will be opened to you. For everyone who asks receives; he who seeks finds; and to him who knocks, the door will be opened" (Matt. 7:7–8 NIV). Kinda cool! Christ died to unlock all the cells in your life, and then He destroyed the keys. Even those who don't know Christ as their personal Savior are not locked out. "Here I am! I stand at the door and knock. If anyone hears my voice and opens the door, I will come in and eat with that person and they with me" (Rev. 3:20 NIV). He lets us know we control that door; it's up to us to open that door and let Him into our lives, and from then on out, every door we need to go through is already unlocked. It's nice to know that none of those cells in our lives are locked and that we can escape that bondage and be free just by pushing open the door. "I can do all this through him who gives me strength" (Phil. 4:13 NIV). It often makes me wonder why I constantly waste so much time trying to find keys to life that aren't there instead of leaning on God's strength and pushing open the door. Don't waste your life looking for keys. Instead, spend that time looking deep into your Savior's eyes.

Love,
Dad

The Mustang

Shortly after I graduated, I bought a '69 Mustang Mach 1 fastback and decided to tear it all down and repaint it. It was black with blue flames and side pipes. And when it was finished, there wasn't another one around that looked like it. Turned heads everywhere I went and probably looked a lot hotter than it was. But I got a better job and decided to buy a newer car, so I parked my Mustang under some trees at my parents' house. Well, it wound up sitting there for almost a year. Then one day, I stopped and told my dad I was going to take the car, and he told me I couldn't. I asked him why. He smiled and said, "Because you don't own it anymore. The birds do, because they're the ones making all the deposits on it." I thought it was kinda funny, till I saw my beautiful car covered with white and purple spots. (Recycled mulberries from the mulberry tree out back.) I was washing the car when I noticed that even though I was cleaning off the bird crap, there were still many of the spots on the car where it had eaten through the paint. Now, this had been the hardest paint you could get; in fact, when I sold it, the guy who bought it wanted to repaint it to look the same and was having a hard time sanding the paint off.

Looking back, I realize we do the same thing with our lives. We give ownership of our lives to God but then we sit around and let Satan put deposits on our life in the form of sin. And no matter how strong a Christian we are, the longer we leave those spots on our lives, the more lasting effects it will have on our beauty as Christians. But the key is not to keep washing the spots the minute they happen, but for the owner to be driving the car so the birds don't get the opportunity. "But in keeping with his promise we are looking forward to a new heaven and a new earth, where righteousness dwells. So then, dear friends, since you are looking forward to this, make every effort to be found spotless, blameless and at peace with him" (2 Pet. 3:13–14 NIV). "But you, man of God, flee from all this, and pursue righteousness, godliness, faith, love, endurance and gentleness. Fight the good fight of the faith. Take hold of the eternal life to which you were called when you made your good confession in the presence of many witnesses. In the sight of God, who gives life to everything, and of Christ Jesus, who while testifying before Pontius Pilate made the good confession, I charge you to keep this command without spot or blame until the appearing of our Lord Jesus Christ" (1 Tim. 6:11–14 NIV). So let God so drive your life that Satan doesn't get the chance to make many deposits on your beautiful finish. When Satan does leave a deposit on your life, which he is bound to do, go to God and get it washed off before it leaves lasting marks on your life. "If we confess our sins, he is faithful and just and will forgive us our sins and purify us from all unrighteousness" (1 John 1:9 NIV). Remember, an idle Christian's walk is probably collecting deposits from Satan's flock.

Love,
Dad

The Skunk

For the two years in high school after I got my driver's license, it seemed like several of my friends and I spent two or three nights a week out driving around. It seemed we were always going to games of friends or going to town after our own games to eat. Sometimes we would just drive around in the country or the small town we lived in, listening to music on the radio or 8-track tapes (that dates me). We just enjoyed hanging out, and from those times many memories of things said and done resurface when we get together and reminisce. This is one of those stories about when, one night, we were driving around in the country close to a friend's house, killing time, before he had to be home. There were four of us in the car, and I was driving near the river on a deserted road. It was a dead-end road with a little field between the river and the road where some of my friends and I many times would swim in the summer. We had often gone there in the winter to spin cookies (slide the car in circles) in the field. I didn't like to do it in the summer because it would tear up the farmers' prairie hay and the ground. But in the winter the ground was frozen, and we didn't figure it was going to hurt anything. We were heading for the field when I drove by a dead skunk in the middle of the road. We braced ourselves for the smell, but it didn't smell. Now, we had driven by a lot of dead skunks before, but no matter how long they had been there, they stunk. So one of the guys suggested that we check it out. I turned around, and we went back and parked by the skunk and all got out to see why the skunk didn't smell. Finally, when we were sure it was dead, we started pushing it to see if moving it would make it smell. Still nothing. It didn't look like it got hit, or it would have sprayed and stunk. It looked to us like it had just lain down in the middle of the road and died.

Then one of us got the bright idea of taking it into town. I said there was no way I was putting it in the car, so we decided that we would pull it in to town with a string one of the guys had in his pocket. Guess you can say we were pretty bored. Anyway, we had tied the string to the tail of the skunk and I was tying the string to the bumper of the car when one of the guys decided to grab it by the tail and shake it around. The smell made our eyes water, so I quickly finished tying the string to the bumper and we all jumped in the car. We headed to town trying to decide where we would leave this find. At first, we thought the school, but none of us wanted to risk getting caught, so we decided that we would put it downtown by one of the local bars. On the way into town, I was watching in the rearview mirror, and I thought I saw something fall off. The guys in the back told me that the fur was peeling off but the skunk was still there. After a five-mile trip to town, we pulled in behind the bank across main street from the bar. When we got out to look at the skunk, it looked more like a hairless cat or a rubber chicken than a skunk. No fur on the skunk whatsoever, totally naked, dead skunk (not a pretty sight). We decided who was going to pull the dead skunk over to the bar with the string, and the guy who had shaken the skunk to make him smell was going to do the same thing right before the runner took off. But while

I was trying to untie the string from the bumper, the one guy started shaking the skunk and kept shaking it. I finally just cut the string because the smell had gotten so strong I thought I was going to lose my lunch. The runner took off, leaving the dead skunk right by the front step of the bar. Then we waited and watched as different guys would come to the door, look around, trying to figure out where the smell was coming from, and walk back in, shaking their heads.

Yep, life in a small town in Nebraska was just full of thrills. Once again you ask, What does this have to do with anything at all? And once again, you will be amazed at how this warped and twisted mind works. Maybe by the time I'm through with this project, you'll be used to it, although I'm still not, and I've lived with it my whole life. Well, here it goes. I was reading in Romans the other day, chapters 7 and 8, and this story of the skunk came to mind and helped me make a little more sense of it. Scary, right? Well, hold on. Here it goes. "I do not understand what I do. For what I want to do I do not do, but what I hate I do. And if I do what I do not want to do, I agree that the law is good. As it is, it is no longer I myself who do it, but it is sin living in me. I know that good itself does not dwell in me, that is, in my sinful nature. For I have the desire to do what is good, but I cannot carry it out. For I do not do the good I want to do; but the evil I do not want to do—this I keep on doing. Now if I do what I do not want to do, it is no longer I who do it, but it is sin living in me that does it. So I find this law at work: Although I want to do good, evil is right there with me. For in my inner being I delight in God's law; but I see another law at work in me, waging war against the law of my mind and making me a prisoner of the law of sin at work within me. What a wretched man I am! Who will rescue me from this body that is subject to death? Thanks be to

God, who delivers me through Jesus Christ our Lord!" (Rom. 7:15–25 NIV). Kind of dizzying, isn't it? Chapter 8 goes on to elaborate and explain it a little bit, but this is how I see this passage and how it relates to my story. The second book of Corinthians 5:17 says, "Therefore, if anyone is in Christ, the new creation has come; the old has gone, the new has here!" (NIV). Now the skunk was dead, just like we are dead in sins, but when God gets ahold of our lives, He creates something that takes on a whole different look. With us our thoughts and desires begin to change; with the skunk his appearance changed. "I will give them an undivided heart and put a new spirit in them; I will remove from them their heart of stone and give them a heart of flesh. Then they will follow my decrees and be careful to keep my laws. They will be my people and I will be their God" (Ezek. 11:19–20 NIV).

The longer we let God control our lives, the more our desires change, and the farther we dragged the skunk, the less he looked like a skunk. Although the skunk was dead and didn't look like a skunk, even though he wasn't actively producing or trying to spray us with his stink, the minute we shook him, the fact that he was a skunk became very obvious. Even though our desires change and we strive to take on the nature of our Lord and Savior, the fact that we were born in sin and still fall becomes very evident when life shakes us up. No matter how much our desires change, when life gets rough, we tend to stink it up. What gives us hope is the notion that just like the skunk, which because he was dead he was no longer reproducing his smell, we are, because of our changed desires, less apt to perpetuate evil. And if we had continued to shake the skunk eventually, we would have shaken most of the smell out of him. God also does the same thing for us. "Endure hardship as discipline; God is treating you as his children. For what children are not disciplined by their father? If you are not disciplined—and everyone undergoes discipline—then you are not legitimate, not true sons and daughters at all. Moreover, we have all had human fathers who disciplined us and we respected them for it. How much more should we submit to the Father of spirits and live! They disciplined us for a little while as they thought best; but God disciplines us for our good, in order that we may share in his holiness. No discipline seems pleasant at the time, but painful. Later on, however, it produces a harvest of righteousness and peace for those who have been trained by it" (Heb. 12:7–11 NIV). "Consider it pure joy, my brothers and sisters, whenever you face trials of many kinds, because you know that the testing of faith produces perseverance. Let perseverance finish its work so that you may be mature and complete, not lacking anything" (James 1:2-4 NIV). So when bad things in our lives happen, we can think of it as God taking us by the tail and shaking the stink right out of us. Or if nothing else, at least we can understand a little better why we have such a hard time doing what's right, even though we deeply desire to.

Love,
Dad

Out of Control

Brandon and Yvette, when you were four and two, I was laid off a job that I had just a short time before told someone in passing, "My job is secure. They would about have to shut the place down to lay me off, and we're doing record sales." Four months later, we went from a sixteen-million-dollar month to a two-hundred-thousand-dollar month and immediately laid off the majority of the workforce. Eventually, they closed the plant, but I was laid off about six months after I had made the statement that my job was secure. I took a job working for a farmer close to our home. I probably learned more life lessons in the eight months I worked for that farmer than in any other year in my life. The first being my security is not found in my job or anything else I do or have. And I am not in control. "Lord, I know that people's lives are not their own; it is not for them to direct their steps" (Jer. 10:23 NIV). "In their hearts humans plan their course, but the Lord establishes their steps" (Prov. 16:9 NIV). And James 4:13–15 says, "Now listen, you who say, 'Today or tomorrow we will go to this or that city, spend a year there, carry on business and make money.' Why, you do not even know what will happen tomorrow. What is your life? You are a mist that appears for a little while and then vanishes. Instead, you ought to say, 'If it is the Lord's will, we will live and do this or that'" (NIV). If losing the job didn't make that real to me, what happened a little later did.

I was making only about a quarter of what I was making before ($3 an hour), so things were tight. The farmer, in an effort to try to help us out a little, let his hired hands drive his pickups home so we didn't have to drive our own cars. The pickup awarded to me was an old, beat-up Ford used primarily for irrigating. Now, the farmer lived about half a mile from the farm of a family of which I was very close to three of the kids around my age. I spent lots of time out there, so I was very familiar with the roads, and the route I drove to the farmer's house was the same road I took to theirs all through high school. Coming from town after turning onto the gravel road, I would drive about two miles, then there was a hill sloping down into a sort of valley. At the bottom of the hill, there was a small bridge and then two more bridges after that, all about a mile apart. Now, when I was in high school, I used to drive that road fairly fast because we always liked going across the bridges—they were raised up like short little hills—because it always felt like the bottom was dropping out from under you. Sort of like a roller-coaster ride. Now, I was so used to driving that road fast that I didn't think about how fast I was going when I was driving the old pickup.

One day, the other hired hand and I were going into town, and I took all the bridges fairly fast. He made a comment about slowing down because the poor old truck would fall apart on me. I didn't think much about it. I had driven that road that way for months, and the old beater had held up well. But that day, after we had finished what we had to do in town and were headed back out to the farm, I decided to slow down a little so he wouldn't be so nervous. Just as I was getting to the hill that dropped down onto that first bridge, I realized that I had no steering at all. He thought I was kidding until I spun the steering wheel around in circles, then he immediately said we were going to die. Now, I can't explain it, but I don't remember feeling scared or nervous; in fact, I don't remember feeling anything. It had to be God helping me keep my head. As we headed down the hill, I knew I couldn't step on the brakes, or the truck might pull to one side and roll or hit the bridge. I had taken my foot off the gas, but we were picking up speed going down the hill, so all I could do was let God take care of it and trust that He would do what was best. Now, the bridge was immediately at the bottom of the hill, with a nice, quick drop on the other side of the bridge. There were concrete slab rails about eight feet long on both sides of the bridge, an access road into the field on one side right after the bridge, and after that, ditches on both sides. Now, these ditches were a good six feet deep and steep, and I knew that we would probably roll if we went in the ditch. When we hit the bottom of the hill, we were doing about sixty-five miles per hour, and there was nothing I could do. When the pickup dropped off the other side of the bridge, the wheels turned just enough that I headed toward the ditch on the side of the access road. Right at the edge of the access road where the ditch started, the pickup drifted over and hit perfectly the slope that went into the ditch from the side of the access road and funneled us down the ditch. The weeds were almost as tall as the truck, and when I could see the sides of the ditch on both sides, I stepped on the brakes and stopped the truck.

When I went back to look at where we had entered the ditch, I realized that I had never even noticed the slope from the access road before, because it was always grown up in weeds. I also knew that I couldn't have done anything to get us into the ditch even if I had been able to steer it. That was the only place that we could have gone off the road that wouldn't have totaled the truck and seriously hurt or killed both of us. Some would say we were lucky, but I have to say, God was driving the truck. It's amazing how we think we are in control of our lives until, all of a sudden, something like this lets us know that we are never truly in control—we only think we are. Now, we are prone to worry and try to fix things. We trust our jobs, our bank accounts, our friends, our family, our education, and the list goes on and on. We need to remember these following verses and let God have control of our lives, seeing as how the steering wheel we're holding on to doesn't control the wheels anyway. "Cast all your anxiety on him because he cares for you" (1 Pet. 5:7 NIV). "If you say, 'The Lord is my refuge,' and you make the Most High your dwelling, no harm will overtake you, no disaster will come near your tent. For he will command his angels concerning you to guard you in all your ways; they will lift you up in their hands, so that you will not strike your foot against a stone. You will tread upon the lion and the cobra; you will trample the great lion and the serpent. 'Because he loves me,' says the Lord, 'I will rescue him; I will protect him, for he acknowledges my name. He will call upon me, and I will answer him; I will be with him in trouble, I will deliver him and honor him. With long life will I satisfy him and show him my salvation'" (Ps. 91:9-16 NIV).

Now, I don't think that once Jesus Christ is your Savior and Lord, nothing bad will ever happen to you, but I do think that we can rest in knowing that He is there and in complete control. Jesus Himself made the following statement in Matthew 6:25–34, "Therefore I tell you, do not worry about your life, what you will eat or drink; or about your body, what you will wear. Is not life more than food, and the body more than clothes? Look at the birds of the air; they do not sow or reap or store away in barns, and yet your heavenly Father feeds them. Are you not much more valuable than they? Can any one of you by worrying can add a single hour to his life? And why do you worry about clothes? See how the flowers of the field grow. They do not labor or spin. Yet I tell you that not even Solomon in all his splendor was dressed like one of these. If that is how God clothes the grass of the field, which is here today and tomorrow is thrown into the fire, will he not much more clothe you—you of little faith? So do not worry, saying, 'What shall we eat?' or 'What shall we drink?' or 'What shall we wear?' For pagans run after all these things, and your heavenly Father knows that you need them. But seek first his kingdom and his righteousness, and all these things will be given to you as well. Therefore do not worry about tomorrow, for tomorrow will worry about itself. Each day has enough trouble of its own" (NIV).

But how often we refuse to give Him control and then wrestle with the consequences of our actions. We have to remember to follow close to the Father and, instead of worrying about our lives, trust Him with them like a small child trusts his parents. It also amazes me how little today's church gives God complete control the way He deserves. For example, some of the biggest worriers I know are the leaders in churches, and many of them are obsessed with money or the size of the church. Many pastors are complete control freaks, expecting to have everything done their way without question. We, as a whole, seem to trust our money more than we trust God, and I think the main reason we do is that we feel more in control of what is happening. It is kind of ironic that our money says, "In God we trust," but we trust our money instead of God. We in America definitely have control issues. Maybe that is why Jesus said in the verse right before His statement in Matthew 6, "No one can serve two masters. Either you will hate the one and love the other, or you will be devoted to the one and despise the other. You cannot serve both God and Money" (Matt. 6:24 NIV). I believe our greatest sin is not sexual immorality, or any of the other sins we point at in our nation today, but it is our trust of money. And the church is not only some of the worst offenders; we also try to justify it by saying we are being good stewards. I will leave that for another time. For now, I want to talk about control and how that should be modeled.

I believe we can turn to how Jesus sent out his disciples in Matthew 10:7–20, "As you go, proclaim this message: 'The kingdom of heaven has come near.' Heal the sick, raise the dead, cleanse those who have leprosy, drive out demons. Freely you have received, freely give. Do not get any gold or silver or copper to take with you in your belts—no bag for the journey, or extra shirt, or sandals or a staff; for the worker is worth his keep. Whatever town or village you enter, search there for some worthy person and stay at their house until you leave. As you enter the home, give it your greeting. If the home is deserving, let your peace rest on it; if it is not, let your peace return to you. If anyone will not welcome you or listen to your words, leave that home or town and shake the dust off your feet. Truly I tell you, it will be more bearable for Sodom and Gomorrah on the day of judgment than for that town. I am sending you out like sheep among wolves. Therefore be as shrewd as snakes and as innocent as doves. Be on your guard; you will be handed over to the local councils and be flogged in the synagogues. On my account you will be brought before governors and kings as witnesses to them and to the Gentiles. But when they arrest you, do not worry about what to say or how to say it. At that time you will be given what to say, for it will not be you speaking, but the Spirit of your Father speaking through you" (NIV). He goes on, but I think you get the point.

I have heard pastors say they want to see God move, see His miracles, experience His power. Guess what? It will never happen without our giving God complete control. Our missionaries aren't even sent by the church until they have raised all their support so that all their expenses are covered. Far cry from the way Jesus sent out His disciples. On occasion, I will hear of someone doing like missionaries of times past and just going to some country because God said to go, taking nothing with them. It is amazing how God provides and moves in their lives and the impact they have. We don't want to give God control because it might get uncomfortable. Jesus talks about them being rejected, getting beaten, and I would imagine, going hungry once in a while, but they would not only see but also perform great miracles. We sacrifice seeing God's power and greatness for comfort and control. I always thought I was in control of what happened in my vehicle, that I was the one that kept me safe with my driving skills, until that day in that pickup. Because I didn't try in some way to help my situation and trusted God to keep me safe, I believe God saved my fellow worker, me, and even the pickup from harm. Now I wish I could say that since then I let God take over in every situation in my life, but I can't. Just like everyone else, I'm a control freak. It's hard for me to let go and let God take care of me and my problems, and unfortunately, it is usually only when He takes away all my control that I give up and let Him do what I should have been letting Him do all along. Maybe all the time God has been trying to tell us, "Don't worry, be happy." I think it would be best if we took to heart Matthew 6:33, "But seek first his kingdom and his righteousness, and all these things will be given to you as well" (NIV).

Love,
Dad

Cootie

As I get older, I'm finding more and more that it is the little, seemly insignificant things in my past that bring me some of the fondest memories. Like playing Cootie (a game where you put together a bug) with my aunt or when my father would buy us boys a pop when we were working tearing down an old building or maybe cutting down trees. You might say, "Why would those simple things be so special to you?" When we went back to visit my grandparents while my aunt was still there, she was ten to fifteen years older than all my brothers and me, yet she would take the time to play games with us, even a game like Cootie, which was great fun for me but probably enough to bore any college-age person to death. She could have left the house, found some of her friends, but she chose to stay with us. When she got married, I figured it would end, but my uncle was just as kind. He always had time to throw the football with me, or one of them would play tennis with me. It always was special to me to know that they would do that for me. And my father buying us a bottle of pop, well, we had very little money growing up, and pop was not a luxury we enjoyed often. But occasionally, even though he couldn't afford it, we would take a break from whatever we were doing and he would buy us a pop. And I can still envision him during that time, drinking his pop, talking to the local store owner. Now, you're probably asking yourself, What does this have to do with anything at all?

Well, I have fond memories of those times not because the pop and the game Cootie are so special but because I knew that the ones who were sharing them with me loved me and really cared about me enough to do those little things for me. We many times want to do big, important things for people to have an impact on our world and show them we love them. But to be honest, it's many of those small acts of kindness and love that are offered to us in grace and humility, without all the grandstand giving, that are many times remembered as the big gifts and acts of kindness. In Matthew 10:42, Jesus said, "And if anyone gives even a cup of cold water to one of these little ones who is my disciple, truly I tell you, that person will certainly not lose their reward" (NIV). In Matthew 25:34–40, Jesus says, "Then the King will say to those on his right, 'Come, you who are blessed by my Father; take your inheritance, the kingdom prepared for you since the creation of the world. For I was hungry and you gave me something to eat, I was thirsty and you gave me something to drink, I was a stranger and you invited me in, I needed clothes and you clothed me, I was sick and you looked after me, I was in prison and you came to visit me.' Then the righteous will answer him, 'Lord when did we see you hungry and feed you, or thirsty and give you something to drink? When did we see you a stranger and invite you in, or needing clothes and clothe you? When did we see you sick or in prison and go to visit you?' The King will reply, 'Truly I tell you, whatever you did for one of the least of these brothers and sisters of mine, you did for me'" (NIV). God recognizes these small gifts and acts of love and says when we do these things for people, we do them for Him. My aunt was not only playing Cootie with me, but she was playing Cootie with God as well, and God remembers it as fondly as I do. My father not only bought me a pop, but he was giving God a pop as well, and God remembers it as fondly as I do. Never think that your acts of kindness, no matter how small, go unnoticed by God. I'm certain they are fond memories that He cherishes as much as the one you bestowed them on does. That is how you must show your love to those around you and to God. Remember, your love and devotion to God and those around you are made evident by the little everyday acts of kindness, not by the few big ones that come once in a while.

Love,
Dad

Most Embarrassing Moment

The most embarrassing moment of my life was when I was about eight. Mom and Dad had invited a family over. These friends of my parents had four girls about the same age as my brothers and me. The eight of us were out on the merry-go-round in our backyard. We had gotten it spinning pretty fast, and I decided I was going to stop it, so I planted my feet in the dirt and the seat slid underneath me and planted a big wood splinter deep into one of my cheeks (and I'm not talking about my face). I started to cry and headed to the house, holding my butt. Already embarrassed because I cried in front of the girls and my butt was bleeding. I knew now one of my parents was going to have to see my butt to get the splinter out, and I didn't want anyone looking at my butt. Anyway, I got my dad and told him what happened, and he took me to their bedroom and had me pull down my pants. He tried to pull the splinter out, but it wouldn't budge, so he had me lie facedown on the bed and called my mom to bring a needle. So there I lay with my bare butt in the air, and in came my mom, followed by their friends, followed by their girls and my brothers. Everyone was staring at my wound in a very private place while my mom and dad worked for ten minutes to get the splinter out. All their poking and prodding hurt, but it was more embarrassing than it was painful, and it hurt a lot.

You're probably wondering what the point of this story is. We all have splinters in our lives, in the hidden, private corners of our souls, and we need someone to help us remove them from our lives. Now, my mom and dad, they belonged in the room, they loved me, they had been there when I was sick, they had loved and cared for me my entire life. But their friends didn't belong there; they didn't know me, were just concerned adults. The girls and my brothers didn't belong there; they were just spectators. In life, people are living with the hurt and the pain of deep, painful splinters, and they have no one close to them that they can trust to help them pull their splinters. We need to love people where they're at, being true friends willing to sacrifice our time and ourselves. In John 13:34–35 Jesus says, "A new command I give to you: Love one another. As I have loved you, so you must love one another. By this everyone will know that you are my disciples, if you love one another" (NIV). Only when we have become a part of their lives will we earn the right to see into the private corners of their lives and help them pull their splinters. We know people who are hurting; we see them every day. For some, the pain becomes too great and they commit suicide and we are shocked, never having been involved enough to even know the extent of their pain. We don't seem to realize how much weight our love and involvement with others carries with our heavenly Father. "Some men came, bringing to him a paralyzed man, carried by four of them. Since they could not get him to Jesus because of the crowd, they made an opening in the roof above Jesus by digging through it and then lowered the mat the paralyzed man was lying on. When Jesus saw their faith, he said to the paralyzed man, 'Son, your sins are forgiven'" (Mark 2:3–5 NIV). Now, Jesus went on to heal the man, but it is important to note that this man trusted these friends completely, or he wouldn't have let them lower him from the roof to Jesus. Also, his friends loved him enough that they would not be stopped from getting him to Jesus. But the most important part of the story, something that I had never noticed before, was the fact that it says, "When Jesus saw [their] faith," He forgave his sins and healed him. How many people in your life trust you that completely? How many people do you love so much that nothing would stop you from bringing them to Jesus to have their hurts and hearts healed and forgiven? And how many times has God healed or intervened in someone else's life because of your faith? I fall miserably short in this area, and unfortunately, the church as a whole does also, or we would be making more of an impact on our country. There are way too many concerned Christians and way too many spectators and not enough true friends willing to get involved and serve one another in today's church. Remember, living for Christ is not a spectator's sport, and someone out there needs your help to pull a splinter or two.

Love,
Dad

Patience

I once prayed for God to teach me patience so I could be a better father and husband. When I prayed for this, I didn't think it through very well, because I wasn't expecting what it takes to learn patience, even though James 1:2–4 says, "Consider it pure joy, my brothers and sisters, whenever you face trials of many kinds, because you know that the testing of your faith produces perseverance. Let perseverance finish its work so that you may be mature and complete, not lacking anything" (NIV). Shortly thereafter, I was laid off my job and started working for a farmer who, along with corn, raised pigs. When I first started working for the farmer, the first thing he told me was that it was hard to herd a pig anywhere. They will go everywhere except where you want them to go. The more you try to force them in one direction, the harder they try to go the other. In fact, he said I would swear God put the head on the wrong end. And he was right. It was the ultimate test of my patience. I had always heard that they were very intelligent animals, but they were an unbelievable source of frustration for me. One day we were trying to load pigs onto a truck, and they just would not go up the livestock chute into the truck. I was so angry I was ready to shoot them all and forget the whole thing. The farmer just smiled and said, "Let me show you something." He took straw and scattered it around the pen, up the chute, and around in the bed of the truck, then left the gate on the chute and the truck open and said, "Let's go home and come back in the morning." In the morning, when I got to the pen, one of the pigs was in the truck. We went to the far side of the pen, waved our hands, and all the pigs ran up the chute into the truck. We shut the gate and went to market. Those pigs would not go into a place they were not familiar with. They resisted going into something they didn't know. When they were given time alone to become familiar with the truck, it was easy to get them into the truck, but it took time and patience.

Now, people are very much like those pigs. People resist being forced into certain molds or lifestyles; they fear what they don't understand. It is important for each of us to find our own way to the Father of Life (Jesus). It is very hard for me to stand back and let you find your own way. I desperately want to push everyone I know into that place that works for me because I like to think I know best. But only you can find that walk with Christ that meets your deepest needs, and I know I will only make it take longer if I try pushing you. Now, you have to step out on your own with one thing in mind. Know that Jesus loves you, and even though He is God, He never forces you to follow Him; He only made it possible for you to find Him and be with Him. The rest is your choice. "The Lord is not slow in keeping his promises, as some understand slowness. Instead he is patient with you, not wanting anyone to perish, but everyone to come to repentance" (2 Pet. 3:9 NIV). If I love someone, I have to allow him or her to find their way into the life God has set aside for them. But that does not mean I do nothing. It only means that I have to be patient and find ways to make Christ more accessible to them, so they know they don't need to fear what they don't understand. "But in your hearts revere Christ as Lord. Always be prepared to give an answer to everyone who asks you to give the reason for the hope that you have. But do this with gentleness and respect, keeping a clear conscience, so that those who speak maliciously against your good behavior in Christ may be ashamed of their slander" (1 Pet. 3:15–16 NIV). Like the pigs, if we start getting pushy, people will resist and go the other way, but with the proper attitude and the patience to love someone right where they are at, we can be that person that makes the path to Christ well traveled by our friends and family.

Love,
Dad

What One's Worth

A few years after Doreen and I got married, I decided to sell my car. With two kids, a two-seater just wasn't going to work. As I was getting it all fixed up to sell, I remember telling my dad that it was worth a certain amount of money, and he said that it wasn't. I immediately said that I had seen cars like mine for sale for even more and that it was at least worth what I was asking. Again, he said it wasn't. Then, with a little smile, he said, "Something is only worth what someone is willing to pay." My car was only worth about half as much as I thought it was because that was all I could get out of it. It was a long time later that I really began to realize the wisdom of those words. You hear of baseball cards and many other collectible items, like paintings, being sold for outrageous sums of money. They rarely cost much to make, and yet they are worth millions because people were willing to pay that for it.

It then occurred to me, Why do we shuffle around and conduct ourselves as if we are someone's leftover trash? Are we sinful and undeserving of God's love? By all means, we are. By the standards that were set, we could never measure up. Just like those collectibles could never be considered that valuable in and of themselves. But God made us priceless by giving up all that He had, even His life, to purchase us. Think about it! How can you put a price on all the power that was His and the kingdom that was His? "Who, being in very nature God, did not consider equality with God something to be used to his own advantage; rather, he made himself nothing by taking the very nature of a servant, being made in human likeness. And being found in appearance as a man, he humbled himself by becoming obedient to death—even death on a cross! Therefore God exalted him to the highest place and gave him the name that is above every name, that at the name of Jesus every knee should bow, in heaven and on earth and under the earth, and every tongue acknowledge that Jesus Christ is Lord, to the glory of God the Father" (Phil. 2:6–11 NIV). Not only did He pay a huge price for us, making us extremely valuable to Him, but He also treats us in the same manner as that collector would treat that baseball card or painting.

You were a huge investment for Him, and He treats you with the same care. "Therefore, brothers and sisters, we have an obligation—but it is not to the flesh, to live according to it. For if you live according to the flesh, you will die; but if by the Spirit you put to death the misdeeds of the body, you will live. For those who are led by the Spirit of God are children of God. The spirit you received does not make you slaves, so that you live in fear again; rather, the spirit you received brought about your adoption to sonship. And by him we cry 'Abba, Father.' The Spirit himself testifies with our spirit that we are God's children. Now if we are children, then we are heirs—heirs of God and co-heirs with Christ, if indeed we share in his sufferings in order that we may also share in his glory. I consider that our present sufferings are not worth comparing with the glory that will be revealed in us. The creation waits in eager expectation for the children of God to be revealed" (Rom. 8:12–19 NIV). So, kids, hold your heads high and dedicate yourselves to bringing glory to the one who has given you yours.

Love,
Dad

What's My Name?

When I was growing up, I spent the first nine and half years of my life in a very small town in the sandhills of Nebraska. But in my class, it just happened that there were two Joels. The other Joel was much bigger than I was, and we became very good friends. We even went to the same church, so from kindergarten on, he was called Joel and I was called Joey. My parents started calling me Joey. Even aunts, uncles, and cousins started calling me Joey. It was really kind of strange. I signed all my papers Joey. It was like after a year or so, my name had just changed.

Then we moved to another town. There weren't any other Joels in my class there, but I was still signing my name and going by Joey. It wasn't until the eighth grade when I decided Joey sounded like a little boy and I didn't want to be called that anymore and I started going by my real name, Joel. I've noticed it in people's nicknames also. People are called one thing till their midteens, and then suddenly it's too childish, so they expect to be called something else more mature or cool.

It's amazing how when pride kicks in, we suddenly have to be called something that makes us seem bigger or feel more important. It goes against our nature to be humble and accept a title that is less than what we think we deserve. That is why it's so amazing that God would humble Himself, give up His title and His throne to become a man, live a lowly life, and die a disgraceful death for us. "Once you were alienated from God and were enemies in your minds because of your evil behavior. But now he has reconciled you by Christ's physical body through death to present you holy in his sight, without blemish and free from accusation—if you continue in your faith, established and firm, and do not move from the hope held out in the gospel. This is the gospel that you heard and that has been proclaimed to every creature under heaven, and of which I, Paul, have become a servant" (Col. 1:21–23 NIV). Maybe in light of that, Saul became known as Paul. Instead of wanting his name changed to something more prestigious, he went from a proud name to a humble name. Maybe it's time we as Christians follow suit.

You know, what's amazing is how good it makes me feel when I hear someone calling me Joey. My aunts, uncles, and cousins many times still call me Joey. The last letter my dad wrote me was written to Joey. The one who named me Joel knew me as Joey and wrote that special letter I cherish to Joey. I am so thankful that I wasn't insistent on everyone calling me Joel. Because now I get this special feeling inside knowing those who know me as Joey have known and loved me longer than anyone else. It's no longer embarrassing—I look forward to it. God has given us a name as well. "For this is what the Lord says: "To the eunuchs who keep my Sabbaths, who choose what pleases me and hold fast to my covenant—to them I will give within my temple and its walls a memorial and a name better than sons and daughters; I will give them an everlasting name that will endure forever" (Isa. 56:4–5 NIV). "The gatekeeper opens the gate for him, and the sheep listen to his voice. He calls his own sheep by name and leads them out" (John 10:3 NIV). "I have come that they may have life, and have it to the full. I am the good shepherd. The good shepherd lays down his life for the sheep" (John 10:10–11 NIV). Christ knows your name, and if you know Him and His voice, it truly is a sweet thing to hear Him call your name. Listen closely!

Love,
Dad

Looking Back

I remember watching many of my favorite shows when I was young and how great they seemed. They were so funny or so cool, and I would watch reruns and usually couldn't wait to see the next show even if I had seen them before. But many years later, I sat down to watch shows that I thought were so great as a kid, and my anticipation always seemed to turn to disappointment. They suddenly seemed really dumb and a waste of time. I didn't find any pleasure in them. Now I rarely watch shows that were so exciting for me as a child, because I want to remember them the way they made me feel then and not spoil it by seeing it from an adult's perspective.

It is always so easy to look back on what I would call mountaintop experiences, stages in your life when, like those TV shows, you were totally caught up in the moment and everything seemed so great. You want to stay right there and relive it over and over like a rerun. But we can't stay there. Growing up in Christ requires moving ahead, facing new challenges, becoming more equipped to handle things that come our way. "When I was a child, I talked like a child, I thought like a child, I reasoned like a child. When I became a man, I put the ways of childhood behind me" (1 Cor. 13:11 NIV). Unfortunately, we many times try to either stay where we are, which leaves us trying to be like Peter Pan, refusing to grow up and sacrificing the joy of experiencing all God has to offer out of selfishness or fear. Or we try going back to relive an experience, only to suffer a real letdown, finding that all those things God has been taking us through have changed us and we don't find the same fulfillment in them as before.

My advice to you is to enjoy each experience to the fullest and then look ahead to the next, anticipating the growth that comes with each new experience. "Not that I have already obtained all this, or have already arrived at my goal, but I press on to take hold of that for which Christ Jesus took hold of me. Brothers and sisters, I do not consider myself yet to have taken hold of it. But one thing I do: Forgetting what is behind and straining toward what is ahead, I press on toward the goal to win the prize for which God has called me heavenward in Christ Jesus. All of us who are mature should take such a view of things. And if on some point you think differently, that too God will make clear to you. Only let us live up to what we have already attained" (Phil. 3:12–16 NIV). Remember, you can't move ahead if you are always looking back. Take each day, learn what you can, and move forward. Those who live in the past usually aren't going anywhere.

Love,
Dad

My Helper

When Brandon was small, he used to like to help me when I worked on the house. The one time I remember the most was a time when I was framing a window in a bedroom and he wanted desperately to pound the nails in with the hammer, but he wasn't strong enough to get the nail to go in. I wasn't terribly patient, and I was just going to go ahead and do it myself, but he looked so sad, like I had just broken his favorite toy. I started feeling really bad for him, so I decided I didn't need to be in such a hurry. I went to get a drill and drilled a hole about half the size of the nail everywhere we needed a nail. Then I started the nails, and he went around and pounded in all the nails. The look on his face was priceless to me. He was smiling, as if he had just conquered the world. I wouldn't have traded that moment for anything, and to think I almost missed it by being in too big of a hurry to finish the job. It did take more time to let him help. It was more work for me to have him help than if I had done it myself, but when he had to tell Mom what he had done or burst, that excitement was well worth the extra effort.

I think that our heavenly Father does much the same thing for us. Everything He commands us to do, He could do much quicker and much better, but He chooses to make things so we can do them, so that we can have a part in building His church. E. V. Hill once said at a Promise Keepers Conference in Boulder that Christ, while He was on earth, did only the things that He also enables us to do. That is not an exact quote, but I think it is truth. God didn't ask us to live a life that He hadn't already endured; He lived it before us. Jesus prays in John 17:15–23, "My prayer is not that you take them out of the world but that you protect them from the evil one. They are not of the world, even as I am not of it. Sanctify them by the truth; your word is truth. As you sent me into the world, I have sent them into the world. For them I sanctify myself, that they too may be truly sanctified. My prayer is not for them alone. I pray also for those who will believe in me through their message, that all of them may be one, Father, just as you are in me and I am in you. May they also be in us so that the world may believe that you have sent me. I have given them the glory that you gave me, that they may be one as we are one—I in them and you in me—so that they may they be brought to complete unity. Then the world will know that you sent me and have loved them even as you have loved me" (NIV).

In His life, in His Word, He gives us the tools and the example, clearing the way, drilling pilot holes, so we can do the job that needs to be done. He now limits Himself in the building process, so we are needed and important in His building plan. Isn't it great that God never waits for us to be as strong as Him (like that will ever happen) before He has us help? "Then Jesus came to them and said, 'All authority in heaven and on earth has been given to me. Therefore go and make disciples of all nations, baptizing them in the name of the Father and of the Son and of the Holy Spirit, and teaching them to obey everything I have commanded you. And surely I am with you always, to the very end of the age'" (Matt. 28:18–20 NIV). He is with us, helping us, making the job we need to do just easy enough so we can do it, but never so easy that it requires no effort on our part, and He is basically doing it for us. That way, when the task is done, we can enjoy a sense of accomplishment and satisfaction knowing we were a part of His plan. Paul said in Philippians 4:13, "I can do all this through him who gives me strength" (NIV). Isn't it great we can accomplish everything He has called us to do?

Love,
Dad

Selling Our Savior

It seems we, as Christians, are driven by greed as often or maybe even more so than the world is. Of any place on this earth, the church should be the most prone to experience financial parity. The rich should be helping those without, and those with knowledge and expertise should be teaching those who have none. The first church operated in much the same way, but I am not talking about selling everything and starting a commune. Today it seems the rich are too busy accumulating and keeping what they have accumulated to even hear and understand the problems of the poor. The poor are too busy trying to attain a lifestyle they don't have or crying about how they are owed or deserve somehow what others have. Wealthy Christians will use the parable of the talents to say that they are walking in God's will by being financially responsible with their money and by making a lot more money. Then giving some of it to the church. What they fail to see is that Christ was not teaching financial responsibility. In Matthew 25, Jesus tells the parable of the talents, but right after that, He goes on, and that usually is where you get the gist of what the parable means. This is what He says right after. He starts talking about the judgment and what will be said. "Then the King will say to those on his right, 'Come you who are blessed by my Father; take your inheritance, the kingdom prepared for you since the creation of the world. For I was hungry and you gave me something to eat, I was thirsty and you gave me something to drink, I was a stranger and you invited me in, I needed clothes and you clothed me, I was sick and you looked after me, I was in prison and you came to visit me.' Then the righteous will answer him, 'Lord, when did we see you hungry and feed you, or thirsty and give you something to drink? When did we see you a stranger and invite you in, or needing clothes and clothe you? When did we see you sick or in prison and go to visit you?' The King will reply, 'Truly I tell you, whatever you did for one of the least of these brothers and sisters of mine you did for me'" (Matt. 25:34–40 NIV). He then also tells what happens to those who don't do these things exactly like He did with the talents. The talents were a parable of investing what the master gives you for the master, not for yourself. So what Christ was saying is, if we truly are good servants, we will invest all our energies into what is important to Him. What is important to Him are people, and He will be able to tell the servants that love and respect Him by the way they treat the least of these people. The poor, the sick, the hurting, etc.

To carry this even further, this is the same Christ who told the rich man to give all that he had to the poor and come follow Him. "'All these I have kept,' the young man said. 'What do I still lack?' Jesus answered, 'If you want to be perfect, go, sell your possessions and give to the poor, and you will have treasure in heaven. Then come, follow me.' When the young man heard this, he went away sad, because he had great wealth" (Matt. 19:20–22 NIV). That man left shaking his head. I am sure that man had given lots of money to the church, but his lifestyle was more important than following Christ. He was serving a different God. When asked by the Pharisees about paying taxes, Jesus said in Matthew 22:20–

21, "And he asked them, 'Whose image is this? And whose inscription?' 'Caesar's,' they replied. Then he said to them, 'So give back to Caesar what is Caesar's and to God what is God's'" (NIV). The religious leaders would have preferred that the money be given to the church, which ultimately was them and made them rich and comfortable. If God wanted their money, Christ would have taken these opportunities to say so. He made no claim on their money, for He was asking for their hearts and devotion. Once He received those, He knew that their possessions would follow willingly. We equate blessings with cash flow and godliness with prosperity when Christ, in Matthew 5:3–12, tells us who are blessed: the meek, the poor, the hurting, the persecuted. A far cry from the rich and prosperous.

Oh, those servants who were given the talents to make more for the master. Nowhere is it stated that they quit being servants or that they got to keep any of the money. That they got wealthy, bought big cushy houses, and lived a life of luxury equal to that of the master. It was not their bank accounts that grew; it was the master's account. It was his money to start out with, and everything they made was his as well. They only received his money to start out with, and everything they made was his as well. They only received praise and more responsibility, which seemed to be reward enough. Today I hear preachers preaching on tithing and giving to the church, and it reminds me of the Pharisees asking about the taxes. Christ didn't ask for 10 percent of their money, and if we really follow the standards set forth in those parables, we would not be giving 10 percent to the church, because a servant never makes more than his master. So if we really lived out this parable, we would be giving 80 to 90 percent of what we make to God and keeping what we presently give God. But we wouldn't be giving it to the church; we would be giving it to the poor. Didn't Christ say, "If you have given it to the least of these, you have given it to Me"? How much of our time is spent making our lives more comfortable and our bank accounts bigger? We say it is all for God, but we are the ones enjoying all the benefits. How many of us neglect the important things of God in the pursuit of wealth or trying to keep our wealth?

How many of us take time out from our busy schedule to help someone who is hurting or just listen to someone who needs to talk? We are usually too busy being blessed or, should I say, blessing ourselves to be a blessing to others. We, many times, don't even have time for our own families, much less the family of God. Now, if Christians were really making money for God and believed it was His, then when they died, they would not have a bank account of any significant size, because it would have all been given to their master's business, invested in his work and not just a church. I think too often we throw our money at things instead of investing what we have in things that will make a lasting difference. For example, if we feed the poor but don't provide them with work, we only make them dependent on someone else. Where are the businessmen that will not only give money to meet the immediate need but also invest their money and talents in ways that make those charities and mission fields self-supporting, along with the people they are trying to help.

Our faith most often is not in God but in our bank accounts, our savings for retirement, and the possessions that make our life comfortable. If our faith truly were in God, we would go out like the disciples did, keeping nothing to claim as our own. As we scurry around, trying to maintain our blessed lifestyle, we often stop long enough to tell our brothers and sisters in Christ we love them, yet we have no time for them. We really love ourselves and our lifestyle too much to follow Christ and His example. He gave up far more than we have ever had to. He gave up His life, His kingdom, and all the glory that went with it to come and save us. I am not implying that everyone should sell everything and wander around the country, sing gospel songs, and preach, but what I am implying is that all of us, rich and poor, need to re-evaluate what we are really serving in life and take steps to change our attitudes. We need to recognize that God's salvation was not a money rope that He threw down to pull us from our sin and, in turn, feed our greed. It was a selfless sacrifice of all that He was and all that He had.

I believe many times God calls us to do things that are financially stupid so we can see his power and glory and so He can see where our treasure really is. In Mark 14:3–11, when Mary poured out the oil on Christ's head and feet, she lavishly wasted all that she had on Christ. Some of the disciples, seeing that she had wasted her life savings on Christ, were quick to criticize the waste and point out that there were wiser ways to spend the money. Judas, the man who managed the group's money, immediately left, apparently upset by the waste and Christ's approval of it. Because he left and went straight to the Pharisees and betrayed Christ, selling our Savior for thirty pieces of silver. Are we, the church, doing the same thing by always doing the practical, sensible, comfortable thing? What are we selling Christ for? This is not a call to be irresponsible but for us to be more accessible. To follow God, whether it makes sense or not. "'For my thoughts are not your thoughts, neither are your ways my ways,' declares the Lord. 'As the heavens are higher than the earth, so are my ways higher than your ways and my thoughts than your thoughts' (Isa. 55:8–9 NIV). I hope it will be said one day that my family was a part of a church and a people whose passion was for God always, not just when God made sense. "Do not store up for yourselves treasures on earth, where moths and vermin destroy, and where thieves break in and steal. But store up for yourselves treasures in heaven, where moths and vermin do not destroy, and where thieves do not break in and steal. For where your treasure is, there your heart will be also" (Matt. 6:19–21 NIV). Many times it seems to me that we treat God like the great gumball machine in the sky. Shove a quarter in, if we say the right prayer or have the right kind of special faith, and he will rain down glory gumballs, give us everything we want, and make our life easy. Is our treasure really stored in heaven, or is it in the nearest bank? When was the last time you did something for God that made no sense to you at all, and you only did it because you felt God told you to do it? Your life is an adventure; spend it believing in more than money.

Love,
Dad

Tell Me You Love Me

Each year, as I watch each of my kids, especially on the holidays, when everyone is together, I am amazed at how grown-up you've become. You are both adults now and suddenly seem so mature. I can't seem to fathom where all the time went. I keep going back and remembering both of you when you would wait at the screen door for me to come home. Brandon said his first word one of those times, "Dad." I was so proud, and it completely made my day. Your mom, on the other hand, was pretty disappointed. I guess every mother wants the first words out of their baby's mouth to be *Mom*. The other time I remember most is coming home from work. Yvette was waiting at the door, and I had just been told I was being laid off. I was pretty down, but everything somehow seemed better when I walked up on the porch, and though she was barely talking and walking, she smiled a great big smile, and without even saying hi, she said, "I love you, Daddy." It still makes my day when I hear "I love you, Dad." It's what I look forward to the most, knowing that those I love the most love me enough to let me know.

We know a couple that every so often you would hear her say, "Tell me you love me," and he would always smile and say, "I told you I loved you when we got married, and if anything changes, I'll let you know." Now he was just teasing her, but how often do we have that kind of attitude with our heavenly Father? We say we love God, yet we're too busy to talk to Him and tell Him we love Him or spend time with Him. We, in essence, say, "God, I told You I loved You when You saved me, or at church on Sunday, and if something changes, I'll let You know." Jesus quoted Isaiah 29:14 in Matthew 15:8–9, "These people honor me with their lips, but their hearts are far from me. They worship me in vain; their teachings are but rules taught by men" (NIV). I think God wants what my children gave me at the door when I came home from work and not all the things we, as mature, screwed-up adults, want to give. Maybe that is why in Matthew 19:14, Jesus said, "Let the little children come to me, and do not hinder them, for the kingdom of heaven belongs to such as these" (NIV). I don't think that anything can be more sincere than a little child whose life is totally consumed with you, wanting to be with you, trusting you, looking up to you, always wanting you around, saying, "I love you." It's as genuine as it gets, honest adoration expressed to you in the simplest, purest form. I think we all need to hear "I love you" in one way or another from those we love. I am so thankful that God keeps finding new ways to let me know how much He loves me. Hope I can find new and different ways to tell Him I love Him. I also hope that you never quit telling God you love Him and that we keep telling one another "I love you" as well.

Love,
Dad

Hiding Sticks and Discipline

When I was young, I was in church every time the doors opened, mostly because my dad was the pastor and we could only pretend we were on our deathbed once in a blue moon. So there my brothers and sister and I sat every Sunday morning, Sunday night, and Wednesday night. Now, I was not a good sitter, nor was I a good listener, and I drove my mother crazy, I'm sure. I remember very few services when I was not ushered outside by my mother to receive certain incentive stimulation to make sitting a little less comfortable but much more inviting. In fact, I was known to do such things as turning sanctuary lights on and off during the service, escaping under pews, and running down aisles, even in one instance biting my Sunday school teacher. Some of which even prompted my father to stop his sermon long enough to see that I had received a little more personalized instruction. Now, looking back, I'm amazed that I remember anything my father said in his sermons, but be assured, I remember my parents' personalized instruction to this day. In fact, I would even go around before church and hide any sticks or other instruments that could be used for this personalized instruction. It never helped—there was always something to be found.

Now, there are people out there who would say I was abused and that I just needed the proper motivation. But I can assure you, a good spanking was a good motivator. "He who spares the rod hates his son, but he who loves him is careful to discipline him" (Prov. 13:24 NIV). "Discipline your son, and he will give you peace; he will bring delight to your soul. Where there is no revelation, the people cast off restraint; but blessed is he who keeps the law. A servant cannot be corrected by mere words; though he understands, he will not respond" (Prov. 29:17–19 NIV). "Do not withhold discipline from a child; if you punish him with the rod, he will not die. Punish him with the rod and save his soul from death" (Prov. 23:13–14 NIV). "Folly is bound up in the heart of a child, but the rod of discipline will drive it far from him" (Prov. 22:15 NIV). My parents cared that I was being a brat enough to correct me and tried to teach me how to be around other people, to respect them and obey God. I always knew I was loved because I knew they hated it more than I did. But today I am so thankful they did spank me. In some cases, there are alternatives to spanking. But that child who has never been spanked by a parent who loves him and is trying to teach him right from wrong has never been truly loved by a parent. Because a parent who loves their child will correct them early and often so that it won't be so painful and destructive to them when they learn those lessons on their own later. "And you have forgotten that word of encouragement that addresses you as sons: 'My son, do not make light of the Lord's discipline, and do not lose heart when he rebukes you, because the Lord disciplines those he loves, and he punishes everyone he accepts as a son' [from Prov. 3:11–12]. Endure hardship as discipline; God is treating you as sons. For what son is not disciplined by his father? If you are not disciplined (and everyone undergoes discipline), then you are illegitimate children and not true sons. Moreover, we had human fathers who disciplined us and we respected them for it. How much more should we submit to the Father of our spirits and live! Our fathers disciplined us for a little while as they thought best; but God disciplines us for our good, that we may share in his holiness. No discipline seems pleasant at the time, but painful. Later on, however, it produces a harvest of righteousness and peace for those who have been trained by it" (Heb. 12:5–11 NIV).

To be honest, I think those who believe a child should not be spanked promote child abuse. I believe, if you correct a child quickly and soundly and do so because what the child is doing is wrong and must be corrected, you will spank the child long before you are angry, long before the child has taken your sanity from you. You will be doing it out of love, and it will be hard for you to do. Allowing your child to drive you and push you until you explode is what causes parents who truly care about their children to be abusive. I realize some parents don't care about their children, only themselves; that will show up as abuse, either by a parent taking out all their aggression physically, sexually, or verbally on a child. This is a totally selfish and cruel place for a child to be living in. But some people, because they don't want to do anything that's hard for them or because they are so busy with themselves and their own problems, they totally ignore their child and fail to teach them the lessons they need to learn. This is probably the most prevalent form of child abuse out there today, and not only accepted, but in some cases, also encouraged or mandated. I believe this is what Paul speaks to in Ephesians 6:4, "Fathers, do not exasperate your children; instead, bring them up in the training and instruction of the Lord" (NIV). I hope that you will remember, when you have kids, that to love them means doing what needs to be done even when it's hard to do. I remember my parents always saying, "This is going to hurt me more than it hurts you." And I remember thinking, *Yeah, right, it's my butt that's sore, not yours.* I determined never to say that to my kids when I spanked them because they wouldn't believe it anyway—I didn't. But spanking you, in fact, anytime I had to discipline you in any way was the hardest thing I ever had to do. It doesn't hurt physically, but to see my kids hurt just made me want to curl up and die, and believe it or not, it hurt more than words can describe. In fact, I had to almost detach myself from the situation and tell myself it was something that just had to be done and force myself to do it. If you ever have to spank or discipline your child, that is a good way to check if you are doing it in a godly and loving manner. If it hurts your child more than it hurts you, then you had better stop and pray that God will change your heart and your attitude.

We have to remember that disciple is about teaching and correcting, not about punishment. Punishment is rendered as payment for an offense by a, hopefully, impartial judge or jury. In Hebrews quoted above, chapter 12 verse 6 says the Lord disciplines and punishes, which tells me that they are different, and 1 John 4:18 says, "There is no fear in love. But perfect love drives out fear, because fear has to do with punishment. The one who fears is not made perfect in love" (NIV). Discipline is correction and teaching coming from someone who cares for an individual enough to do what it takes to correct actions that, if left unchecked, can cause that person harm. A loving parent will want it to hurt them more than it hurts their child and will gladly endure that pain for the sake of their child. They will also be big enough to admit when their attitude is not right and ask their child and God to forgive them. I know that you will be good and godly parents to your children when that time comes. I just hope I'm a good grandpa. Never done that before.

Love,
Dad

Build His House

People today, not unlike the religious leaders of the past, are content to keep the traditions and the comfort of always operating in repetition rather than doing those things that involve oneself in a more intimate manner. I am reminded of a time when a friend from work was building a new house and I, along with about fifteen to twenty more friends of his, helped him frame in his house on a Saturday. At about two o'clock in the afternoon, everyone was sitting on a wood-pile, taking a break, and one of the men asked the man if he wanted him to help him the next day. He said that Sunday he was playing in a tennis tournament but that he could cancel out of it if he still needed help. Before my friend could reply, his pastor, who was also there helping, very sharply informed the man that they didn't work on Sundays, that they had church and that it was the Lord's day. Then he leaned back with this satisfied look that I would interpret as a "Look how I just witnessed to all these people." My friend, appearing a little embarrassed by the way his pastor had talked to his friend, politely told him he had relatives coming to town for his baby's dedication and that he wouldn't be working on the house.

Now, the more I thought about the incident, the more upset I got. Here was a man who had probably spent money to enter a tournament, doing something he obviously enjoyed on his day off, yet he was willing to sacrifice it all to help his friend. Yet he was being chastised by a man who would most likely preach a sermon (which was the job he was being paid to do, meaning he was working), eat a leisurely meal, perhaps take a nap, then prepare to preach an evening sermon. I wonder who was making a greater sacrifice and who was demonstrating greater love for his friend. I would venture to guess that if that church had a picnic on a Sunday after church, it might have been attended by one hundred people or more, and it would have been an acceptable function. But I have to ask myself, if that same church had a Sunday-afternoon workday in which they painted a widow's house, would ten people have shown up? Or would many, including the pastor, likely condemned it as wrong? Yet if it is truly the Lord's day, why is it we take the day off to lounge around? "Going on from that place, he went into their synagogue, and a man with a shriveled hand was there. Looking for a reason to accuse Jesus, they asked him, 'Is it lawful to heal on the Sabbath?' He said to them, 'If any of you has a sheep and it falls into a pit on the Sabbath, will you not take hold of it and lift it out? How much more valuable is a man than a sheep! Therefore it is lawful to do good on the Sabbath.' Then he said to the man, 'Stretch out your hand.' So he stretched it out and it was completely restored, just as sound as the other. But the Pharisees went out and plotted how they might kill Jesus" (Matt. 12:9–13 NIV).

How many times was Christ chastised by the Pharisees for healing someone on the Sabbath? If Christ was busy doing His Father's work on the Sabbath, shouldn't we do the same? Shouldn't we dedicate that day to serving God, and we demonstrate service to God by meeting the needs of those around us? "When they had finished eating, Jesus said to Simon Peter, 'Simon son of John, do you truly love me more than these?' 'Yes, Lord,' he said, 'you know that I love you.' Jesus said, 'Feed my lambs.' Again Jesus said, 'Simon son of John, do you truly love me?' He answered, 'Yes, Lord, you know that I love you.' Jesus said, 'Take care of my Sheep.' The third time he said to him, 'Simon son of John, do you love me?' Peter was hurt because Jesus asked him the third time, 'Do you love me?' He said, 'Lord, you know all things, you know that I love you.' Jesus said, 'Feed my sheep'" (John 21:15–17 NIV). The reality is, in life we are all guilty of many times praying to God, expecting Him to do many of the things we were put here to do while we are watching from a distance, being careful not to get too close or too involved. Be careful that your faith is a lot more show and a lot less blow.

Love,
Dad

Walking on Water

Sometimes in life, I find we get a little overconfident in ourselves. Those things we were sure we would never do, we find ourselves up to our eyeballs in them. We like to think we're doing really well, then suddenly we crash and burn. We really like to think we got God's number and that He is pretty lucky to have us on His team. Even if we will never own up to that attitude, if we are honest with ourselves, we all get cocky and prideful in what we know or think we know at some point in our life. We like to look at Peter's life and think somehow we would have done better, we wouldn't have sunk, or we would have never denied Christ three times. We like to point at Peter and say his faith was weak, but if you read the account in Matthew 14:22–33, he was the only one who got out of the boat at all! The fact that he took his eyes off Jesus and started to sink is not even relevant to the others because of where they were at. Many times you will step out of the boat and sink, and your only critics will be the people whose butts are still firmly planted in the boat, because the people who have dared to venture out of the boat will sympathize with you, not criticize you. I hope you venture out of the boat often, but I hope you learn to eliminate the sinking part.

In the meantime, a good chapter to take to heart is Psalms 91, and verses 14–16 are good verses to memorize.

"'Because he loves me,' says the Lord, 'I will rescue him; I will protect him, for he acknowledges my name. He will call upon me, and I will answer him; I will be with him in trouble, I will deliver him and honor him. With long life will I satisfy him and show him my salvation'" (NIV). Remember also when Peter said he would die for Christ and then denied Him. We again want to point and say what a spineless fool, yet we forget that in the garden, when they came to take Jesus away, he cut off the servant's ear. He had drawn his sword even with all the soldiers there and was going to die defending his master. He was good to his word; he was willing to die to save his Savior. He was trying to save the one who came to save him. He was trying to save someone when he couldn't save himself. He thought Jesus needed him when he really needed Jesus. But when things didn't go the way he planned or in a way that he could understand, he freaked out. What Christ did made no sense to him, and it completely unnerved him. He then fell apart and did what he swore he would never do: deny Christ. Now, how can any of us say we can understand all the things God does or allows? When things like that happen, we lose confidence and fall flat on our faces. We find out most of our faith is more in ourselves and the plans we've conjured up in our minds (which, incidentally, are pretty puny compared to God's plans) instead of in an all-knowing, all-powerful God. Man, we can be so pathetic sometimes. But I guess that's why we need His grace so much. I am sure that is why Jesus told Peter right before his betrayal in the garden in Mark 14:38, "Watch and pray so that you will not fall into temptation. The spirit is willing, but the flesh is weak" (NIV). Peter promptly fell asleep again and was not even remotely prepared for what was coming. How can we know God's plan if we're not talking to Him? I'm writing this not only so you can begin looking at yourself, and hopefully see your tendencies, so you can head off some of your problems before they hit, but also so when you see the failures of others out there trying to serve God and continually fumbling around and falling down, like Peter did, you can help them up. Remember, if you criticize instead of sympathize, you're probably still sitting in the boat.

Love,
Dad

The Three Things People Need

One night, I was asked to do sound at a meeting for the college group from the church we attended at that time. The college pastor made a statement that night that I found fascinating. I spent a lot of time thinking about the statement, and I think the conclusions I've come to are worth passing on; right or wrong, hopefully it will cause you to think. The college pastor said, "There are three things people need: they need to know, they need to be right, and they need to win." I think the statement describes what seems to drive people perfectly, but I don't believe we need these things. Instead, I believe that a more accurate statement would be that the three things people want are to know, to be right, and to win. But in that statement, I can find very few positive reasons for our intense desire to achieve these things. Every time I tried, I kept coming up with pride being the driving force behind our desires for these things. Even though it seems we all are driven by them. So I want to take each one and look at the positive and the negative, and hopefully we can avoid the pitfalls of these three prominent vehicles to a prideful life. Let's start with the "need to know" and see how much trouble we can get into with just the first one.

Let's start out at the beginning. What was the first temptation of mankind? "Now the serpent was more crafty than any of the wild animals the Lord God had made. He said to the woman, 'Did God really say, "You must not eat from any tree in the garden"?' The woman said to the serpent, 'We may eat fruit from the trees in the garden, but God did say, "You must not eat fruit from the tree that is in the middle of the garden, and you must not touch it, or you will die."' 'You will not surely die,' the serpent said to the woman, 'For God knows that when you eat of it your eyes will be opened, and you will be like God, knowing good and evil.' When the woman saw that the fruit of the tree was good for food and pleasing to the eye, and also desirable for gaining wisdom, she took some and ate it. She also gave some to her husband, who was with her, and he ate it. Then the eyes of both of them were opened, and they realized they were naked; so they sewed fig leaves together and made coverings for themselves" (Gen. 3:1–7 NIV). The very first temptation of man was the need to know. "You'll be like God, know good and evil." Eve's reason for taking the fruit was not that it looked good. There were lots of trees with good fruit in the garden. She took it because she wanted to know more than what she already knew, more than God had desired for her to know. Adam was there with her, so it wasn't like she twisted his arm. He wanted to know as well. They weren't satisfied with what God wanted them to know. To only know good and not evil wasn't enough; they wanted to know everything, and it cost all mankind dearly. "What good is it for a man to gain the whole world, yet forfeit his soul" (Mark 8:36 NIV). Adam and Eve gained knowledge of evil, but with it they sacrificed their soul and their closeness to God. Is all knowledge bad? The knowledge God gave them was good. "Then the Lord said to Moses, 'See, I have chosen Bezalel son of Uri, the son of Hur, of the tribe of Judah, and I have filled him with the Spirit of God, with skill, ability and knowledge in all kinds of crafts—to make artistic designs for work in gold, silver and bronze, to cut and set stones, to work in wood, and to engage in all kinds of craftsmanship'" (Exod. 31:1–5 NIV). God gives us all the knowledge we need to complete what He has for us to do in life. In Proverbs, Solomon talks about all that wisdom and knowledge can do for you, but he is careful to let you know where true knowledge and wisdom begin. "The fear of the Lord is the beginning of knowledge, but fools despise wisdom and discipline" (Prov. 1:7 NIV).

But we have to also consider what Solomon, considered the wisest man ever, says when he writes these thoughts in Ecclesiastes. "I, the Teacher, was king over Israel in Jerusalem. I devoted myself to study and explore by wisdom all that is done under heaven. What a heavy burden God has laid on men! I have seen all the things that are done under the sun; all of them are meaningless, a chasing after the wind. What is twisted cannot be straightened; what is lacking cannot be counted. I thought to myself, 'Look, I have grown and increased in wisdom more than anyone who has ruled over Jerusalem before me; I have experienced much of wisdom and knowledge.' Then I applied myself to the understanding of wisdom, and also of madness and folly, but I learned that this, too, is chasing after wind. For with much wisdom comes much sorrow; the more knowledge, the more grief" (Eccles. 1:12–18 NIV). This was his starting place. Now, check out his conclusion. "Not only was the Teacher wise, but also he imparted knowledge to the people. He pondered and searched out and set in order many proverbs. The Teacher searched to find just the right words, and what he wrote was upright and true. The words of the wise are like goads, their collected sayings like firmly embedded nails—given by one

Shepherd. Be warned, my son, of anything in addition to them. Of making many books there is no end, and much study wearies the body. Now all has been heard; here is the conclusion of the matter: Fear God and keep his command-ments, for this is the whole duty of man. For God will bring every deed into judgment, including every hidden thing, whether it is good or evil" (Eccles. 12:9–14 NIV).

The quest for knowledge didn't bring Solomon hap-piness, only fleeting pleasure. We are fulfilled, not by how much we know, but by how we use what we know and whom we use it for. Wisdom and knowledge are not bad things; in fact, they are good. It all seems to come down to what we are using it for. "My son, if you accept my words and store up my commands within you, turning your ear to wisdom and applying your heart to understanding, and if you call out for insight and cry aloud for understanding, and if you look for it as for silver and search for it as for hidden treasure, then you will understand the fear of the Lord and find the knowledge of God. For the Lord gives wisdom, and from his mouth come knowledge and understanding. He holds victory in store for the upright, he is a shield to those whose walk is blameless, for he guards the course of the just and protects the way of his faithful ones. Then you will understand what is right and just and fair—every good path. For wisdom will enter your heart, and knowledge will be pleasant to your soul. Discretion will protect you, and understanding will guard you" (Prov. 1:1–11 NIV). Both the statements in Ecclesiastes and Proverbs were written by the same man, yet they have totally different outcomes. Self-enlightenment only brings emptiness, whereas the search for godly wisdom and knowl-edge brings fulfillment. The search for truth and knowledge is an adventure that stimulates the senses, and with every revelation, a sense of accomplishment. Unfortunately, it is usually followed by a sense of pride, which, if left unchecked, puffs us up and turns us into fools. "We know that we all possess knowledge. Knowledge puffs up, but love builds up. The man who thinks he knows something does not yet know as he ought to know. But the man who loves God is known by God" (1 Cor. 8:1–3 NIV).

This leads us into the second of the three needs: people need to be right. We all know someone who thinks he knows everything and is compelled to let you know how much he knows, or how little he knows, depending on your point of view. It is funny how we all tend to gravitate to this behavior, although some tend to be more obvious and annoying. When I was eighteen, I thought my dad was stupid and I was sure to know more than he knew in a few years. It is amazing how much my dad learned in the next couple of years. As every day goes by, I feel more foolish and find more wisdom in the things my father told me. Once again, it is pride that causes us to foolishly feel that if we are not right, then, somehow, we are not as important or as good or that, somehow, we're less of a person. One time, when I was in the seventh grade, I remember totally bombing a test in history class. I think I got a 37, and after we got our test back, I was crushed. I had never gotten that bad of a score, so I went back and tried to figure out where I had screwed up. At home that night, after supper, my dad asked me how school was, and I told him about the bad test score, expecting him to get upset, but he didn't. My dad asked me if I knew what I did wrong and what the answers were to the questions I had missed. I said yes and told him what the questions were and what the answers were. He then asked me what the answers were to the questions I got right. I could not remember even one of the questions I had gotten right, much less the answers. What he told me next, I have never forgotten, and I try to live my life in this manner. My dad told me that many times in his life, the knowledge he retained the best was the stuff he screwed up first and then went back and figured out what he did wrong. Those instances made more of an impression than being right all the time. He said that being wrong can be a good thing if it causes you to go back, find the answer, and commit it to memory. As I look back after that, I wasn't as afraid to make mistakes, because with each mistake I learned something new. Now, that doesn't mean I like making mistakes; I still want to get it right the first time, but I don't have to be right all the time. Success or failure doesn't define who I am. Even if failure humbles you sometimes, it is only part of the learning process.

It is very much like all these little parables I am writing. I would be happy if even part of what I say makes sense and is right; that is why I try to put so much of God's Word in them. Even if what I say is stupid or wrong, I fully believe that God's Word is truth, and you should be able to find what is right in what is pure and true. I totally identify with Paul when he says in Corinthians 13:8–12, "Love never fails. But where there are prophecies, they will cease; where there are tongues, they will be stilled; where there is knowledge, it will pass away. For we know in part and we prophecy in part, but when perfection comes, the imperfect disappears. When I was a child, I talked like a child, I thought like a child, I reasoned like a child. When I became a man, I put childish ways behind me. Now we see but a poor reflection as in a mirror; then we shall see face to face. Now I know in part; then I shall know fully, even as I am fully known" (NIV). Paul recognized that he didn't know all there was to know. But even if he didn't know everything and wasn't always right, it was more important to love and to know that to love was better than maybe being right. For him to love was the only way to be sure he was right. Churches and even nations are divided because people have to be right. To know the truth is important, but if you show me a man who always has to be right, I'll show you a man that is a prideful, arrogant fool. Philippians 2:1–5 says, "If you have any encouragement from being united with Christ, if any comfort from his love, if any fellowship with the Spirit, if any tenderness and compassion, then make my joy complete by being like-minded, having the same love, being one in spirit and purpose. Do nothing out of selfish ambition of vain conceit, but in humility consider others better than yourselves. Each of you should look not only to your own interests, but also the interests of others. Your attitude should be the same as that of Christ Jesus" (NIV). If we only lived that way, there would be a lot less fighting and feuding.

The last thing people need is probably the most misused and misunderstood. This is, of course, the need to win. Now, you would have been hard-pressed to find someone more competitive than I was growing up. If I did something, it had to be as fast and as hard as I could do it, and I wanted to keep doing it until I won. If I won, I wanted to win by more. I never wanted to stop until I couldn't go anymore. Now, I can't say that the desire to win is all wrong, but I would say that my perspective on winning has changed over the years. When I got a little older, suddenly, winning was if I could hold my own with the young pups. Then after a little longer, winning was if I didn't get totally embarrassed by the youngsters. Now I'm just happy if I can still walk when it's all over. So we have to ask ourselves what winning really is. Paul in 1 Corinthians says this about his walk of faith. "Do you not know that in a race all the runners run, but only one gets the prize? Run in such a way as to get the prize. Everyone who competes in the games goes into strict training. They do it to get a crown that will not last; but we do it to get a crown that will last forever. Therefore I do not run like a man running aimlessly; I do not fight like a man beating the air. No, I beat my body and make it my slave so that after I have preached to others, I myself will not be disqualified for the prize" (1 Cor. 9:24–27 NIV). Paul is talking about training to win a prize, but to win that prize meant beatings, prison, and eventually, death, much like the very one he was serving. We like to think of winning as being successful, popular, and better than the competition. That's not winning in Paul's eyes or God's eyes.

By our standards of winning today, Christ and His followers were total losers. They were killed for something they didn't do, they had nothing, and any praise they received was only fleeting. Today, winning means being better than something or someone, but we can't even claim that if we believe what Solomon says in Ecclesiastes 9:11, "I have seen something else under the sun: The race is not to the swift or the battle to the strong, nor does food come to the wise or wealth to the brilliant or favor to the learned; but time and chance happen to them all" (NIV). But Solomon, right before he made that statement, writes in verse 10, "Whatever your hand finds to do, do it with all your might, for in the grave, where you are going, there is neither working or planning nor knowledge nor wisdom" (NIV). Right before that bleak picture of "We're going to die and the better man doesn't always win," he says, whatever you do, do it with all your might. Now, if winning was most important, then his advice would have been, "If the best man doesn't always win, why bother? Save your energy. Woe is me." But I think he recognized that the most important part was the journey. Doing your best, giving it everything you have, is the reward, not winning. Maybe giving your best is winning.

We like the praise, the adoration, the feeling of being better than someone else. Which in some way makes us proud and bolsters our self-esteem. This tells us how poor our self-esteem is. If we are confident in who we are in Christ, we will be able to lose with joy, knowing that we did all we could do, and if we don't think we did all we could do, then we will look for ways to do it better. We can also, in spite of all our hard work, be the better person and still not win. Yet we can be happy if we have competed to the best of our abilities. I get tired of coaches complaining about the other team running up the score. Personally, I want someone to beat me as bad as they can so I know where I really stand. I prefer to compete against someone much better because it makes me work harder and makes me better. The more humbling the defeat, the more it should spur you on to work harder. Our society hinges our self-worth on our success and the "Look at me, I'm somebody because of what I have accomplished" factor.

I'm somebody because of what Jesus Christ did for me, not because of what I've done. Winning the race is not coming in first; it's how you grow along the way and how you achieve the goal. It's all about accomplishing the purpose you were put here for. Christ won not because He defeated death and conquered the grave; He won because He endured all that He endured to accomplish the purpose that He came for, which was to die for us. That is why He could say in John 19:30, "When he had received the drink, Jesus said, 'It is finished.' With that, he bowed his head and gave up his Spirit" (NIV). "It is finished" was not "I'm defeated and I'm going to die now"; it was "I have completed my mission. I have won." This is one of my favorite passages, and I think it sums up what I want to be about. "Not that I have already obtained all this, or have already been made perfect, but I press on to take hold of that for which Christ Jesus took hold of me. Brothers, I do not consider myself yet to have taken hold of it. But one thing I do: Forgetting what is behind and straining toward what is ahead, I press on toward the goal to win the prize for which God has called me heavenward in Christ Jesus" (Phil. 3:12–14 NIV). So the three things people need are really the Father, the Son, and the Holy Spirit, without whom nothing else works right, anyway. Desire wisdom and knowledge, desire to know the truth, and be right. Desire to win. Just remember, there is God's way and a wrong way. I hope you will achieve the goal and the purpose God has for you.

Love,
Dad

Life's Choices

Today so many people I observe—in fact, most people I observe, including me—don't like to face responsibility for their choices in life. And our legal system seems to encourage the pass-the-buck syndrome. Smokers are awarded millions because they got cancer from smoking even though the label on the package tells of the risk. A woman spills coffee on herself at McDonald's, and the courts award her a big sum of money because she wasn't told it was hot. Now they have a caution label on the cup. Now, the smokers want to blame someone else for the consequences of their choice to smoke, yet the first time they smoked, they coughed, and if they were told to work in an area that had smoke from a fire, they would complain it wasn't healthy. This woman who, if the coffee was cold, would have returned it and expected it to be hot wanted someone else to bear responsibility for her clumsiness. It's nothing new; it started with Adam and Eve in the Garden. "The man said, 'The woman you put here with me—she gave me some fruit from the tree, and I ate it.' Then the Lord God said to the woman, 'What is this you have done?' The woman said, 'The serpent deceived me, and I ate'" (Gen. 3:12–13 NIV). Adam said, "It's Eve's fault because she gave it to me, and it's Your fault, God, because You gave me Eve." Yet in Genesis 3:6 it says, "She also gave some to her husband, who was with her, and he ate it" (NIV). Now, Adam makes it sound like he was nowhere around; she brought him this piece of fruit, and he ate it. Only he was there through the entire encounter, and if anything, he should bear even more responsibility because he knew better yet didn't try to stop her. Eve said, "It's the serpent's fault because he told me to eat it." He deceived her was what she said, yet God had told her not to eat from the tree and she hadn't forgotten it, because she told the serpent what God had said. I know it doesn't say so, but I can imagine the serpent (if he were human) saying, "The devil made me do it." A phrase I've heard so many times in my life time. But somehow, I think the snake was the only one who recognized that he couldn't fool God into believing something else, and bore responsibility for its actions. (Just a thought.)

Anyway, we have to recognize that everything is a choice. If we choose to play with matches and get burned, we actually choose to get burned, because it is a consequence of our choice. If you choose to have sex outside of marriage, whether you get pregnant or get AIDs or not, you choose those things because you choose to take that risk. If you choose to drink then drive, and whether you kill someone or not, you took that risk, and so you choose the worst-case scenario. I have a problem with our legal system because it rewards those who make bad choices and don't get "caught" or get the job done. If you try to kill someone and you're too stupid to get the job done or a really bad shot, you get a lesser sentence than someone who is better at it and actually gets the job done. They both committed the same crime. Their intent was to kill. Because one was successful and one was not doesn't change their choice and intention. If you choose to drive drunk and no one dies, you get a slap on the wrist, a fine, or maybe a suspended license. If twenty-nine children die, you get life without parole or the death penalty. Each committed the same crime, but they were judged on the consequences of the choice, not the choice.

God, however, judges by the choices we make, not the consequences of them. Not just the outward choices people see, but the choices of our hearts that only He sees. "But I tell you that anyone who looks at a woman lustfully has already committed adultery with her in his heart" (Matt. 5:28 NIV). The church, friends, and family are all often basing their thoughts of you by what they see, not what your heart is. Isn't it great that God sees your heart, not the consequences of your choices? "All a man's ways seem right to him, but the Lord weighs the heart" (Prov. 21:2 NIV). We know we are going to make bad choices. "We all stumble in many ways. If anyone is never at fault in what he says, he is a perfect man, able to keep his whole body in check" (James 3:2 NIV). We need to be careful to consider not only the consequences we are choosing and take responsibility for them but also consider what God sees in our heart. Remember, God gives us a choice to accept His salvation, follow Him and live forever or ignore Him, follow your own way, whatever that may be, and face eternal torment. Now, people say a loving God won't send them to hell, and they're right. He died to get them out, but they have a choice, and if they choose not to believe, then they choose the worst-case scenario, which is hell. That might seem to be an either-or situation, and we all have a tendency to say that's not a choice. We want lots of options with varying degrees of consequences, but God's not like that, and we shouldn't be either. Always consider the worst imaginable consequence as the only consequence of your choice, and it will make the right choice much easier to choose. Ever since I heard the song "Get Over It" by the Eagles, I've felt it says something we need to hear. I'm going to quote the song's lyrics. It might offend the sensibilities of some, but I'll risk it, because it says something about our society and its condition, and I think we need to hear it and heed it. So here it is:

"Get Over It"
by the Eagles

I turn on the tube and what do I see
A whole lotta people cryin', "Don't blame me"
They point their crooked little fingers at everybody else
Spend all their time feelin' sorry for themselves
Victim of this, victim of that
Your momma's to thin, your daddy's too fat
Get over it
Get over it
All this whinin' and cryin' and pitchin' a fit
Get over it, Get over it

You say you haven't been the same since you had your little crash
But you might feel better if I gave you come cash
The more I think about it, Old Billy was right
Let's kill all the lawyers, kill 'em tonight

You don't want to work, you want to live like a king

But the big, bad world doesn't owe you
a thing

Get over it
Get over it
If you don't want to play, then you might
as well split
Get over it, Get over it

It's like going to confession every time I
hear you speak
You're makin' the most of your losin'
streak
Some call it sick, I call it weak
You drag it around like a ball and chain
You wallow in the guilt, you wallow in
the pain
You wave it like a flag, you wear it like a
crown
Got your mind in the gutter, bringin'
everybody down
Complain about the present and blame
it on the past
I'd like to find your inner child and kick
its little ass
Get over it
Get over it
All this bitchin' and moanin' and pitchin'
a fit
Get over it, Get over it
Get over it
Get over it

It's gotta stop sometime, so why don't
you quit
Get over it, Get over it

We have become a society that somehow thinks we
are entitled to the good life. That our country and our God
somehow owe us wealth and happiness. We forget that our
freedom only guarantees us the opportunity to pursue happiness and God without fear of government interference.
People who lose loved ones sue to try to get money, as if that
will make them happy and make the pain go away. People
who lose everything in tragedy sit around and whine, wanting someone to come around and fix it for them. Now, don't
get me wrong; I am all for helping people. But if someone is
not willing to help themselves, then they just want a handout.
I see people pitching in and working together to weather a
storm, then rebuild. Then I see others who, when bad things
happen, use it as an excuse to plunder, destroy, and even
kill their neighbors, then sit around, waiting for someone
to rebuild and give them money. They don't want to actually do anything themselves. We have government officials
who promise the moon to get these votes but don't plan on
keeping any of them. Many things like economy, prejudice,
fairness can't be changed through the government, because
they require people's attitudes to change. For example, the
economy can be temporarily improved if the government
cuts taxes, which gives people a little more money to spend,
putting a little more money in the economy. But as long as
CEOs and heads of corporations continue to cut pay, move
jobs to China, and take huge salaries, all the money will eventually wind up in the hands of a few and not in the economy.
Their greed for more eventually will kill the economy and
their source of revenue. But their allegiance lies with their

bank accounts, not their country or their employees. I have to say that today in our country, we look out for number one. We are a self-centered society that seeks self-gratification above all else.

If we follow God, then we, above all, should be modeling Christ, which is not at all what I see today. "Your attitude should be the same as that of Christ Jesus: Who, being in very nature God, did not consider equality with God something to be grasped, but made himself nothing, taking the very nature of a servant, being made in human likeness. And being found in appearance as a man, he humbled himself and became obedient to death—even death on a cross" (Phil. 2:5–8 NIV). Following God is a choice, and so is how we live our lives. I hear people saying, "You made me mad" or "I had to do this because you said this or that," then I realize I'm guilty of the same response. When things get bad and don't work out the way they should, or the way we think they should, when life doesn't seem fair, we respond in really ugly ways. It is our nature. It's wrong, but it's what we naturally lean toward. To not respond in anger or spite is a choice. It is also a choice to be happy or sad. We can wallow in pain, or we can choose to see the good God is working and be happy. It is all a choice.

Caleb is a good example of a man who chose to stay upbeat even though he endured forty years of waiting because of others' unfaithfulness. "Now the men of Judah approached Joshua at Gilgal, and Caleb son of Jephunneh the Kennizzite said to him, 'You know what the Lord said to Moses the man of God at Kadesh Barnea about you and me. I was forty years old when Moses the servant of the Lord sent me from Kadesh Barnea to explore the land. And I brought him back a report according to my convictions, but my brothers who went up with me made the hearts of the people melt with fear. I however, followed the Lord my God wholeheartedly. So on that day Moses swore to me, "The land on which your feet have walked will be your inheritance and that of your children forever, because you have followed the Lord my God wholeheartedly." Now then, just as the Lord promised, he has kept me alive for forty-five years since the time he said this to Moses, while Israel moved about in the desert. So here I am today, eighty-five years old! I am still as strong today as the day Moses sent me out; I'm just as vigorous to go out to battle now as I was then. Now give me this hill country that the Lord promised me that day. You yourself heard then that the Anakites were there and their cities were large and fortified, but, the Lord helping me, I will drive them out just as he said.' Then Joshua blessed Caleb son of Jephunneh and gave him Hebron as his inheritance. So Hebron has belonged to Caleb son of Jephunneh the Kenizzite ever since, because he followed the Lord, the God of Israel, wholeheartedly" (Josh. 14:6–14 NIV). Caleb wasn't whining about the fact that he was wandering for forty years because someone else wouldn't trust God. He must have spent all his time preparing for the time when it would finally happen. He believed if God gave them the land, they could not be stopped, no matter what the obstacle, and that it would happen no matter how long it took. Here is a man who watched all his peers die in the desert, except for Joshua. He apparently was training, because he said he was as strong as he was when he was forty.

He also never gave up on his dream, his belief that God was going to give them the land, because he was as pumped up about going to fight and take it as he was when he first saw the land. This guy had spunk; he wasn't asking for a land that was easier to get than the other areas, he was asking for the very best land, the best of the best. It also was going to be the hardest to take, because in those days the best land was occupied by the strongest people. This was no exception. In Numbers 13 and 14, it says that this land was a land where giants lived in fortified cities. He asked for the best, fully knowing that it was also going to require the most faith, commitment, dedication, and hard work to conquer. I love this guy. He was God's stud even at eighty-five, and I hope I have half the passion and determination now as he had at eighty-five. But even that is a choice. We can choose to follow God with passion and zeal, or we can sit around and whine—it is our choice. I hope you will determine to make every effort to make the right choices in life. "Now fear the Lord and serve him with all faithfulness. Throw away the gods your forefathers worshiped beyond the River and in Egypt, and serve the Lord. But if serving the Lord seems undesirable to you, then choose for yourselves this day whom you will serve, whether the gods your forefathers served beyond the River, or the gods of the Amorites, in whose land you are living. But as for me and my household, we will serve the Lord" (Josh. 24:14–15 NIV). Joshua knew what the most important choice in life was, and that choice affects every other choice we make from then on. We make choices every day in life. I hope you choose wisely.

Love,
Dad

When Dreams Die

The other day, on my way to work, going down the highway, I saw a strange and kind of unusual sight. It was a windy October morning, and all of a sudden, about eight tumbleweeds bounced across the road about half a mile ahead of me. Now, seeing tumbleweeds on a windy day in the Midwest is not unusual, but these tumbleweeds were all together and bounced along as if they were a herd of deer or something. They stayed close together across the road, through the ditch, and all the way up to a fence. Then, as if they were jumping the fence, they each, one after another, bounced over the fence and continued across the field. As I drove on to work, I couldn't help but keep thinking about how beautiful and how alive those tumbleweeds were or at least seemed to be. I never in my wildest dreams ever thought I would see them as anything but a stupid weed. Then, it also dawned on me that no matter how beautiful they seemed, the entire time they were bouncing along, they were scattering the seeds to grow more of those obnoxious weeds. Now, that should have been the end of it, but I guess God wanted me to get an object lesson out of it, because it just stuck in mind and wouldn't go away until I realized the following. They were free to go wherever the wind took them because they were dead. Not only did they have to dry up and die, but they also had to be broken off to free them from the roots that held them in place. In the same way, all my life I had dreams of playing sports professionally or, if that didn't work, maybe a rock star or artist.

Never once did I dream of fixing things or of writing. It wasn't part of my dream. I was like that tumbleweed; I had lots of life, and my dreams had lots of life. I thought my dreams were God's dreams for my life, and though they might have been in some areas, there was way too much of me and not enough of Him in my dreams. I was like the weed when it was all green, growing bigger and stronger, and, if weeds can think, thinking that I was going to change the world. My roots grew deeper, and the stem that grounded me grew fatter and stronger. It's funny how, in a way, we begin to think that God is just pretty lucky to get someone so grounded and focused. Then, all of a sudden, it seemed like nothing I did worked, everything I touched turned to crap, and everything I thought I was good at fell by the wayside. Even the good things I did were viewed as crap by those around me. Like the weed dying in fall, it really felt like all my dreams were dying, so I tried harder and got angry with God for toying with me. Surely, if He didn't see my life turning out the way I saw it, then He hated me, or at the very least, He didn't see how much I could do for Him if He just did it my way. God was in the process of killing my dreams because they were my dreams, not His. My kids, my wife, my family, my job, it was all mine, and everything had to fall apart and all my preconceived notions, as well as my dreams, had to die.

But the cool thing is, as everything was dying, all the hard things happening in my life were leaving seeds. Things that could be passed on to you and others that wouldn't have happened if God hadn't let my dreams die. He also broke me off at the stem that rooted me in the one place I felt at home and comfortable. And I now see his Spirit, like the wind, is blowing me to places I never dreamed, allowing me to share things I'd never known, if my dreams hadn't died. Jesus said the same thing twice to his disciples, once in Matthew 10:37–39, and also in Matthew 16:24–26, so it must be important. This is Matthew 16:24–26: "Then Jesus said to his disciples, 'If anyone would come after me, he must deny himself and take up his cross and follow me. For whoever wants to save his life will lose it, but whoever loses his life for me will find it. What good will it be for a man if he gains the whole world, yet forfeits his soul? Or what can a man give in exchange for his soul?'" (NIV).

It is amazing how tightly we hold on to things that don't really make a difference in eternity. It is like God has to kill us, then pry our dreams out of our hands, so He can give us something better to share with the world. Today I finally realize that sometimes dreams have to die for us to experience the best things in life. To recognize that God's plan isn't always my dream and that His plan is always far better. I'm sure if we would learn to hold on to things more loosely, it would be easier for God to transform us into who He wants us to be. "Therefore, if anyone is in Christ, he is a new creation; the old has gone, the new has come" (2 Cor. 5:17 NIV). It is important to remember that the new in us is not always what we envisioned, because we still many times view our life from the old. When dreams die, it is usually a rough time, so it is also important to remember God's promises. "But now this is what the Lord says—he who created you, O Jacob, he who formed you, O Israel: 'Fear not, for I have redeemed you; I have summoned you by name; you are mine. When you pass through the waters, I will be with you; and when you pass through the rivers, they will not sweep over you. When you walk through the fire, you will not be burned; the flames will not set you ablaze'" (Isa. 43:1–2 NIV).

We really can't spread God's seed until we're dead and broken, so don't worry about what you seem to be losing, but look forward to what God's going to be doing and know that He is with you. "'For I know the plans I have for you,' declares the Lord, 'plans to prosper you and not to harm you, plans to give you hope and a future'" (Jer. 29:11 NIV). Too many times we pursue our dreams and not God. If we pursue God, then the rest will fall in line and we will find ourselves being thrilled that things didn't work out the way we planned. "But seek first his kingdom and his righteousness, and all these things will be given to you as well" (Matt. 6:33 NIV). Sometimes God even asks us to give up things He has promised us to see if He is more important to us than the promise. Abraham was promised he would be the father of many nations by God and only received a son when he was a hundred years old. The fact that he had to wait until he was a hundred years old wasn't enough. In Genesis 22, God tells Abraham to sacrifice his promised son, and he prepares to do what God has asked. "Then he reached out his hand and took the knife to slay his son. But the angel of the Lord called out to him from heaven, 'Abraham! Abraham!' 'Here I am,' he replied. 'Do not lay a hand on the boy,' he said. 'Do not do anything to him. Now I know that you fear God, because you have not withheld from me your son, your only son'" (Gen. 22:10–13 NIV). Whether it's His promise or your dreams, God wants to know that you choose him above all else. So hold on to your dreams loosely and hold on tight to God. Oh, and while you're at it, go ahead a try to enjoy the ride.

Love,
Dad

Value

On the radio the other day at work, I heard the DJs of a radio station talk show talking about the gunmen of the Columbine High School shooting. They referred to them as animals and psychos, dirt, and worthless scum. Then said that the other kids were better than that. Heroes, upstanding young people, and that we were all proud of them. Now, what made them think they were better than them? Because right after that, they started talking and making jokes about things that were just plain dirty in my eyes, and somehow that was okay. What they don't seem to realize is that we are all caught in the grip of sin and that we all crawled out of the same cesspool of humanity. "All of us have become like one who is unclean, and all of our righteous acts are like filthy rags; we all shrivel up like a leaf, and like the wind our sins sweep us away. No one calls on your name or strives to lay hold of you; for you have hidden your face from us and made us waste away because of our sins" (Isa. 64:6–7 NIV). Those boys and the men on the radio were in the same boat even though the DJs thought they were better. They thought they were better because they didn't shoot anyone and maybe helped a charity or two, but neither the boys nor the DJs had done anything that God would consider clean. They were all filthy and consumed in their sin, and God can only look on what is clean. "This righteousness from God comes through faith in Jesus Christ to all who believe. This is no difference, for all have sinned and fall short of the glory of God, and are justified freely by his grace through the redemption that came by Jesus Christ" (Rom. 3:22–23 NIV). "For the wages of sin is death, but the gift of God is eternal life in Christ Jesus our Lord" (Rom. 6:23 NIV).

I am reminded of hearing about a collector who paid millions upon millions to purchase the oldest piece of cheese thought to be in existence. Now, as for me, if he offered me that piece of cheese or a fresh one from the supermarket, I would pay more for the one I would eat. No way would I put that old piece of cheese in my mouth. I would view that cheese as a smelly piece of garbage and would never recognize the value that that one collector saw in it. If another person didn't like cheese at all, he would consider all cheese worthless. It depends on your perspective. God paid an enormous price for each one of us caught in this cesspool of humanity. Now, we like to give ourselves more value by looking down on the next guy in an attempt to make ourselves feel better about ourselves. The only problem is, dung is dung, no matter how you slice it, dice it, or package it. We all reek of sin, and it all smells the same to God. I'm so thankful God, in His mercy, could get beyond the smell and see the value in me and pay such a great price to purchase me and give me value. Because it's not us that makes us of great value; it is the price He paid that makes us of great value.

When I was young, there were times kids made fun of me because I wore jeans with patches on the knees and anywhere else that I managed to put holes in them. We were too poor to replace them if they could be fixed at all. So my mom would try to find little patches that looked like they were meant to be there so I didn't get made fun of so much. I always remember her telling me what her mother told her. She would say, "Your grandma always used to say it's not a shame to be poor, but it's a shame to be dirty." Now, I never fully appreciated that statement until now. I believe what my grandmother and mother were saying was that you are able to wash or clean what you have, even if you don't have much. We were able to keep ourselves clean, so if we didn't, it would have been shameful. We didn't have to be ashamed of being poor, because it was all that my dad was paid to preach. Today, what I learned from being poor actually makes me glad that we were poor. But that is not the most significant part of what was being said. We are all spiritually dirty, and we have a way to be clean. We don't have to know a lot about the Bible, and we don't have to be good or rich; all we need is faith in Jesus Christ. "Therefore, there is now no condemnation for those who are in Christ Jesus, because through Christ Jesus the law of the Spirit of life set me free from the law of sin and death" (Rom. 8:1–2 NIV). It is so easy, when you see others who don't seem to stack up to your standards, to forget that we all crawled from the same hole in the ground.

It is a shame if they are dirty; even though our world views them as okay or as trash, it shouldn't hide the true shame of living life without Christ. If we know what it takes to be clean and we don't let them know the shame rests with us, if we let them know and they reject it, then the shame of being dirty is theirs. "Son of man, I have made you a watchman for the house of Israel; so hear the word I speak and give them warning from me. When I say to the wicked man, 'O wicked man, you will surely die,' and you do not speak out to dissuade him from his ways, that wicked man will die for his sin, and I will hold you accountable for his blood. But if you do warn the wicked man to turn from his ways and he does not do so, he will die for his sin, but you will have saved yourself" (Ezek. 33:7–9 NIV). We received a great gift through Christ, but with it comes a tremendous responsibility. "But the one who does not know and does things deserving punishment will be beaten with few blows. From everyone who has been given much, much will be demanded; and from the one who has been entrusted with much, much more will be asked" (Luke 12:48 NIV). We all have a tendency to look at others and value them by what we feel is clean. We all view others from a perspective that makes us feel better about ourselves. If it is easy for us not to do certain things we feel are wrong or do something that we feel is right, then that is what becomes our measuring stick for others.

We rarely value people in a way that makes us feel like we are not measuring up. We like to look down on people, and if you can't look down on them, it's our nature to try to put them down in an effort to build ourselves up. We all come from the same place, and all that makes us clean and brings us value is Christ. "But because of his great love for us, God, who is rich in mercy, made us alive with Christ even when we were dead in transgressions—it is by grace you have been saved. And God raised us up with Christ and seated us with him in the heavenly realms in Christ Jesus, in order that in the coming ages he might show the incomparable riches of his grace, expressed in his kindness to us in Christ Jesus. For it is by grace you have been saved, through faith—and this not from yourselves, it is the gift of God—not by works, so that no one can boast. For we are God's workmanship, created in Christ Jesus to do good works, which God prepared in advance for us to do" (Eph. 2:4–9 NIV). We need to value people as highly as God does, and remember, to value something is to want to see it the best it can be. Nothing is the best it can be or what it should be if it is dirty, so strive to see what God values most clean before Him.

Love,
Dad

Waiting on Wings

When I was in the fifth grade, I remember one day it was pouring rain and blowing hard at lunchtime. My brothers and I were supposed to go home for lunch, so my parents came to pick us up. Now, my dad came wearing a raincoat so he could ride my new ten-speed bike home for me. He knew how important that bike was to me. I had delivered a lot of newspapers and mowed a lot of lawns to earn the money for that bike. So he hopped on the bike and rode ahead of us, and we followed with Mom in the car. He was riding really fast, so I watched the speedometer in the car, twenty miles per hour. Then he turned the corner on a long stretch of road with the wind at his back, and he did something that really shocked me. He let go of the handlebars, opened his raincoat, and with his hands, grabbed the bottom of the coat, spread his arms out on each side, holding it out as far as he could reach so the wind caught his coat like a sail. And when I looked at the speedometer again, we were going almost forty miles per hour. When he got near the end of the street, he pulled his coat back down and finished riding the short distance left home. I think we made it home faster than we ever had. Looking back on that day reminds me of Isaiah 40:29–31, "He gives strength to the weary, and increases the power of the weak. Even youths grow tired and weary, and young men stumble and fall; but those who hope in the Lord will renew their strength. They will soar on wings like eagles; they will run and not grow weary, they will walk and not be faint" (NIV). The King James Version says, "Those who wait on the Lord," instead of *hope*, but both imply something that will come later, not something present immediately.

We always like to read about the new strength, but we don't give much thought to the wait. I think to wait on the Lord is like my dad opening his coat. We might get wet, but why pedal for all you're worth when we could get where we are going much faster by just opening our coat and letting the power behind us push us there? To mount wings as eagles means we are like an eagle who rides the wind currents, waiting and allowing God to propel us along. I think we get weary because, when we should be waiting on God, we're running in circles. And when God is ready for us to go, we've worn ourselves out trying to push God ahead at our speed, in our time, instead of letting God push us ahead at His speed and in His time. Instead of running in circles, wait on God. He'll get you there faster than you ever could by yourself, and you'll have energy to spare.

Spreading your wings leaves you vulnerable, but you can't soar if you don't. We call it faith, and we all like to think that we have enough faith and that we trust God, but we don't, or we would see more of God's power in our lives. This is what Christ said to His disciples when they tried to cast out a demon and couldn't, and then He did. "Then the disciples came to Jesus in private and asked, 'Why couldn't we drive it out?' He replied, 'Because you have so little faith. I tell you the truth, if you have faith as small as mustard seed, you can say to this mountain, "Move from here to there" and it will move. Nothing will be impossible for you'" (Matt. 17:19–20 NIV). Some manuscripts go on in verse 21 to say,

"But this kind does not go out except by prayer and fasting." Faith isn't something that comes unless you are spending a lot of time talking to God. To spend a lot of time talking to God also means you're waiting for answers, that you're actively seeking to hear what He is saying and see and understand where He is leading. It means you're waiting on God and His timing and purpose. Sooner or later, we have to take the risk involved in waiting on God. We have to be ready to do what God is asking even if it seems totally stupid to us. We have to look at Abraham, who was willing to do what God asked even when it seemed totally wrong and foolish, and God rewarded him for it. "So do not throw away your confidence; it will be richly rewarded. You need to persevere so that when you have done the will of God, you will receive what he has promised" (Heb. 10:35–36 NIV). That means sometimes we have to follow God over the cliff if we ever want to get our wings and soar with the eagles.

Love,
Dad

Faithful Forever

I was talking to an FCA leader just back from a Weekend of Champions. He was so excited as he told of how several members of his group gave their hearts to the Lord and how they stood up and told the whole group of their decision the last day at a time called open mic. A time when kids were allowed to go onstage and tell what God had done for them. Then his tone changed. You could see what he was going to say made a real impact on him. He told me of a girl who went to the microphone and, in tears, made this simple but profound statement. She said, "Last year, when I came here, I was a virgin and planned to wait until I was married, but this last year, I gave in and I'm no longer a virgin. I'm here to tell you all, whatever you do, don't give up, because if you're still a virgin, you have what I can never get back. I can never again be like you, but you can always be like me." The truth of that statement struck me hard after the miserable way Doreen and I started out having done pretty much everything wrong. And the only thing I could tell that man is, I guess there can only be one first time.

I thought about what she had said a lot during the next week and how much I regretted my past and that I was unable to offer that gift of the first time to the woman I loved so dearly now. It is never a guarantee that even if you wait, your spouse will do the same, but in life it is not about what others can offer you but what you can offer them. Too many marriages start with both people trying to get something they think they need or trying to fill a hole or something that is missing in their lives. I think it is important to come to a place where you are okay with yourself and that God is the one meeting your needs before you can even begin to consider a relationship with someone else. When you come to that point in life, then your relationship is built on "What can I do for you and how can I meet your needs?" and not "What are you doing for me or someone meet my needs?"

There truly can only be one first time, and that is a beautiful thing to give to someone, but you can never know if that someone is the one until there is a commitment made in marriage. If someone is not committed enough to take a vow that there will be no other until death parts you, then you should not waste the most beautiful thing you have to offer on them. I have often thought that sex is sort of like pie. We are all given a pie that is sweet and beautiful, but there is only one. Now, every time you give a piece away, you give away a piece of yourself that you can't get back. The more people who try your pie, the less you have to give to the one you are going to spend the rest of your life with, and the less special it is, because something isn't as special if lots of people have had the same thing. Also, once you find someone, you and they will have a tendency to be naturally jealous, because they realize someone has been taking what should have been theirs and theirs alone.

The world seems to want to trivialize the seriousness of this, and the church, as a whole, is not being honest with their kids. On one hand, you have churches who make it sound as if body parts will fall off if you get caught in this sin or that God will destroy you with fire. Then kids see their friends doing it with seemingly no ill effect and see no reason for not doing it. On the other side, you have churches that seemingly approve and disapprove at the same time. This is totally confusing. The first time I ever experienced this was when we had some high-school-age kids coming over for supper and then we would talk about things after supper every Wednesday night. One night, some of the girls told us that they had gone to one of their church's youth groups and that they had been talking about sex and how to protect themselves, so they showed all the girls how to put condoms on a banana. Now, I asked immediately why they would do that, because it seemed to me they were condoning sex outside of marriage. The girls told me that the leaders had told them that they should wait, but if they chose not to wait, then they should at least be safe. To this my response was, "First of all, did they tell you that condoms cannot 100 percent protect you from getting pregnant or a disease?" They told me they had not, so then I asked them if they had shown them a condom for their minds.

They were totally confused, so I explained that the greatest part of sex, the most intimate thing that happens during sex, is emotional, and for that there is no protection. The more partners you have, the more you begin to insulate yourself from the emotional, because when it's over between the two, it hurts too much. Even those who insulate themselves to the point of just going through the motions and think they are just acting on urges can never fully stop these feelings. Feelings of being used or of feeling dirty. And at the very least, they have to keep trying something new to keep it exciting because they feel unfulfilled. They will never find the fulfillment they desire. That comes from two people in a marriage sharing something more intimate, emotionally and physically, than is ever possible in any other context. And every time you give yourself away, a part of you emotionally is also gone. "For this reason a man will leave his father and mother and be united to his wife, and they will become one flesh" (Gen. 2:24 NIV). That's pretty close. We know that we don't have the same body, so I think it's a deep emotional connection that actually makes us one flesh and an intimate part of each other. Paul expands on this when he talks of sexual impurity. "'Everything is permissible for me'—but not everything is beneficial. 'Everything is permissible for me'—but I will not be mastered by anything. 'Food for the stomach and the stomach for food'—but God will destroy them both. The body is not meant for sexual immorality, but for the Lord, and the Lord for the body. By his power God raised the Lord from the dead, and he will raise us also. Do you not know that your bodies are members of Christ himself? Shall I then take the members of Christ and unite them with a prostitute? Never! Do you not know that he who unites himself with a prostitute is one with her in body? For it is said, 'The two will become one flesh.' But he who unites himself with the Lord is one with him in spirit. Flee from sexual immorality. All other sins a man commits are outside his body, but he who sins sexually sins against his own body. Do you not know that your body is a temple of the Holy Spirit, who is in you, whom you have received from God? You are not your own, you were bought at a price. Therefore honor God with your body" (1 Cor. 6:12–20 NIV). How can we participate in something of that magnitude and not think that it will have a lasting effect on us?

Now, God is a God of restoration, and I believe that you can still, through His grace and mercy, share in a godly relationship from which you can find love and fulfillment. But there are certain things in those relationships that are gone forever, and the effects from them will never go away. It's sort of like when Adam and Eve sinned, God still loved them and made a way for them to be restored to Him, but Adam now had to deal with weeds and work much harder to survive. Eve, on what was the most beautiful day of a woman's life (having a child), was going to have to endure great pain. They both lost the intimacy they had achieved with God and had to settle for something far less intimate. Speaking from experience, not waiting makes the marriage experience much more difficult. Doreen and I are only together today because of the grace of God and the sheer fact that we are both incredibly stubborn.

Only you kids can truly know how volatile our marriage has been; we have both given each other plenty of good reasons to leave, yet we are still together. Doreen is, without doubt, God's greatest gift to me, and yet we continue to hurt each other with our past sins and how they affect our everyday lives. A few minutes of passing pleasure were not worth the price we now pay, and I hope that you will not make the same mistakes we did, and if you do, don't compound it by continuing in them. I hope you will offer something to your spouse I was unable to give to my wife. Remember, you can only control what you do and not your spouse or future spouse. I believe that if for some reason your spouse was not or even is not faithful to you, and even if they desert you, because you were faithful when they were not, you now carry and share the very scars Christ carries for you. I believe God not only honors, that He rewards and blesses that. I gave you both dog tags one Christmas as a way to challenge you to remain faithful to your spouse long before you ever knew who they were. Here was my reasoning for this and the note I gave you with the tags:

> *In the military, each soldier is given an*
> *identification number printed on metal*

tags along with his name and rank, commonly known as dog tags. They are for identifying his body if anything ever happens to him. Tags show that his body belongs to the United States of America, and the government then takes his identification number and finds the family that the body belongs to. These tags symbolize you giving God control over your body until the day that He finds that special someone for you to love and that loves you and you die to yourself and give your body to His control and then to your spouse when you get married. Only when you have given yourself to someone else in marriage should your tags be given to another. It also is a commitment to God and that person even before you know who they are.

Also, if soldiers were ever tempted to betray their country or their families, they would resort to only giving their name, rank, and serial number. All they were doing was reciting their tags. On your tags are four scriptures that you should memorize and recite anytime you are tempted to betray yourself, your future spouse, or God. Below your name are two scriptures, the first is Ecclesiastes 5:4–5, which is to remind you how important your commitment is, and the second is 1 Thessalonians 4:3–4, which states why you should be committed to this. On the second tag are the words "Faithful Forever," which empha-

size your faithfulness to that special some-one even if you don't know who it is, and also God's faithfulness to you and His willingness to always help you withstand the temptations that come your way. The two scriptures below, 1 Corinthians 10:13 and 2 Thessalonians 3:3, are reminders of God's promise and commitment to you. These are those four verses:

Your promise. "So when you talk to God and vow to him that you will do something, don't delay in doing it, for God has no pleasure in fools. Keep your promise to Him. It is far better not to say you'll do something than say you will and then not do it" (Eccles. 5:4–5).

Why you should make this vow. "For God wants you to be holy and pure and to keep clear of all sexual sin so that each of you will marry in holiness and honor" (1 Thess. 4:3–4).

God's promise and faithfulness to you. "But remember this—the wrong desires that come into your life aren't anything new and different. Many others have faced exactly the same problems before you. And no temptation is irresistible. You can trust God to keep the temptation from becoming so strong that you can't stand up against it for he has promised this and will do what he says. He will show you how to escape temptation's power so that you can bear up patiently against it" (1 Cor. 10:13).

You are so important He made the promise again. "But the Lord is faithful; he will make you strong and guard you from satanic attacks of every kind" (2 Thess. 3:3).

These verses are from the Living Bible Translation, but you should memorize them in the translation you feel most comfortable with.

Love,
Dad

A Dog's Day

In this day and age, I hear many so-called authorities on sex tell teenagers in no uncertain terms that they can't be expected to wait for marriage, that their libidos are too strong. That they should act on their urges, and if they don't, something is wrong with them. But then they say that if the girl says no, then they should stop. This is totally confusing, because they say you can't control this but then they say that in certain circumstances you have to exercise self-control. Which is it? You can't have it both ways. Basically, they are saying you're no different than a dog. You get the urge, then you should act on it. But this morning, as I looked out the kitchen window, I saw three dogs all curled up together to keep warm, and it reminded me of what Solomon said. "Two are better than one, because they have a good return for their work; If one falls down, his friend can help him up. But pity the man who falls and has no one to help him up! Also, if two lie down together, they will keep warm. But how can one keep warm alone? Though one may be overpowered, two can defend themselves. A cord of three stands is not quickly broken" (Eccles. 4:9–12 NIV). The dogs knew that they would stay warm if they slept together. There was nothing in their closeness that was being thought of as sexual, and I realized what we have been told by society is not that we are like dogs but that we are dumber than dogs.

We cannot be expected to care for, love, or desire one's friendship without there being some kind of sexual overtones. If a girl and a guy like being together, then they should have sex. If two guys or two women enjoy one another's company, then they must have gay tendencies. We cannot seem to distinguish between love and lust and have so consumed ourselves with sex and lust that we put ourselves on an island by ourselves, only venturing off when we think we need sex. Anytime we begin to establish the emotional ties we need to uplift, support, and keep us secure, we have a tendency to begin following society's call that says it must culminate in some sexual experience, making us far dumber than the animal that God put in subjection under us. "God blessed them and said to them, 'Be fruitful and increase in number; fill the earth and subdue it. Rule over the fish of the sea and the birds of the air and over every living creature that moves on the ground'" (Gen. 1:28 NIV). So don't allow society to push you into their degrading mold. You were created in the image of a holy, awesome God. Be sure to act that way. Don't fear close relationships; just keep them in God's perspective. They are meant to make you wiser and stronger, not dumber and weaker than dogs.

Now, the church has not been much better. They focus on these as the ultimate sins and, to some degree, abhor not only the sin but also those who struggle with these sins. Yet the sin we look at is the result of something deeper, if not actually God's punishment. We should pity those in these sexual sins because it is God's punishment for denying God His proper place. That is the reason that people deep in things like homosexuality have to have everyone's approval. If you disagree and say that it is wrong, it is a hate crime, yet the very lifestyle is demeaning and harmful. If their life-style were so right, they would be confident enough that it wouldn't matter what people thought. Their argument is that some zealots have killed gays, and that is true, but there will always be people who do things out of hate. People care if they try to stop someone from smoking because it is harmful to their health, yet if someone believes that someone's sexual lifestyle is harmful to them and disagree with it, then somehow they are hateful. The world deep down knows the truth yet chooses to deny it and will continue to resist anyone who disagrees with them, but the church as a whole needs to change its focus. We cannot approve of this sin, but we also need to recognize that it is ultimately not that particular sin God is concerned with. These sins are their punishment; denying him is the root of their sin.

"The wrath of God is being revealed from heaven against all the godlessness and wickedness of men who suppress the truth by their wickedness, since what may be known about God is plain to them, because God has made it plain to them. For since the creation of the world God's invisible qualities—his eternal power and divine nature—have been clearly seen, being understood from what has been made, so that men are without excuse. For although they knew God they neither glorified him as God nor gave thanks to him, but their thinking became futile and their foolish hearts were darkened. Although they claimed to be wise, they became fools and exchanged the glory of the immortal God for images made to look like mortal man and birds and animals and reptiles. Therefore God gave them over in the sinful desires of their hearts to sexual impurity for the degrading of their bodies with one another. They exchanged the truth of God for a lie, and worshiped and served created things rather than the Creator—who is forever praised. Amen. Because of this,

God gave them over to shameful lusts. Even their women exchanged natural relations for unnatural ones. In the same way men also abandoned natural relations with women and were inflamed with lust for one another. Men committed indecent acts with other men, and received in themselves the due penalty for their perversion. Furthermore, since they did not think it worthwhile to retain the knowledge of God, he gave them over to a depraved mind, to do what ought not be done. They have become filled with every kind of wickedness, evil, greed and depravity. They are full of envy, murder, strife, deceit and malice. They are gossips, slanderers, God—haters, insolent, arrogant and boastful; they invent ways of doing evil; they disobey their parents; they are senseless, faithless, heartless, ruthless. Although they know God's righteous decree that those who do such things deserve death, they not only continue to do these very things but also approve of those who practice them" (Rom. 1:18–32 NIV).

Three times it says God gave them over to these sins, so I guess, in a way, when they say God made them that way, they may be partially right. But they initiated the process by denying God. But as I read that passage, it is hard for me to distinguish where the world ends and the church begins. The lines have been blurred. How many believers voted for presidents knowing that their moral character was in question and, in doing, so approved of things that deny the God they supposedly serve? We are punishing ourselves! Instead of casting stones, we need to be sure that we are acknowledging God the way we should. We cannot approve of a life that denies God, but we first must be certain that our lives don't deny Him as well. "You, therefore have no excuse, you who pass judgment on someone else, for at whatever point you judge the other you are condemning yourself, because you who pass judgment do the same things. Now we know that

God's judgment against those who do such things is based on truth. So when you, a mere man, pass judgment on them and yet do the same things, do you think you will escape God's judgment? Or do you show contempt for the riches of his kindness, tolerance and patience, not realizing that God's kindness leads you toward repentance" (Rom. 2:1–4 NIV).

Our job as followers of Christ is not to figure out who did what wrong but to demonstrate His love to others, for it is His kindness that leads others to repentance, not judgment. We can keep ourselves in check by making Him a part of our every action. "Trust in the Lord with all your heart and lean not on your own understanding; in all your ways acknowledge him, and he will make your paths straight" (Prov. 3:5–6 NIV). Jesus gave the church His example of how to deal with sin in John 8:3–11, "The teachers of the law and the Pharisees brought in a woman caught in adultery. They made her stand before the group and said to Jesus, 'Teacher, this woman was caught in the act of adultery. In the law Moses commanded us to stone such women. Now what do you say?' They were using this question as a trap, in order to have a basis for accusing him. But Jesus bent down and started to write on the ground with his finger. When they kept on questioning him, he straightened up and said to them, 'If any one of you is without sin, let him be the first to throw a stone at her.' Again he stooped down and wrote on the ground. At this, those who heard began to go away one at a time, the older ones first, until only Jesus was left, with the woman still standing there. Jesus straightened up and asked her, 'Woman, where are they? Has no one condemned you?' 'No one, sir,' she said. 'Then neither do I condemn you,' Jesus declared. 'Go now and leave your life of sin'" (NIV). Jesus must have been writing down the sins of each man, and that was why they left. And if Christ, who was perfect, did not condemn her, then who are we to condemn anyone? Jesus did not condone her lifestyle, because He told her to go and quit sinning, but He did not condemn her. Jesus does not have to condemn us. We are condemned already, and we all know it. Jesus is all about saving us and directing us in a life that is free of sin. Jesus said in John 12:47–49, "As for the person who hears my words but does not keep them, I do not judge him. For I did not come to judge the world but to save it. There is a judge for the one who rejects me and does not accept my words; that very word which I spoke will condemn him at the last day. For I did not speak of my own accord, but the Father who sent me commanded me what to say and how to say it" (NIV).

Our lives are not to be about condoning or condemning others; they will do that for themselves. If Christ would not condemn and He was perfect, who are we to condemn anyone? We are to be about showing them God and His gift. We seem to think we need to defend God, but in reality, we are trying to defend ourselves. If we truly trust God, He will defend us, and if He is God, I think He can also defend Himself. We need to be able to let God take care of Himself and us, or we will never be able to show the world the forgiveness and kindness needed to lead them to repentance. And let's be honest. When we condemn or condone anything, it is because it threatens us, our way of life, or our comfort. So now here is the game plan if we follow Christ. Don't condemn, don't condone, and don't defend yourself or God. Sounds easy, right? Here is what Christ says we should do. "You have heard that it was said, 'Eye for eye, and tooth for tooth.' But I tell you, Do not resist an evil person. If someone strikes you on the cheek, turn to him the other also. And if someone wants to sue you and take your tunic, let him have your cloak as well. If someone forces you to go one mile, go with him two miles. Give to the one who asks you, and do not turn away from the one who wants to borrow from you. You have heard that it was said, 'Love your neighbor and hate your enemy.' But I tell you: Love you enemies and pray for those who persecute you, that you may be sons of your Father in heaven. He causes his sun to rise on the evil and the good, and sends rain on the righteous and the unrighteous. If you love those who love you, what reward will you get? Are not even the tax collectors doing that? And if you greet only your brothers, what are you doing more than others? Do not even the pagans do that? Be perfect, therefore, as your heavenly Father is perfect" (Matt. 5:38–48 NIV). Not so easy—it was hard for me to even type it. It goes against the very fiber of my being. I don't want to hear it or do it, it is not my nature, and I'm sure it isn't in yours either. So let's strive together to be perfect or at least closer today than we were yesterday.

Love,
Dad

Under the Table

One evening at my parents' house, I was trying to teach Yvette her colors. She was really young but seemed bound and determined to not give me the satisfaction of saying them even though I was pretty sure she knew them. My dad was standing there, laughing at me, so I started to complain to him about how stubborn she was. He proceeded to tell me that I deserved everything she was able to dish out and then some and that she was a princess compared to me when I was her age. You may have already made that same observation based on my earlier stories. My father told me this story about my early years. He said, when my older brother Lee was little and stood up under the kitchen table and hit his head, for weeks he would not stand up under the table. He would either walk all bent over or crawl clear to the middle of the room, well away from the table, before he would even stand up. "Then you came along." He said, "When you were little, you would stand up and hit you head, go down, come back up, and hit your head again and again, every time coming up harder than the time before, until someone pulled you out from under the table." He said that he was never quite sure if there was something mentally wrong with me or if I was just that stubborn. Then he smiled and said he still wasn't sure which one it was. To be certain, there are still a lot of people out there who are still not sure which it is, including myself. But there is no doubt that both my children got their stubbornness from me, so I guess I would have to say it's a little of both.

After Mom, Dad, and Randy died and we got the letters Dad had written us, when I would start to miss them or I felt like giving up, I would sit down and read Dad's letter to me. I was always encouraged to go on, especially when I would read this part: "I never quite got control of your strong will. I have seen from your early childhood you were more competitive than any of my children. Determination under God's control is the most admirable of qualities. Such are never known as quitters." It finally occurred to me after several years that my dad had chosen to look at something that many would consider a bad quality and see the positive side of it. Where some would see an unbearably stubborn and difficult person, my dad saw a competitive, determined person who was not quick to quit. Many times, that encouragement kept me from quitting when others were telling me I was stupid to keep going and that I should give up and quit.

I believe Christ saw the same thing in Peter. Peter was an impulsive man who was always getting himself in trouble by pushing ahead without thinking things through. Yet Jesus said that He would build His church on him and that he would die for his sake. It was Peter who was the first to recognize Christ for who He was and the only disciple to walk on water, even if only for a while. I believe many times we view certain characteristics as undesirable when I believe God built them into us for a reason and, under God's control, will make us exactly what God intended. For example, a stubborn person may hold on too long and be hard to steer in the right direction but, once going in the right direction, will not quit when the going gets tough. An impulsive person may jump into bad situations without thinking things through, but when God tells them to go, they do it, whether it makes sense or not, without analyzing it till the opportunity has passed. An impatient and driven person is one who will have no tolerance for underachievers, but they will also passionately pursue what God has given them to do and will motivate others to go far beyond their potential. The passive and thoughtful may react too slow and not push others to attain greatness, yet God many times uses those to encourage those in pain. They hear and see the pain in people that others are totally unaware of. That space cadet that gets so consumed by what they are doing that they miss opportunities and don't contribute to those around them. But they are focused, and when God gives them a task, they are not easily distracted. Those with a short attention span, the ADD crowd, don't focus, have a hard time getting things done. But they also are not so focused that if God shows them a need, they will drop what they are doing and go and meet that need no matter how insignificant it may seem to others.

I can go on and on, but you get the idea. The amazing thing I see over and over in the Bible is, God used flawed individuals to do great things. Those things that, in our way of thinking, would hinder the work they were chosen to do were in fact the traits that made them perfect for the task. Many times, parents and just people in general have a tendency to focus on the negative aspects of our traits and not the positive, and we begin to look at ourselves as defective screwups. I hope that each of us will begin to start a trend where we see the possibilities of how God can use those different traits for His glory and good. Embrace who God created you to be and strive to bring it under His control.

Love,
Dad

Grandpa's Poem

My grandma had died suddenly when I was sixteen, and I remember my grandpa coming to visit us that next year. My dad had all of us sit around the dining room table. He turned on a tape recorder and asked my grandpa to tell us all about his life and his walk with Christ. My grandfather, for most of my life up to that point, had been pastor of the Harvester Church in Fort Wayne, Indiana. It was a big church that we used play hide-and-seek in when we went to visit. We were always finding new rooms. It seemed like it was always an adventure when we were there. Until that night, I guessed it never really dawned on me that there was a life for Grandma and Grandpa before that. My grandfather told us how he had grown up always wanting to be a farmer and how he had gotten saved at a tent revival meeting. He told us about how he had raised draft horses and how his were the top in the state. I remember listening to him talk about his horses and how you could tell how much he loved those horses and farming just by the way he talked about them. Then he said God told him to sell everything and move to the city and be a preacher. He told how my grandma told him she wasn't going, that she would leave him if he went because she liked the life they had. Grandma went with him grudgingly, which really surprised me, because my grandma was the greatest little kids' Sunday school teacher of all time, and for my whole life, I could see how much my grandma loved the people of the church. He told how he started a church in a run-down neighborhood and a radio ministry. I don't remember many of the facts; I just remember him getting sidetracked, talking about this person or that person and where they were at, where their kids were at, what they were all doing, sometimes even their grandkids.

I just remember realizing later, looking back, that God had replaced the love for his horses and farming with an even deeper love for those people and preaching God's Word. My mom told me a while later that when my grandpa had first gone to that neighborhood, it was far different than when he left. She said his ministry had completely changed the neighborhood for the better. When Grandpa came back for my mom, dad, and little brother's funeral, he looked healthy. When he came back for my little sister's wedding just a few months later, he looked like his health was failing, and I told my wife later that I didn't think he would make it through the year. That fall, he went home to be with the Lord he had served all those years and to be with Grandma, Mom, Dad, and Randy. At the funeral, my uncle read a poem that my grandpa had written in the front of his Bible. I got a copy of it and wrote in the front of my Bible to remind me of the sacrifice and the reward that my grandpa had modeled for me. I hope his legacy and that of my parents and others who have gone before me will someday also be modeled in me. This is the poem my grandpa had written in his Bible.

What I said and what Christ said
I said, "Let me walk in the field." He said,
"No, walk in the town."

*I said, "There are no flowers there." He
said, "No flowers, but a crown."
I said, "But the skies are black, there is
nothing there but noise and din."
And he wept as he sent me back. "There is
more," He said. "There is sin."
I said, "But the air is thick, and fogs are
veiling the sun."
He said, "But hearts are sick, and souls in
dark undone."
I said, "I shall miss the light, and friends
will miss me, they say."
And he answered, "Choose tonight if I am
to miss you or they."
I pleaded for time to be given. He said, "Is
it hard to decide?
It will not seem hard in heaven to have followed the steps of your guide."
Then I turned one look at the field and set
my face to the town.
He said, "My child, do you yield, will you
leave the flowers for the crown?"
Then into his hand went mine, and into
my heart came he.
And I walk in a light divine that path I
had feared to see.*

—author unknown

This poem has been a reminder to me that God many times asks us to give up things that we love to see if we love Him more. But in exchange, He gives us joy and fulfillment that we can never achieve on our own without sacrifice. "Therefore, I urge you, brothers, in view of God's mercy, to offer your bodies as living sacrifices, holy and pleasing to God—this is your spiritual act of worship" (Rom. 12:1 NIV). What we have is not our own, so hold on to it loosely. Spouse, family, children, jobs, our things, and especially our lives are all His, so remember that what God gives us here is only on loan and we should be ready always to give what we have back to its rightful owner. "For Christ's love compels us, because we are convinced that one died for all, and therefore all died. And He died for all, that those who live should no longer live for themselves but for him who died for them and was raised again" (2 Cor. 5:14–15 NIV). Who are you living for?

Love,
Dad

Grandpa's Promise

I remember, when I was young, overhearing my aunt Sandy telling my dad that she couldn't imagine what it was like to lose a parent. She had been talking to my dad about when his father had died. He had died when I was really young, and I really didn't remember my grandpa Lehman. Then I remember Sandy saying that she had been so blessed that she had never had to live through that. Then, when I was sixteen, my grandma died suddenly. I remember seeing Sandy handle that situation with unwavering faith. Then about ten years later, my mom, dad, and little brother died in a car wreck. As I watched, Sandy was a strong pillar even though she had lost both her mom and sister. That fall, my grandpa died, and still, as I watched, I never saw anything that would cause me think she ever doubted God's goodness, and I wondered how she stayed so strong. Then a few years later, my aunt Nancy died in a car wreck in almost the same manner as my mom and at almost the same age as Mom. At Nancy's funeral, they sang "It is Well With My Soul," and I remember seeing everyone trying to put on a face of "We're okay" and "Isn't God great?" But I felt like all of us were faking it because I was struggling with the whole thing. I'm not good at covering up what I think or feel, so I was feeling like I must be failing somehow, but I couldn't see anything but people

saying what they were supposed to say as "good Christians."
And it felt so fake.

My aunt Sandy was there talking to us, and I was
remembering how she had said she had never experienced a
death in her immediate family, and now she was the only one
of her family left. Then she said, "We sang 'It Is Well with
My Soul,' but it's not. It's not well with my soul." She said
a little more that I don't remember; I just remember being
relieved that I wasn't the only one with what felt like a big
empty hole in my soul. And how could it be well with my
soul when I felt that way? I guess, if God knows my thoughts,
He knows exactly how I'm feeling at that moment. I can't
imagine a loving God expecting a perfect response from an
imperfect people. Right or wrong, I struggled with that for
several years. It seemed like such a waste. Then God gave me
this passage in Hebrews 11. While Paul is talking about those
who suffered for the faith in verse 38, he says, "The world
was not worthy of them" (NIV). Suddenly, I realized that they
were faithfully serving, and God had decided for reasons
unknown to me that this world was no longer worthy of their
physical presence. Who am I to second-guess the God of all
creation? But there was more Paul goes on. "These were all
commended for their faith, yet none on them received what
had been promised. God had planned something better for
us so that only together with us would they be made perfect.
Therefore, since we are surrounded by such a great cloud of
witnesses, let us throw off everything that hinders and the sin
that so easily entangles, and let us run with perseverance the
race marked out for us" (Heb. 11:39–12:1 NIV).

It's not too surprising that God has planned something
better than I could. It's sometimes hard to see it or trust him
with the lives of our loved ones. But what is even better is
now those who have gone on before me are a part of my

cloud of witnesses. My grandparents, parents, brother, and aunt Nancy are now a small part of my cloud of witnesses. Together with me, they are being made perfect, so I don't have time to feel sorry for myself. I have a race set before me to run. And because they are my witnesses, I know that not only God is with me, but they are also there, cheering me on. It makes me think that I'm in a huge stadium and I'm running a race—only the whole stadium is filled with my family and friends, all wanting me to win. To accomplish the task set before me and, through my life, achieve another phase of the plan and promise that had been given to my grandparents, my parents, and those before me who had not seen their entire promise fulfilled. I could finally say it was well with my soul.

A year or so later, at the Eicher reunion, my uncle John was giving a devotional, and he read this passage from Isaiah telling us it was Grandpa's promise, the one he had claimed from God as his own. "'As for me, this is my covenant with them,' says the Lord. 'My Spirit, who is on you, and my words that I have put in your mouth will not depart from your mouth, or from the mouths of your children, or from the mouths of their descendants from this time on and forever,' says the Lord" (Isa. 59:21 NIV). As I looked around, I saw no one in the room that day that didn't claim Christ as Lord, which made me aware of God's faithfulness to keep what He had promised my grandpa. My aunt Sandy still loved the Lord and was still the grounding force in demonstrating what my grandparents were all about, and it was apparent that the word God had given to my grandpa was still active not only in his children and grandchildren but also in his great-grandchildren. What a legacy my grandpa had left through his faithfulness!

I, too, claim that promise for my children and their descendants. I have always struggled with Isaiah. I would always hear great, insightful passages from the book of Isaiah, but every time I would read it, it confused me and I just didn't get a lot out of it. So I decided that since the main promise I was claiming was in Isaiah, I should get a better feel for the book, so I decided to read it until I understood the book, and that was all I was going to read. I spent a year and a half reading Isaiah, and I am still not sure I completely understand what all is being said, but God gave me some great things from that time. One was, I had always looked at the verse my grandpa claimed and had been a little relaxed in the way I thought about the statement "My Spirit, who is on you." I always concentrated on "And my words that I have put in your mouth." I guess because my grandpa was a preacher teaching God's Word, I had figured that it was God's Word that would remain in grandpa's descendants forever and that all would believe in Christ and His sacrifice. The more I would read it, though, the more it bothered me, because I not only wanted to represent God's Word accurately but also portray His Spirit properly as well. Then God showed me what his Spirit was about, and it was only a few chapters away in Isaiah 61:1–4. "The Spirit of the Sovereign Lord is on me, because the Lord has anointed me to preach good news to the poor. He has sent me to bind up the brokenhearted, to proclaim freedom for the captives and release from darkness for the prisoners, to proclaim the year of the Lord's favor and the day of vengeance of our God, to comfort all who mourn, and provide for those who grieve in Zion—to bestow on them a crown of beauty instead of ashes, the oil of gladness instead of mourning, and a garment of praise instead of a spirit of despair. They will be called oaks of righteousness, a planting of the Lord for the display of his splendor. They will rebuild the ancient ruins and restore the places long devastated; they will renew the ruined cities that have been devastated for generations" (NIV). I remember that Spirit in my grandparents and my parents, and I hope that my children remember that Spirit in me. We each have our own race to run, but we are all to have the same Word and Spirit. We all are a part of the fulfillment of the promise God gave my grandpa.

Love,
Dad

Love, American Style

When I was in high school, I remember watching a TV show called *Love, American Style* and how my dad would complain about the morals of the show, or maybe it would be more accurate to say it's lack of morals. Now, this show was several short stories fifteen to twenty minutes long shown in the hour-long show. They were goofy encounters of people falling in love, or maybe you could say falling in lust. These stories were usually funny, and though I can't remember a single story or plotline, the intro and the ending of each story have always stuck in my mind. When I think of the show, I think of a bunch of fireworks covering the screen like a Fourth of July fireworks display. Every show ended with fireworks going off to signify that they had fallen in love. It's amazing to me that we bought it. We seem to think, if we wait long enough or try out enough partners, we will have this fantastic, fireworks-going-off-in-our-heads kind of experience that lets us live happily ever after without any difficulties. We want love to be glamorous and exciting, but then this love, like the fireworks, always seems to fade away, so we quit on that experience and go try to find a new one.

Now, there is another high school experience with fireworks that I believe more accurately describes what love should look like. We used to always find ways to buy pop bottle rockets; even though they were illegal, we always seemed to have them. They were the best if they were the ones with the reports. But just putting them in a bottle and standing back got boring, so we started holding the bottle to better aim them. Then we started holding them in little tubes to aim them better. Then we started having bottle rocket fights. We would drive around in cars and shoot bottle rockets at one another. In order to improve my accuracy, I started just holding the tail, lighting the rocket, pointing it until it started to pull, and then letting go. Nobody else would do it, so I had the advantage and got to where I hit just about anything I was aiming at. One day, we were having one such war, and I was the shooter, so my driver was driving by the local grocery store, looking for our classmates in the other car, when we saw some underclassmen walking to the store with their backs to us. So I shot a rocket at one of them, my goal being to hit him in the butt. Not only did I hit him in the butt, but I also hit him right between the cheeks in the crease of his jeans, and he couldn't shake it. So we laughed as he danced around, trying to get away from it, with rocket tail wagging around and following him everywhere he went until the report went off. Then we laughed even harder when he looked at us and, in a wavering voice, said, "Guys, that wasn't funny." All we could say was, "From this end it was hilarious!"

Right now, you're thinking that if the bottle rocket tale more accurately describes love, this guy must be one romantic guy. Or maybe not. But as I look at the love Christ showed us, and if it is my guide to follow, then romantic or not, the bottle rocket story demonstrates more what love is to be like. Christ's love was intentional and focused. His love propelled Him to us, and He would not be distracted in any way from the object of His love. Like I chose a target, His love and its direction toward us was a choice. It just didn't happen by chance with all the emotional fanfare that we equate with love. We were not even aware of His love, and our salvation was not available to us until His life, like the rocket, was totally spent. Like the report of the rocket signified that the rocket was spent, Christ's words "It is finished" echoed through eternity that His life was spent and we are what He bought with his life. "Once you were alienated from God and were enemies in your minds because of your evil behavior. But now he has reconciled you by Christ's physical body through death to present you holy in his sight, without blemish and free from accusation" (Col. 1:21–22 NIV).

Now, the church today in America, as I see it, seems to have changed God's love and His call to be like Him to love American-style. Most believers in America can tell you all about the love chapter (1 Corinthians 13), and many can quote John 13:34–35, "A new command I give you: Love one another, as I have loved you, so you must love one another. By this all men will know that you are my disciples, if you love one another" (NIV). Many can quote John 15:9–17, "As the Father has loved me, so have I loved you. Now remain in my love. If you obey my commands, you will remain in my love, just as I have obeyed my Father's commands and remain in his love. I have told you this so that my joy may be in you and that your joy may be complete. My command is this: Love each other as I have loved you. Greater love has no one than this, that he lay down his life for his friends. You are my friends if you do what I command. I no longer call you servants, because a servant does not know his master's business. Instead I have called you friends, for everything that I learned from my Father I have made known to you. You did not choose me, but I chose you and appointed you to go and bear fruit—fruit that will last. Then the Father will give you whatever you ask in my name. This is my command: Love each other" (NIV). But I'm not sure that any of us are paying attention. The minute we hear the word *love*, our minds change it to love American-style. No sacrifice, just warm, fuzzy feelings that say everybody and everything is okay.

We rarely exercise self-discipline or self-control, and we find our spiritual lives emulating the commercial for Chase credit card that says, "I want it all, and I want it now." We want to be mature Christian leaders without ever having to endure hardship or having ever learned to follow. I heard more than one person say that they felt like Job because their life wasn't going well, and I always thought to myself, How could anyone in America compare themselves to Job? This is a man that had everything a man could want and lost it all in one day, and his response was this, "At this, Job got up and tore his robe and shaved his head. Then he fell to the ground in worship and said: 'Naked I came from my mother's womb, and naked I will depart. The Lord gave and the Lord has taken away; may the name of the Lord be praised'" (Job 1:20–21 NIV). When we worship God, we have music and fireworks, praise-and-worship time, complete with all the warm, fuzzy feelings. When was the last time your worship came from the pit of grief or despair, and when was the last time you heard anyone refer to their hardships as a time of praise and worship?

We worship the Lord when things are good, and when they're not good, we whine. We treat God like we treat our parents nowadays. We say we love Him, which I am not doubting that we do in an American-style way. As children, we have grown up expecting our parents to meet our needs, with little regard to the sacrifices that they make, and if we, at some point, have a hard time in life, it's our parents' fault—they failed us somehow. We ignore all their sacrifices. Then like a spoiled child, we focus on ourselves and what they could have or should have done to make our lives better. The more we focus on ourselves and our problems, the worse our parents failed us. We love them American-style. If everything is good, we honor and respect them, but when life takes a turn for the worse, they have failed us and we forget their sacrifice. Sure, we want to please them as long as it doesn't inconvenience us too much, and even if it's for our own good, we had better like it, or they suddenly hate us and are doing their best to ruin our lives. We treat God that way. We expect Him to make our life good and give us what we want out of life; after all, life and love are all about the fireworks.

How often do we choose sacrifice over success? When was the last time you counted it joy to have bad things happen to you or for being mistreated, because it gave you an opportunity to be Christ to those around you? When was the last time you did without or put your needs on hold to help someone else? How many times have you gone hungry so someone else could eat? I'm sorry to say, I don't love the Lord like He loved me, because I sacrifice very little for Him. Love is like the rocket, focused, committed, and intentional. The title *The Passion of the Christ* for the Mel Gibson movie was completely accurate. Because of His passion for me, He was focused on me to the point of enduring a horrible death to set me free. But my passion for God, like the passion of many of my American brothers and sisters, is better described as a passing fancy or a childhood crush. We are too passionate about me to be focused on God. We are not committed to our God, our country, or our fellow man the way we should be! We should be willing to sacrifice all we have to see any one person saved and, in that, honor God and the sacrifice He made for us. If we are passionate about our God, then we will be passionate about what He is passionate about—people. We should ask ourselves every day, is our love focused and intentional? How committed are we to the cause of Christ? And what will people say we are passionate about, if anything at all?

Love,
Dad

Waiting for the Mailman

For all his life, my father was a pastor of small churches. There were many times that I remember my father going several months without getting paid, and he didn't get paid much to start out with, so he relied on odd jobs to get us by. We cut down trees, tore down buildings, and planted a large garden. Dad did home repairs and was a substitute rural mail carrier. Shortly after I graduated high school, my father was offered the mail route full-time, and he took it. So he carried mail full-time while being a full-time pastor as well. After Doreen and I got married, we lived across town from the folks, but the rural carrier delivered in town also, so my dad was our mailman. Now, I worked nights, so I was home during the day, and sometimes I would wake up early, and if it was anywhere close to the time that my dad was to deliver mail, I would find both of you kids waiting at the front window. I knew what you were looking for, but a lot of times I would ask what you were doing anyway. I always got the same response: "Waiting for Grandpa." When my dad would pull up in his mail Jeep, you would say, "Grandpa's here!" and run out the door. You both would hug my dad and sometimes crawl into his Jeep to talk to him. Then before he left, he would give you a piece of candy. Now, most of the kids on my dad's mail route waited at the mailbox for him because he carried a big bag of candy, and he gave every kid that waited a piece of candy.

I never thought much about it until years after my parents' accident, when I was in a shop where I was getting the wheels and tires balanced and aligned on our car. The young man who was working there had graduated with Brandon, but he didn't recognize me. When I went to pay and he saw the last name on the check, his face lit up and he asked if I was related to Brandon. I told him I was his father. Then he asked if I was related to Sam Lehman, to which I told him that Sam was my dad. I then asked him how he knew my dad. He told me Dad was his mailman and he and his sister would wait by the mailbox every day in the summer to get a piece of candy and that my dad was the best mailman ever. I thanked him and left, but it wasn't until later that I realized the difference between those kids and my children and what they had said they were waiting for. You kids were waiting for Grandpa; the candy was just something that Grandpa gave you. The other kids were waiting for the candy, and my dad was just the one who would give it to them.

I see that in Christians today. Rarely do I hear people say, "I can't wait until I die so I can meet Jesus and thank Him face-to-face for all that He did for me." I hear, "I can't wait until I get to heaven. This life sucks." Or "I hope Christ comes back soon." (Which for me is saying, "Forget all those people that would ultimately be going to hell and have no chance of knowing who truly loves them. I just don't want to die.") Or "I can't wait to get to heaven, then I can fish or ride horses and do all the things I love to do." Then there's the one I have been most guilty of: "I can't wait until I get to see my mom, dad, and little brother, along with all the others I love that have gone on before." My children were looking for Grandpa, the man who loved them, and the candy was just a gift to the ones he loved. Do we truly recognize God's love, and do we really love God if we view him as the man with the candy? If we are not waiting to see and spend time with God, then we are waiting for candy. I have to ask myself, Am I a child of God if He is an afterthought? Am I just after a way to see my parents again? I must be certain that what I am waiting for is God and not my own selfish desires. Salvation is not a get-out-hell-free card; it is recognizing our separation from God and our inability to be restored to that relationship. And then desiring to be with Him so much that we would be willing to do anything, even humble ourselves and accept Christ's sacrifice so we can be restored. I constantly hear of books about the rewards God gives and how we should work for rewards, and it drives me crazy. People have gotten to a place where they feel they should be rewarded or paid for serving God. We have been given a gift from God that we can neither earn nor buy; it is a debt we can never repay, yet we want to be rewarded for doing God's work. We have become a nation of allowance junkies.

When I was in junior high, it was not cool to take your lunch to school, and I liked what the school served most of the time. Because we were poor, our lunches consisted of mainly peanut butter sandwiches or bologna and cheese. Now, one day the school had sent home paperwork for free lunches. Because of my dad's income, we qualified, so I took them to my dad, thinking this was my chance to get school lunches. My dad looked at the paperwork and said no. I was upset and asked why not, and he told me that someone had to pay for it and we would trust God to meet our needs, not the government, and that I was getting all I needed already. If I wanted to eat at school, I would have to pay for that with the money that I had earned myself, because it was something I wanted, not something I needed. So then I went at it with a different angle and told my dad that a lot of the kids in my class got an allowance. I did a lot of chores around the house, so why couldn't he give me an allowance that I could use for my lunches? All my dad said was, "You're part of this family, aren't you? It is your responsibility to do part of the work." That was the end of the discussion. Now, looking back, I see what my father was saying. As part of a family, we have a duty to work for the common good of the family. Every person needs to help out to make a family function as a family. If I benefit from the family, I should contribute to the family, and those who get paid for their work are really only hired hands and not really part of a family. Even if we are born into a family, it is that contribution of work that truly makes us part of the family, and if we expect to get paid for it or for someone else to pay for it, we are not really valuing the family the way we should. We either want something for nothing or we want to be paid to be part of the family as Christians today. "Therefore, brothers, we have an obligation—but it is not to the sinful nature, to live according to it. For if you live according to the sinful nature, you will die; but if by the Spirit you put to death the misdeeds of the body, you will live, because those who are led by the Spirit of God are sons of God. For you did not receive a spirit that makes you a slave again to fear, but you received the spirit of sonship. And by him we cry, 'Abba, Father.' The Spirit himself testifies with our spirit that we are God's children. Now if we are children, then we are heirs—heirs of God and co-heirs with Christ, if indeed we share in his sufferings in order that we may also share in his glory. I consider that our present sufferings are not worth comparing with the glory that will be revealed in us" (Rom. 8:12–18 NIV).

If we are truly followers of Christ and God's children, then we have an obligation to strive to live a life pleasing to God and to endure suffering and hardship as part of belonging to the family. We should labor and endure not for a reward but for the privilege of being part of the family. I watched my father and father-in-law labor for years, having to work side jobs, and many times other full-time jobs, just to make ends meet, all the time being full-time pastors as well. Yet they visited more sick people in the hospital, dedicated more time to God than many pastors who are only pastors, receive a very good wage, and have lots of paid assistants. I know where their hearts are. They serve and have served because of the privilege they were given to be part of the family. When a pastor starts talking about receiving God's blessings and rewards, I cringe, because most of the time they are talking about an allowance. They are hired hands, and when you begin to observe their lives, they take more than they give. A Christian in a paid position who gets paid for forty hours and only spends forty hours working for God is not part of the family—he is a hired hand. I see pastors in America who pray on the clock and also who teach on the clock. Most pastors I have met of late take two days off during the week and consider Sunday their workday, yet all the people who come to worship have worked all week, and when they come on Sunday, it is a sacrifice of their time off. "To the elders among you, I appeal as a fellow elder, a witness to Christ's sufferings and one who also will share in the glory to be revealed; be shepherds of God's flock that is under your care, serving as overseers—not because you must, but because you are willing, as God wants you to be; not greedy of money, but eager to serve; not lording it over those entrusted to you, but being examples to the flock. And when the Chief Shepherd appears, you will receive the crown of glory that will never fade away" (1 Pet. 5:1–4 NIV). How can our leaders in the church lead by example and demonstrate

Christ's selfless sacrifice if their congregation sacrifices more of their free time than they do? If you are not giving more than you are taking, then you are a hired hand, and you have to ask yourself, Am I really part of the family? Do I long to see the Father, or am I looking for the gifts He gives?

Love,
Dad

The Concert

When I was a junior in high school, I was constantly butting heads with my dad. I thought I was smarter than I was and that he was not as wise as he was. It's amazing how the older you get, the wiser your parents get and the dumber you feel. Anyway, this time Dad had made the statement that if I was going to live there, it would be on his terms and his rules had to be followed. Now, to be sure, I was beginning to stretch the boundaries that Dad had set and had determined that if everybody thought I was a black sheep, no matter how hard I tried to do what was right, well, I would go ahead and prove them right. I'm sure my father saw this attitude and was trying to correct it. But with that statement at that time in my life when I was feeling that no one was giving me the credit I deserved, I decided that I would leave. So I, without telling anyone, began to pack up my things and hide them in my closet. I was just waiting until I had made a little more money, and then I would pack my car when everyone was gone and leave. I had determined that I was never coming back. I would go until I found a place where someone respected me for who I was and wouldn't always be criticizing me. I know that even as I write this, it was an extremely selfish thing to think and consider doing after all my parents had sacrificed for me, but that was my plan. One day, I walked into my room, and my mom was standing in my closet, crying, and I knew what she had found. Now, I knew my mom hadn't been snooping in my stuff, because the closets were really deep and she would store other stuff in the back. She had come upstairs to get something from the back of my closet and had found all the stuff I had packed. She asked me when I planned on leaving and why, and she never tried to talk me out of it. But she did tell me that she and Dad loved me and that she really didn't want me to go. She said Dad didn't know how to deal with me because I was so different from the other kids and that he knew that he had made mistakes with me but that he was doing the best he knew how. Then she left. Dad never said anything to me, so I don't think she ever said anything to him. But because I could see how much it hurt her, I unpacked my stuff and stayed.

Now, I still continued to ignore my father's advice and do my own thing. I just didn't do it openly. It wasn't until I had done all the things I shouldn't have and found out for myself why you shouldn't do them that I started to realize maybe I was wrong. And then when I had kids of my own, I suddenly realized how foolish I had been, but my relationship with my father was still strained. I was trying to prove that I was just as wise as him because I had seen his failures and I wasn't going to do the same things. Slowly, mainly because I'm a slow learner, I began to realize that God had told us to honor our parents, not because they are perfect, but because they are our parents and that they would always be my parents. "Honor your father and mother"—which is the first commandment with a promise—"that it may go well with you and that you may enjoy long life on the earth" (Eph. 6:2 NIV). That's right; it was one of the Ten Commandments. "Honor your father and mother, as the Lord your God has commanded you, so that you may live long and that it may go well with you in the land the Lord your God is giving you" (Deut. 5:16 NIV). No matter how old I get, my parents will still be my parents and deserve my honor and respect no matter what. So I began to actually listen to my father and ask for his advice. I still didn't agree with everything he would say; it didn't mean that he was always right and that he didn't make mistakes. It meant that because he was my father, I needed to listen and respect him. We seem to think respect and honor are earned, but they are given. Many people are given honor and respect, and from my perspective, they don't deserve it—still they receive it. But what was amazing to me was when I began to respect and honor my father, our relationship changed. Not only that, but I also began to feel like God was revealing Himself to me in ways that I had never known before.

About six months before my parents' death, Doreen and I paid to have a band from Lincoln, Nebraska (about two hours away), come in and put on a concert for the kids in Shelton. Our youth group showed up, and that was it. So there were about ten kids, and to my surprise, my father walked in and sat down. Now, my music had always been a point of contention between my father and me. He never liked that rock stuff because it was devil music, and it had always bothered him. He knew that we were now listening to Christian rock and trying to get young people to listen to it. He had even let my little brother go with us to some of the festivals that we would take kids to. But he had never gone to any of the concerts himself, and I knew he didn't care for that style of music. So I went over and sat down beside him and thanked him for coming, but I told him I knew he didn't care for this style of music and that he didn't need to stay on my account. I will always treasure what he told me as one of the most special moments in my life as far as my relationship with my father is concerned. He told me he was going to stay for the whole thing because he wanted to see what he was supporting. For the first time in my life, I felt that my father was affirming my heart for the kids and me even if he didn't care for the medium we were using. I don't believe that moment would have ever happened if I hadn't humbled myself and given my parents the honor and respect God has commanded us to give our parents. In John 8:49, 50, and 54, Jesus speaks to Jews who are questioning His authority, and this is His response, in verse 49: "'I am not possessed by a demon,' said Jesus, 'but I honor my Father and you dishonor me. I am not seeking honor for myself; but there is one who seeks it, and he is the judge.'" Then in 54, Jesus replied, "If I glorify myself, my glory means nothing. My Father whom you claim as your God, is the one who glorifies me" (NIV). Jesus modeled the pattern that we are to follow, and if we fail to emulate Christ with our parents, I don't believe we can do it with God. Now, I received honor and respect from my father only after I had learned to honor him, and I believe that it wasn't until then that I could honor and respect God the way I should. I didn't realize how much honor and respect my father had given me until after my parents' death, when I received the letter he had written for us for Christmas and hadn't given us. The last line my father closed the letter with was this:

Keeping your family high in your priorities has also encouraged me. I'm proud to call you my son, and I love you as an equal.
Christmas Blessings on You and Your Family

Now, I'm honored that my father would consider me his equal, but I will never consider myself his equal. He will always be my father, and I will always honor and respect his authority over me. Even if he is gone, his words still continue to teach me. I believe the son can never be greater than the father, or the servant greater than the master, as long as the son is the son and the servant is the servant. Whether our parents are bad parents or good parents, the position of your parent was God-given, and to dishonor and disrespect them is to dishonor and disrespect God. Now, be sure, I am not saying that if your parents are harming you to stay and allow it—only that you must respect the position God has given them in your life. "Your attitude should be the same as that of Christ Jesus: Who, being in very nature God, did not consider equality with God something to be grasped, but made himself nothing, taking the very nature of a servant, being made in human likeness. And being found in appearances as a man, he humbled himself and became obedient to death—even death on a cross! Therefore God exalted him to the highest place and gave him the name that is above every name, that at the name of Jesus every knee should bow, in heaven and on earth and under the earth, and every tongue confess that Jesus Christ is Lord, to the glory of God the Father" (Phil. 2:5–11 NIV).

Lucifer was second only to God but wanted to be greater than God, and the result will ultimately bring Him not glory but disgrace. Christ could have demanded glory, being in nature God, but instead He humbled Himself and became a servant, and because of that, He is exalted to a position of glory above all others, and His glory brings glory to the Father. Proverbs 3:34 is repeated in James 4:6 and 1 Peter 5:5, which speaks directly to this issue. Peter is speaking to elders in chapter 5 verses 1–4, then in verses 5–6 he says,

"Young men, in the same way be submissive to those who are older. All of you, clothe yourselves with humility toward one another, because 'God opposes the proud but gives grace to the humble.' Humble yourselves, therefore, under God's mighty hand, that he may lift you up in due time" (NIV). If you're prideful and looking for glory, honor, and respect, you will never find it or receive it (at least not the kind worth having). Only when you put yourself aside and, in humility, begin honoring and respecting others will you ever receive what you desire. The only problem with this scenario is, if you are truly being humble, you won't desire to be exalted. My dad once said of a disagreement he had with someone on something in the Bible, "When we both get to heaven, if I'm right, I won't even be able to say, 'I told you so,' because I will love with a perfect love and that's not loving." He was basically saying he would no longer be operating in a prideful, selfish manner but in true, perfect humility. Whether it is money, honor, or respect, never give expecting something in return, or it is worthless and means nothing.

Love,
Dad

Engineers

The other day, I was talking to your mom's father and uncle about recalls and how grudgingly they fixed those things that were of a faulty design. Some things were poorly designed, yet if they think they can get away with it, they will even charge you to fix it right. You all have heard my less-than-complimentary grips directed toward engineers who design things with little regard for the ease and expense of repairing it when it fails. Things designed that don't work right or have to have a custom tool to work on it. Then there is the most irritating thing of all for me. That is when something is put together in such a way that it leaves you no room to work on the problem and you have to spend more time dismantling the machine to make room than you do fixing the problem. Isn't it great that God created us the right way, right from the start, and designed our bodies to actually repair themselves? I've never driven a car that, when it breaks down, fixes itself. But if I cut myself, in a week or two, you can't tell it was ever cut. Our bodies were designed to grow, change, and repair themselves. It's pretty amazing, if you really think about it. "For you created my inmost being; you knit me together in my mother's womb. I praise you because I am fearfully and wonderfully made; your works are wonderful, I know that full well. My frame was not hidden from you when I was made in the secret place. When I was woven together in the depths of the earth, your eyes saw my unformed body. All the days ordained for me were written in your book before one of them came to be" (Ps. 139:13–16 NIV). The master engineer created each one of us to perfectly fit His plan. Yet we still complain and whine about the way He designed us.

What is even more amazing, after designing us perfectly, He has still conducted the largest recall ever known to man. In this day and age, engineers and companies rarely fix their own faulty design, but I have never heard of anyone fixing something for free that was designed and built right but that you broke. If you break it and it was your fault, you can plan on paying to fix it. But God has paid for what man broke even though His design was perfect and we deserved to pay for it. "For all have sinned and fall short of the glory of God" (Rom. 3:23 NIV). But He sent His Son to die and then announced this great recall. Bring me your sinful/hell-bound soul and I'll replace it with a heaven-bound one. Bring me your broken, messed-up life and I'll fix it and make it right. "Therefore, if anyone is in Christ, he is a new creation; the old has gone, the new has come! All this is from God, who reconciled us to himself through Christ and gave us the ministry of reconciliation" (2 Cor. 5:17–18 NIV). What a deal! Unfortunately, with any recall, what is broken and bad won't be replaced until you turn in the old one. And God's recall is no different. I cannot begin to understand how some can choose to keep their old broken lives when God has put such a great recall in effect and made it so easy to receive a new life. "Come to me, all you who are weary and burdened, and I will give you rest" (Matt. 11:28 NIV). Now, my opinion of many of today's engineers is less than favorable, but God is one engineer that I can never begin to repay or praise enough.

Love,
Dad

Jacob

I first met Jacob when he and a friend of his came to the door and asked if we believed that Jesus was the Messiah. I said yes, and we struck up a short conversation, and he handed me a book, asked if I minded looking it over, and that he would come back and discuss it with me. I said I would, and he handed me a booklet and left. It was a booklet on what the Jehovah's Witnesses believe. So I sat down and looked through it, finding many things that I felt were wrong, and set out to disprove them biblically. The next week, when he returned, we began to discuss our differences over what was written in the booklet and what we believed the scriptures were saying. He very patiently listened to everything I had to say, asked questions, and stated why they believed the way they did. At a later time, I hope to write to you about what I found and what they believe compared to what I believe Scriptures say. But as he left, I noticed that I was feeling a little cocky about how well I had defended my beliefs, and I found that I was thinking that next week I would even be more prepared. It was then it felt like God just slapped me upside the head with a "Could your attitude be any more arrogant and selfish?" I was trying to prove I was right and he was wrong. I wasn't truly seeking the truth, or I would have seen God's love and heart in my attitude. When you truly seek God's truth in His Word, he will also reveal His heart.

After that, Jacob and I met many times, and I began to pray for him, and I still do, even now after he quit coming back. His knowledge about the Bible and his ability to share his religion impressed me, and I learned a lot about why they believe the way they do. But it saddened me to think that my friend was missing the heart of God. I am so glad God, in His grace, cut through my pride and stupidity to let me see that without His heart His words can be manipulated to make anyone feel he is right and to justify almost anything. And I have noticed that it is that way with every religion out there. There are many different views on what different passages of the Qur'an mean and how they are interpreted depending on the person and what they want. Every quoted author, religious leader, or person of importance has had people view what he had to say from different sides of the fence. Every one of us has a tendency to do the same thing.

We, as Christians in America, may be the worst. We use the Scriptures to justify where we are at and to condemn those who don't believe like we do. In our pride and selfishness, we miss the heart of God. If what we believe is right, it will produce the heart of God in us. A heart of love, compassion, and sacrifice with a passion for what God is passionate about. If it doesn't produce those things in us, then we have not really grabbed ahold of God's Word. We've just read a good book. Paul writes to Timothy in 1 Timothy 1:3–8, "As I urged you when I went into Macedonia, stay there in Ephesus so that you may command certain men not to teach false doctrines any longer nor to devote themselves to myths and endless genealogies. These promote controversies rather than God's work—which is by faith. The goal of the command is love, which comes from a pure heart and a good conscience and a sincere faith. Some have wandered away from these and turned to meaningless talk. They want to be teachers of the law, but they do not know what they are talking about or what they so confidently affirm. We know that the law is good if one uses it properly" (NIV). If someone is teaching God's Word yet not living a life of service, sacrifice, love, and faith, then everything he says is meaningless talk. Sounds like most Americans to me. It is time for our nation of believers to stop all the meaningless talk and begin to grab ahold of the heart of God. And maybe in turn our nation will see the heart of God and turn back to Him. It has to start somewhere; maybe it should start with us.

Love,
Dad

Sam's Son

When I was young, I used to have a paper route, and I also worked at a grocery store for several years, along with mowing and raking leaves in the summer. It seemed that every time an adult would ask who I was, when I told them my name was Joel Lehman, their response was, "Oh, you're Sam's son." It kind of bothered me at first, then it began to make me proud. I was proud to be associated with my father, and it meant that I belonged to a family and I was recognized for my father's accomplishments. This week, with the passing of Doreen's uncle Leo, it became even more evident to me how much our parents' lives are extended in our lives. As I watched Leo and Rosalie's children and saw the pictures of them when they were younger, it amazed me how much their children looked like and acted like their parents. I had gotten to know Leo and Rosalie far better than the cousins, so it was incredible how much of their parents I saw in them. Then it got me to thinking about the different kids I had known that had been adopted by a family, and after a little while, you would actually forget they were adopted. They started acting and even looking so much like their parents you would almost swear they were born to them. I guess it was all the time spent with them. How they smile, laugh, talk, their gestures and mannerisms all, somewhere during life, are passed on, just like the genes of natural-born parents. Before Leo went to be with the Lord, for almost two years, every time we left the house after visiting them, Doreen would always say, "Man, Uncle Leo looks like Grandpa."

Thinking back, I always liked being around my aunts and uncles, because they reminded me of my parents in so many different ways. I now realize that my aunts and uncles were not like my parents. All those brothers and sisters were a reflection of their parents, and I am seeing all the little pieces of my grandparents that made up who my parents were, just glued together in different ways. I guess, if I really wanted to know my grandparents intimately, even though they are gone, I could just observe all the children and have a fairly good idea of what my grandparents were really like in life before we were there. I am little bits and pieces of my parents all stirred together, with a little of my own experiences, choices, independence, and character poured in on top to make me who I am. It's like that with our spiritual lives as well. The things that we get from our parents, influences, and the physical things around us are the pieces that make up the religion part of my faith, because those influences are not pure and live in the sinful nature. But when I gave my life to Christ, I was adopted into His family. "For all who are being led by the Spirit of God, these are the sons of God. For you have not received a spirit of slavery leading to fear again, but you have received a spirit of adoption as sons by which we cry out, 'Abba! Father!' The Spirit Himself testifies with our spirit that we are children of God, and if children heirs also, heirs of God and fellow heirs with Christ, if indeed we suffer with Him so that we may also be glorified with Him" (Rom. 8:14–17 NAS).

Now, religion and the things of this world come easy for me because that is what I was born into. When I was born to my father and mother, I got their name and physical characteristics. I started to take on the other characteristics because of all the time I spent with them. If my perspective of who God is and what He desires comes from my parents and what the world or the church says, then it is them I have learned from, and I become a mirror of the world, not God. If I rely on my parents' relationship with God or others around me, I will never be a pure reflection of God, only a reflection of God as seen through my parents. Most people today take the name of Christ but not the adoption of God. To be a Christian by name only is like me being recognized by strangers by my name. They did not truly know me or my parents, only the name and what they had either heard or thought they knew of us. Now others who knew my parents well, when they are around me, will say, "You look like your mother" or "You act like your father." Every person has a different perspective and observation, but they see a part of what they saw in my parents in me. Now, today, my hope is that people recognize me as a son of my heavenly Father, that when people see me and know me, their first thought is of my Father in heaven. What an honor and privilege that would be! Something to strive for. But that will only come when I spend so much time with God that I begin to act like Christ and I begin to mirror His passions, His heart, and all He desires. It is not natural to me, because I was born of this world. The only way this can happen is if I become a part of the family and immerse myself in Him. Jesus even prayed for this to happen in us in John 17. I hope you will read the whole chapter, but in verses 20–23, He prays, "My prayer is not for them alone. I pray also for those who will believe in me through their message, that all of them may be one, Father, just as you are in me and I am in you. May they also be in us so that the world may believe that you have sent me. I have given them the glory that you gave me, that they may be one as we are one: I in them and you in me. May they be brought to complete unity to let the world know that you sent me and have loved them even as you have loved me" (NIV).

In you kids I see a lot of your mom and me, but I hope it is your desire as well to be a purer reflection of God and His nature so He becomes a major piece of who you are. I never want you to rely on who God is to me or your mother to shape the reflection of God in your life. Spend lots of time with Him. I know He will cherish the time as much as I cherish the time you spend with me.

Love,
Dad

The Great Abortion

When I was in the eighth grade, our biology teacher gave a little quiz for fun. We were told that certain animals were named for their description with a combination of Latin words. So we were given not the words but what the words meant and a list of animals. We were to combine word definitions and assign them to each of the animals, then we exchanged papers, and the teacher was going to read off the answers. He told us he had been giving that little quiz for years and no one had ever come close to getting them all right, and he also said that it was a standing offer that he made every year. If anyone got all the answers right, he would buy them a steak dinner. We began to check the answers as he read them off. Halfway through, he asked if there was anyone who had all the answers correct so far, and only one person raised their hand. It was the one checking my paper. Everyone else had missed at least two already. He said that no one else had ever made it that far, so after that, with every answer given, he asked if I had it right. He had asked whose paper she had, so now it was checking to see if I was maybe going to win a steak dinner after every answer. It came down to the second-to-the-last answer, and I still had all of them right. The teacher said he was getting a little nervous. He gave the answer, and I had turned the descriptions around. I had switched half of the description of the last answer with half of the answer of the second-to-the-last one. But after that, every year the biology class of that year would come up to me and say, "I hear you almost won a steak dinner in Holley's class." Even after I got out of school, for years I would have kids I knew come up and say that they took Mr. Holley's test and he told them that I had almost won a steak dinner and nobody had ever come as close. Mr. Holley was still teaching when both of you kids went to school, and it amazed me when you came home and said, "I hear you almost won a steak dinner from Mr. Holley." I never minded being remembered for coming closer than anyone else ever came to winning Mr. Holley's steak dinner. But I wasn't so fond of how I was remembered from my ninth-grade physics class.

In Mr. Evert's physics class, we were getting ready to do a lab that involved putting sodium in water to watch the reaction, but I and the other guys in our lab group were talking and not listening to the instructions. When it came time to do the lab, I had heard something about corking the beaker, so I put a cork in it. Should have done that during the discussion, because there was a loud pop and everything blew up in my face. Next thing I know, I have my head pushed under the faucet by the teacher, washing the solution out of my eyes. It was pretty embarrassing, and for the next two years, the biology class would say, "Hear you almost won a steak dinner from Holley," then shortly after that, the physics class would say, "Hear you blew up your sodium experiment." I'm sure you can imagine which one I didn't mind hearing about. At the end of my junior year, Mr. Everts took another job and moved, so even though I liked Mr. Everts I knew since he left, I wasn't going to hear from the physics class about having my experiment blow up. Funny how we like to be recognized for our accomplishments even if they were pure luck, not talent, but don't like the recognition for our screwups. We hope it goes away or people forget, and sometimes we want to cover it up, hoping no one will notice.

Abortion is much the same. It is someone who has made a mistake, has made a poor choice, or got caught doing something that is wrong. It doesn't matter how you say it; it is just something you don't want to face and be recognized for. Now, abortion seems like a logical way to hide the situation, and some will say that it should be a woman's choice. Think of how many innocent lives are lost to abortion. Now, you can pretend that it's not really a life, yet the legal system can't seem to make up their minds. They will charge someone with two counts of murder for killing a pregnant woman, charge a woman with child abuse for taking drugs or alcohol during the pregnancy, and even include the unborn child in a tragedy death toll, but not call it murder if a doctor does it. But it occurred to me, in abortion the only true innocent person in the situation is the one who dies to cover up the sins of the parents. The babies never even get a chance to make a mistake. They are perfect, without spot.

It also occurred to me that we, as Christians, get all angry and condemn people for making that choice when we are as guilty of killing the innocent as they are. We killed a man who was as perfect as these babies, yet He had to die to cover up our sin and take away our shame. I can, in no way, condone abortion, but neither can I condone the hypocrisy of thinking we are any different. Our entire faith is, in fact, an abortion of sorts. The innocent dying for the guilty. We shouldn't be angry because they want to hide their guilt and shame or cover up their sin. We should be finding ways that we can introduce them to the one perfect soul that had a choice yet willingly gave up His life to not just cover up sin or hide it but also take it away and give us lasting peace. Abortion only covers up the sin and takes away a problem. It can't take away the guilt and shame. In fact, anytime you sin, to hide sin it only increases the guilt and shame. Christ's death not only covers the sin; it also removes the guilt and shame that only forgiveness can.

When your mother and I started out, Brandon, you were already born, and, Yvette, you were on the way. Not the ideal way to start out. I am so thankful that your mother had the courage to stand and face all the criticism and the shame that was heaped on her because of our mistakes and have you kids. She never, ever considered not having you, and she put you above her own comfort. You can never say she doesn't love you, because she made great sacrifices just to have both of you. I know your mother carries deep scars from what she endured for you. I hope you always honor and thank her for her love for you. Those who have sinned don't need to be condemned; they already feel the weight and the shame of their sin. They need love and forgiveness. "For God so loved the world that he gave his one and only Son, that whoever believes in him shall not perish but have eternal life. For God did not send his son into the world to condemn the world, but to save the world through him. Whoever believes in him is not condemned, but whoever does not believe stands condemned already because he has not believed in the name of God's one and only Son" (John 3:16–18 NIV). We would do more to stop abortion by loving those caught in shameful situations and introducing them to the one who loves them enough to willingly be aborted for the removal of their sin. We should try to bring about the stop of abortion, but if we meet the heart's need for a savior in mothers-to-be, then there won't be a demand for it anyway. Every child is a gift from God. I am truly thankful for the two gifts God and your mother gave to me.

Love,
Dad

The Slingshot and the Magpie

When I was six or seven, we were still living in the sandhills of Nebraska, and my dad was the pastor of two little country churches about ten to fifteen miles outside of the little town we were living in. One Sunday, we would go to one, and Wednesday the other, and then would switch. So in the summer, we would get to go to two vacation Bible schools within a couple of weeks of each other. That summer was no different. I was a perfect angel at these like I always was, always being careful to do everything my father told me not to do. Okay, maybe that's a little exaggerated, but it did seem like I had a hard time doing what I was told. So one day at vacation Bible school, during our playtime, I had gone over to an old abandoned country school building close to the church where I saw some magpies. Magpies are a black-and-white bird with long tail feathers, and they were not afraid of me at all, so I could get fairly close to them. Me, being the great white hunter I was, started throwing rocks at them, thinking I could get one and then my brothers would be impressed with my hunting abilities. I was late getting back for class, and my dad told me I was not allowed to go over there without permission and I wasn't to be over there alone. But I wanted to get one of those cool birds, and because I'm a little stubborn, I decided that I was going to get what I wanted. So I borrowed, without his knowledge, my brother's wrist rocket (a modern marvel of a slingshot that was almost as great an invention as the BB gun or the bow and arrow) and hid it in the station wagon that night, just in case the opportunity to disobey my father happened to present itself. It was amazing how the next day an opportunity just happened to present itself. It must have been a sign!

So since Dad wasn't outside at lunchtime, I got the wrist rocket and headed over to the old schoolhouse. I found the magpie, picked up a rock, and took careful aim and shot. I almost hit it, but it only flew a little way and perched on another tree. I did that a couple of times, seemingly getting closer every time. This time, I was closer; no way I could miss this time. So I went to pick up a rock, but there were no rocks close, just a broken bottle. So I grabbed a piece of glass and took careful aim. All of a sudden, one of the straps on the wrist rocket broke and the glass came flying out the sling pocket and put a huge gash in my finger. Now my finger was dripping blood, and I couldn't get it on my shirt or pants or I was sure to be caught. So with my finger dripping, I sneaked over to the station wagon, put the wrist rocket away. There was a box of tissues under the seat, so I wiped up any evidence, wrapped my finger up, and headed to the back door of the church. If I could just get down the back stairs into the basement, there was a bathroom right at the bottom of the stairs. I could wash it up and hopefully the bleeding would stop by the time I had to go back to class. No such luck. It wouldn't stop bleeding, and I could open it up and see the bone. No matter how tight I wrapped it, it still soaked up the paper towel with blood fairly quickly.

Now, I was late for class, and I knew it was only a matter of time before Dad came looking for me, and my finger would be the least of my worries. The spanking I was sure I would be getting was sure to hurt worse than my finger hurt, and the anticipation of it was worse than the spanking. About that time, there was a knock on the door, and I answered. It was my father. He asked if everything was okay and if he could open the door. I said yes, and when he saw my finger, he asked me what happened. I think he already had a pretty good idea but he just listened to me and shook his head. He looked at my finger and asked if I had washed it out. I said yes, and he just said, "The bleeding will probably clean the dirt out, so when you get it to stop bleeding, get to class." And he left. But I could see the disappointed look on his face. It is the first time I can recall seeing that look, and even though I still figured I was going to get spanked, the thought of the spanking didn't bother me anymore. All I could think about was how I had disappointed my dad and the look on his face.

I finally got the bleeding to stop as long as I kept it wrapped, so I made it through the rest of the day, and on the way home, nothing was said. So when we got home, I went to my room and waited for the inevitable. But it never came, and nothing more was ever said. Now, I don't know if Dad figured the gash on my finger was enough to make an impression, or if there was another reason, but I would have rather had the spanking than the look he gave me. I knew that he required my obedience and that I should have been spanked, and because I didn't listen, I had gotten hurt. But that was the first time I saw the pain it caused my father, and after that, the pain that I endured because of my stupidity was always nothing compared to the knowledge that I had done something to disappoint or hurt my dad. As I look back, every time I am selfish, it brings me trouble and shame. I am convinced that if the love of money or greed is the root of all kinds of evil, like it says in 1 Timothy 6:10, then every evil thing that comes from our heart in our entire life is born out of selfishness. I believe selfishness is the root of all evil, and because of it we endure many things, hurting ourselves and others, but what we seem to forget is the pain we cause our heavenly Father. A selfish person serves only themselves, and I think that is what Christ said in Matthew 6:19–24, "Do not store up for yourselves treasures on earth, where moth and rust destroy, and where thieves break in and steal. But store up for yourselves treasures in heaven, where moth and rust do not destroy, and where thieves do not break in and steal. For where your treasure is, there your heart will be also. The eye is the lamp of the body. If your eyes are good, your whole body will be full of light. But if your eyes are bad, your whole body will be full of darkness. If then the light within you is darkness, how great is that darkness! No one can serve two masters. Either he will hate the one and love the other, or he will be devoted to the one and despise the other. You cannot serve both God and Money" (NIV). Our selfishness is what fuels our greed and love of money and the things it buys. So if this is true, we cannot serve God and live a life of selfishness. We can't say we love God or say we are serving Him while selfishness is allowed to rule in our lives. I would encourage you to read what He says after that, but it is important for me to stay focused on what our selfishness brings us. Because I believe the darkness consumes us when we are selfish.

As I watched all the news coverage on the death of Michael Jackson, I began to see a pattern in his life that is very similar to all of us that live in America. I found that when he was younger, in his interviews he talked about his music (his love), but as he achieved greater success, he began to talk more and more about what he was cheated out of, how he was a victim. Even though everything he had was because of how his life had played out to that point, all he could think of was what he had missed out on, not all he had been given. His stories and behavior became more extreme and bizarre. I don't think he could distinguish between fact and fiction anymore. I believe it related directly to his focus on himself instead of others or his music. He was consumed with himself, and there was room for nothing else. Everyone I have seen or met who gets to that point is usually miserable. And his death and the way he died was his final selfish act. Some cases are not so extreme, yet it is selfishness just the same. I remember the year that Princess Di and Mother Teresa died, and it still amazes me how much you still hear about Princess Di in the news and how little you hear about Mother Teresa in the news. Then they tried to compare them to each other and how much good they both did. The media showed little bits and pieces of Mother Teresa's funeral, but like Michael, the news was consumed with Princess Di. Princess Di had lent her name to several charities, yet she died in a limousine, leaving a fancy hotel where she received the finest of everything, fleeing the paparazzi. Mother Teresa died with nothing, surrounded by those she had dedicated her entire life to. Giving everything she had to the thousands of people that she loved and that loved her in return for her sacrifice. "Jesus sat down opposite the place where the offerings were put and watched the crowd putting their money into the temple treasury. Many rich people threw in large amounts. But a poor widow came and put in two very small copper coins, worth only a fraction of a penny. Calling his disciples to him, Jesus said, 'I tell you the truth, this poor widow has put more into the treasury than all the others. They all gave out of their wealth; but she, out of her poverty, put in everything—all she had to live on'" (Mark 12:41–43 NIV). But that's not all Christ said about this kind of giving, going back to Matthew 6:1–4: "Be careful not to do your 'acts of righteousness' before men, to be seen by them. If you do, you will have no reward from your Father in heaven. So when you give to the needy, do not announce it with trumpets, as the hypocrites do in the synagogues and on the streets, to be honored by men. I tell you the truth, they have received their reward in full. But when you give to the needy, do not let your left hand know what your right hand is doing, so that your giving may be in secret. Then your Father, who sees what is done in secret, will reward you" (NIV).

There are a lot of rich people giving to a lot of charities for these very reasons. If they truly believed in the things they are giving to, they would dedicate their lives and make great sacrifices for them. But many give for selfish reasons, like it makes them feel good, it gives them political clout, it eases a guilty conscience, it gives them a tax break, because it seems like a good thing to do, or because maybe it will earn them favor with God. None of these reasons are bad, but the underlying problem is. It is for themselves, not out of true love and compassion for those in need. We know Christ loves us because He gave up everything for us, including His life. How is God supposed to know we love Him if everything we do for Him just happens to benefit us as well? Where is the true sacrifice that tells God nothing in life is more important than you? No wonder we live our lives angry, depressed, and alone. The reward in true sacrificial giving is a joyful heart, because my focus is not on myself but on others. I won't be feeling cheated or like I'm a victim because I will be busy trying to help others. I won't care what others think of me because my focus will be on what I think and do for others. If we truly recognize what we have been given, it should cause us to want to give what we have to God. But because we are selfish, we tend to be more worried about what God is doing for us. So we have to ask ourselves every day, How does God know that I love Him? And remember to see the selfishness in the things we do. I still have the scar on my finger to remind me of the look on my father's face and how I disappointed him. I also carry many other scars to remind me of how many times I have hurt and disappointed my heavenly Father with my selfishness. I hope you can learn to live an unselfish life, without having to carry so many scars to remind you of how many times your selfishness has hurt the very ones you are supposed to love.

Love,
Dad

Third and One

The other day, I was reading the June 26, 2009, Friday edition of *The Denver Post*, and an article caught my eye. I think it's important enough to share the whole article with you. It is entitled "A Final Toast to WWII Marines," by Colleen O'Connor:

> The first men to drive amphibious tractors in World War II are now gathering for their last reunion: a final toast of Old Grand Dad whiskey poured into 15 shot glasses emblazoned with the Marine Corps emblem. That bottle of whiskey has been with them since their first reunion, back in 1982. The plan was to save it until there were only two of them left standing. But with some now well into their 90's and some too ill to travel, they decided to make this the final salute.
>
> "The combat situation is a lifetime experience," said Jim Boring, 83, the youngest member. "I'm closer to some of these Marines I was in the war with than I am with my regular friends," he said.

"It's a relationship that can't be duplicated any other way."

On Saturday night at the Inverness Hotel, these 15 Marines of the 2nd Amphibian Tractor Battalion will gather for a banquet, with performances by the U.S. Marine Corps Color Guard and the Douglas County Young Marines Drill Team. The meeting has changed locations every year, traveling to cities where members live. They chose Denver for the last gathering, because Boring's daughter lives in Colorado. These are the last remnant of a generation fast disappearing. World War II veterans are dying at a rate of about 1,100 a day, according to the U.S. Department of Veterans Affairs. Most are octogenarians. One is 96. They use canes and wheelchairs and hearing aids.

"I'm going to miss these very much," said Boring, who became a preacher after the war and now serves as their Chaplin. Back then they called him "Kid". He was 17, and their first mission together was in 1943 at the Battle of Tarawa in the Gilbert Islands. It was the first test for the Alligator Amphibian tractors, designed by Donald Robeling, whose grandson also attends these reunions. "It was just like being in hell," said Dwight Hellums, 88, who now lives in Mississippi. In that three-day battle, all but 146 of 5000

Japanese were killed. One thousand Marines were killed, and nearly 2,300 were wounded. As the amphibian tractors made it over the reefs, they were mowed down by Japanese artillery. "I was in the first wave," said Boring, who was 17 at the time, "I didn't even make it to the beach. They blew mine out the water before it got there." He bailed out, swam to a reef, got on another tractor and went right back in. "The resistance from the beach was tremendous," he said. "I don't know how anybody lived through it. I was just in a daze all the time I was there." As the men told war stories, they were interrupted by Clay Evans, the Longmont Humane Society's development director, who'd seen their battalion sign in the hall as he passed by for a conference. "Were you guys on Tarawa?" he asked. "My grandfather was Alexander Bonnyman, who was killed there." Ralph Barber, 86, leaned forward on his cane, and stared intently. Like the other Marines, he knew all about Evans' grandfather, who'd received a posthumous Congressional Medal of Honor for storming a Japanese stronghold. "Your always surprised who comes in here," said Hellums, shaking his head.

After the war, these soldiers carved out new lives: lawyers, farmers, policemen. Not until 1982 did they gather together for the first reunion, in Tulsa, Okla. At first they brought their journals and memorabilia, stained newspaper clippings about places they'd served, from Tarawa to Saipan. They now travel lighter. "It's getting to the point if you can bring yourself and your own clothes and make it here, you're doing well," said Marie Darnell, wife of Robert Darnell, who now uses a wheelchair.

The soldiers and their wives treasure their memories of reunions gone by. "Every year, they fight World War II," Marie said, "and every year they win." (Colleen O'Connor, *The Denver Post*, June 26, 2009)

It is amazing the bond of friendship formed in these men during their life-and-death struggle in a war so long ago. They were different in every way possible, but they fought for one another's survival and became brothers forever. They survived all the killing and death and, together, were willing to sacrifice everything for their country and one another. "Greater love has no man than this, that he lay down his life for his friends" (John 15:13 NIV). They shared in something that few experience outside of the fray of the battle. The life-and-death struggle wipes away all the silly disputes and petty differences and causes one to hang on to one another. They needed one another if any of them were to survive and accomplish their objective. They could not win their fight if they were fighting one another. They had a common enemy and a common goal, and that was all that mattered, and they would die to achieve it. The Bible says we also are at war in 2

Corinthians 10:3–5, "For though we live in the world, we do not wage war as the world does. The weapons we fight with are not the weapons of the world. On the contrary, they have divine power to demolish strongholds. We demolish arguments and every pretension that sets itself against the knowledge of God, and we take captive every thought to make it obedient to Christ" (NIV). In Ephesians 6:10–18, Paul talks about the war we wage and the weapons we use, yet we don't come together as Christians, as if our very survival depends on it. A friend had shown me a breakdown of where all the different religions and denominations came from and asked what I thought of it, and as I looked at it, all I could see was how fractured the followers of Christ were. Of all the religions listed, the Christian faith was the most divided into little sections. If we were really aware of the battle around us, we would be more concerned about the cause of Christ than our doctrine. If you go to the gospels and study what Christ told his disciples, it was, in a nut shell, to love God, love one another, and tell others. Yet Christians tear one another down and beat one another up because they are a little different in what they believe. We are not focused on our common enemy and somehow don't seem to recognize that we won't survive without one another. "No one serving as a soldier gets involved in civilian affairs—he wants to please his commanding officer. Similarly, if anyone competes as an athlete, he does not receive the victor's crown unless he competes according to the rules" (2 Tim. 2:4–5 NIV). Paul was saying, whether we look at it as a war or a game, it has to be looked at the same. You can't win a war if everyone isn't in it together, and you can't win a game if you're not playing as a team. Don't get me wrong—every individual has to do certain things differently and some things the same. But if the whole is not working together, there is complete chaos.

When I was in high school, I loved sports with a passion, and my favorite by far was football. To be a college or professional player would have been a dream come true, but there was only one problem. As a five-foot-six, 150-pound senior in high school I had to work my tail off to earn even a little playing time, so there are very few highlights in my career. But the absolute greatest moment in my football days was as an outside linebacker when the opposing team had the ball on our forty-five-yard line and it was third down and one yard to go for the first down. The ball was snapped, and a hole in the line began to open up in front of me. The tackle took the defensive end out, the guard blocked down on the nose tackle, and the other guard pulled through the hole and took out the middle linebacker, leaving a hole in our defense. I could see the quarterback turning to hand the ball to the running back as I ran toward the hole. I met the running back at the hole just as the back got the ball, and I leveled him with the best solo tackle of my career. It wasn't anything incredibly fantastic; he didn't fumble the ball, and it wasn't like he could have gone around me, because I hit him at the same time he got the ball. But they still had to punt the ball. Now, you've had to endure a trivial football story about a not-so-great football player, namely me, so that I could make this point. Even though it was just a small gap in our defense, if I had not been prepared to step into it, there is no telling how far that runner might have gone—it might have even cost us the game. In our Christian walk, we are called to stand in the gap before God for our teammates and even our country. In doing so, God has promised that He will give us victory. "So I sought for a man among them, who would make a wall, and stand in the gap before me on behalf of the land, that I should not destroy it: but I found no one" (Ezek. 22:30 NKJV). It is important for us to remember that God is looking for someone to step up to the gap and take on the responsibility for those around us, and we may be all that stands between them and losing.

God has a spot and a time for each one of us on His team in this game. We must be prepared to fill it. Remember, "a chain is only as strong as its weakest link, and a team is only as good as its worst player." We, as a church, can build dividing walls that won't let anything out or anything in, or we can build the walls of unity that allow access in and out, then stand in the gap, defending those who belong to Christ and actively attacking the gates of hell and pulling those we are put here to deliver from its very clutches. Sounds kind of dramatic, but it is not just a game you play and everything will be okay even if we lose. Like war, there are lives depending on us to take responsibility for them and stand in the gap for them. Maybe if we quit fighting among ourselves and start fighting for what really matters, God will even preserve our country.

Love,
Dad

Tearing Down, Building New

When we were kids, we always used to help my dad tear down old buildings. We saved the bricks and the lumber. It was always an adventure. We never knew what we would find. All kinds of little treasures, antique bottles, coins, etc. We would find stuff in walls, in floors, and in ceilings. One time we even found a room that had been completely walled off. The doors had been walled off so we didn't even know it was there until we started tearing out the walls. It had been like that for years, and we found all kinds of old stuff in there. No one had been in there for years. When we first found it, I almost expected to find a dead body or something. Why else would you waste the space? We would tear down the buildings, and it was always interesting to see what the owner would build in its place and what we would build with the stuff from the old building. In fact, the addition to the house in Shelton was built largely from salvaged lumber from buildings we tore down.

Like those building, our lives all have rooms, compartments, and stuff. We are constantly building or tearing down walls that create who we are. But along with the big open, inviting rooms we build in our lives that everyone sees as who we are, there are these little walled-off rooms in our lives that no one has access to. No one gets into that part of our life, and that part of our life is never let out. It's those parts we want to forget are there, and it is easier to leave them buried. But those parts can never be cleaned or used because nothing goes in and nothing gets out. It's easy to think we're protecting ourselves, but like that room in that building, it becomes wasted space or wasted life. When I was in the seventh grade in school, one of my closest friends was an eighth grader that was popular and everything I was not. I'm still not sure how we became such good friends, but we did over the summer before I started seventh grade. That Halloween, he and his girlfriend were hit and killed by a car as they walked home from a party. The next two years, two kids that were a little older than my little brother, Randy, died. I used to give them piggyback rides, push them on the swings, play with them like I did with Randy and the other little kids. Then one died in a car accident and the other drowned. When I was sixteen, my grandma Eicher died suddenly, and a few years later, Grandma Lehman died. Every time someone in my life died, a little piece of my life was walled off—nothing evident to anyone on the outside, yet those walls were being built along with hurts I experienced in school or just those things that every kid goes through. Your mother and you kids came along, and everything seemed to be falling in place.

Then Mom, Dad, and Randy died, and the walls I had built to protect me from that pain were crushed, amplifying the pain and the loss of Mom, Dad, and Randy. That fall when Grandpa Eicher died, it seemed like it would crush me. I'm sure that life with me was painful as I struggled through that, yet it seemed like every time I was getting a handle on the hurt, someone else would die, whether by car wreck, murder, or suicide, and it would feel like I was having my heart ripped out. Then four years after Mom, Dad, and Randy died, Aunt Nancy, mom's sister, was also killed in a car wreck. So I started rebuilding walls that had been broken down and making them thicker, stronger. Making more rooms that nothing was going to penetrate. The parents of two friends from high school that had remained constant friends through our entire lives had become like secondary parents during high school, and two years ago, I attended the funeral of the last one living. She was the only one to see any of her grandchildren graduate, and she only saw one graduate. Three years ago, your aunt Trish died.

Every time someone died, to cope, I built another wall to keep it from being quite as painful. It is easier to build those walls than it is to tear them down, because everything left in those walled-off rooms of your life are still there exactly like you left them. Sometimes it might help to wall them off for a little while, but eventually, if you want to live life to its fullest, the way God intended, you will have to pull down those walls and face those hurts and all that ugly stuff in that room. It actually is like having a dead body in that room; you may not have to deal with the body, but the stench of that decaying part of your life eventually becomes evident, and you will see it seep out in anger, frustration, and bitterness. The only way to get rid of the stink is to tear down the walls and bury that part of your life. Face it, deal with it, and learn from it. "There is a time for everything, and a season for every activity under heaven: a time to be born and a time to die, a time to plant and a time to uproot, a time to kill and a time to heal, a time to tear down and a time to build" (Eccles. 3:1–3 NIV).

As I look back at your lives, I see different points in your lives where you both began building walls and how they changed your lives. There are times I have poked at those walls to see what comes out, and like me, nothing beautiful comes out, only ugly. I think I taught you how to build the walls but didn't do a very good job teaching you how to tear them down and face what's behind them. For the walls built because of me, I am eternally sorry, and I'm also sorry for being so busy building my own that I was not aware of the walls you were building and then teaching you how to tear them down. God can help you rebuild your house so every room can be inhabited and full of joy. The ultimate remodel job. "The thief comes only to steal and destroy; I came that they may have life, and have it abundantly" (John 10:10 NAS). Don't let the pains of the past steal your future joy. Make it a point to tear down the walls one at a time, and revel in what God can do with the space.

Love,
Dad

Dirt

Our house in Shelton, where you grew up, was small, and you remember some of the changes we made. Some of the remodeling was done when you were small, and you may not remember it. But even with all the changes and the work to change it and make it nicer and more efficient to live in, we still always had a problem with dust. The house always was dusty, no matter how much we cleaned. It was an old house. We had pulled walls out and cleaned out layers of dirt before putting in insulation, always expecting it to cut down on the dust but never seeing any improvement. Finally, after we moved, I decided I should replace the ceiling upstairs. I started to pull down the ceiling tiles, and much to my dismay, the rafters were clear full of dirt. Every time I would pull down more tiles, the room would get so dusty that I couldn't see, even with fans trying to draw it out. In fact, the fans got so much dirt in them that they stopped and I had to stop and clean them out just so they would run. I was amazed to find that the entire floor was covered with dirt about a foot and a half thick. Once the ceiling was down, I was wading through all this dirt with a corn scoop, shoveling dirt out a window.

It was then that I realized why our house was so dusty. No matter how much we cleaned, every time the wind blew or the house would shake even a little, the dirt in the rafter would sift through cracks in the tiles and float down through our whole house. The house would have always been dirty until I cleaned the dirt out of the rafters. Our lives are very much the same way. We remodel, we clean, we try all sorts of different things to make our lives neat and clean, yet we still keep finding dirt in our lives. We try to hide it; we clean till we think we got it, only to turn around and find it dirty again. Our lives can never be clean as long as we have dirt in our rafters. Every time we're shaken a little in life, all this dirt comes filtering out where we can see it. It will never stop until we clean out our ceiling and clean the rafters of our heart and mind. David says it best in Psalms 51 as he confesses his hidden sin of adultery with Bathsheba and the murder of her husband. "Have mercy on me, Oh God, according to your unfailing love; according to your great compassion blot out my transgressions. Wash away all my iniquity and cleanse me from my sin. For I know my transgressions, and my sin is always before me. Against you, and you only, have I sinned and done what is evil in your sight, so that you are proved right when you speak and justified when you judge. Surely I was sinful at birth, sinful from the time my mother conceived me. Surely you desire truth in the inner parts; you teach me wisdom in the inmost place. Cleanse me with hyssop, and I will be clean; wash me, and I will be whiter than snow. Let me hear joy and gladness; let the bones you have crushed rejoice. Hide your face from my sins and blot out all my iniquity. Create in me a pure heart, O God, and renew a steadfast spirit within me. Restore to me the joy of my salvation and grant me a willing spirit, to sustain me. Then I will teach transgressors your ways, and sinners will turn back to you. Save me from bloodguilt, O God, the God who saves me, and my tongue will sing of your righteousness. O Lord, open my lips, and my mouth will declare your praise. You do not delight in sacrifice, or I would bring it; you do not take pleasure in burnt offerings. The sacrifices of God are a broken spirit; a broken and contrite heart, O God, you will not despise. In your good pleasure make Zion prosper; and build up the walls of Jerusalem. Then there will be righteous sacrifices, whole burnt offerings to delight you; the bulls will be offered on your altar" (Ps. 51 NIV). Hidden sin in our lives will always show up sooner or later, and it will affect you all the rest of your life even if it isn't obvious to you or anyone around you.

Love,
Dad

The Last Christmas

In November of 1986, I had determined that I wasn't going to rush around for Christmas that year. Every year, we would go to my parents' on Christmas Eve, then hurry around and open presents at home, either after we got home from my folks late Christmas Eve or early Christmas morning, before we went to your mom's parents' for Christmas Day. So we made plans to go skiing in Colorado early that year instead of January. So we gave our gifts to our parents early that year, and it was all set. Only one problem: I started to feel guilty. I think maybe God was convicting me, because I really started to feel like I was being really selfish. Not because I wanted a relaxed Christmas with just us, but because I knew how much it meant to our parents to have us there at Christmas. So we canceled the Christmas ski trip and stayed for Christmas, and I thank God every Christmas that He put that on my heart and that I listened, because that was our last Christmas together with my parents and Randy. They died in the accident on February 8, 1987. You kids probably don't remember much about that Christmas, but the memories of that night, I will treasure forever, along with all the other simple memories that keep my parents close to me. Now, that Christmas was just as difficult as any other Christmas, trying to juggle our time between families, but to think I almost missed out on our last opportunity to celebrate Christmas with Mom, Dad, and Randy to have an easier Christmas is hard for me to comprehend. I think it is unfortunate that we lose so much in life and relationships because we are lazy or selfish.

It is like the man or woman that complains about being overweight yet won't rake the yard or dig a hole or park farther away from the door at the shopping mall. We look for the easiest way of doing everything in this country, and our families, our friendships, our work, and even our country suffer for it. Easier is not always better; sometimes doing things the hard way causes you to value what you have more than the easiest, fastest way. Loving someone means that you don't take the easy road; it means you are willing to endure difficult things and work hard to be a part of their life. In most cases, if it is easy, it probably isn't any good or it won't last. I think that was what Christ was alluding to when right after talking about the Father giving gifts in Matthew 7:7–12, He says in Matthew 7:13–14, "Enter through the narrow gate. For wide is the gate and broad is the road that leads to destruction, and many enter through it. But small is the gate and narrow the road that leads to life, and only a few find it" (NIV). If you are not working hard on your relationships with others and with God, then there probably won't be much substance to your relationships. Some of my most vivid memories of my parents are when they were working hard. I can still see my mom in a white cotton dress with light-blue stripes at the kitchen counter, kneading bread dough for her homemade bread and brushing the sweat and hair out of her eyes with the back of her hand because her hands were all covered with dough and flour. I can still see my dad in a worn thin plaid button-up shirt, unbuttoned and hanging open so you see the white T-shirt he always wore, stopping for a drink or to wipe the sweat off his face while he worked in his garden or in the garage. Kids, never settle for what is easy. If it is not worth working hard for, it is not worth having, and if your relationships are not worth pouring everything you are and have into them, then they are not relationships worth keeping.

Love,
Dad

The Bicycle Story

When I was about twelve, my brother Larry and I used our paper route money to buy new ten-speed bikes. We rode them to school and on our paper routes; I guess we rode them pretty much everywhere. After the bikes were out in the rain and snow for the winter, the chains were getting pretty rusty, so we decided to do our own repair and oil up the chains on the bikes, and if a little is good, then a lot has to be better, right? I was so happy with how much better it rode that I was feeling pretty good about ourselves and how well we had fixed the bikes, until I looked up at Larry's back as he rode up ahead of me to make a turn. There was this black streak running from his butt all the way up to the top of his head, and it was getting blacker by the minute. It was about then that I realized our fix-it job was probably all up and down my back as well. So I had Larry stop and check my back, and sure enough, I had a streak up my back to match his. We turned around, rode home, and showed my dad. He gave us a rag to wipe the chains on our bikes down, and then we went in to take showers. I had to wash my hair several times to get the oil out of it, and I'm sure Larry probably had to do the same.

Life is much the same way. There have been so many times in my life when I think I know what I'm doing, only to find out that I was only partly right and what I didn't know or that thing that I forgot to do has made a total mess out of things. Sometimes you make the same mistake over and over, always hoping for different results, but only proving that you are a complete and total fool. It is strange how all your good intentions don't equal wisdom. I believe that God has to be incredibly patient to keep loving us through all the messes we make. I do think He looks at our heart and our intent and not the results. There will be people who are not so kind, and I'm sure you have encountered them. Some people will start a fire on your oil slick and laugh as they watch you burn. Others will see the fire that others have started and, whether out of ignorance or spite, pretend to care but throw water on the fire, causing the fire to spread. Only the people who knock you down and roll you around on the ground really care. It is strange, but the people who sometimes appear to be the least kind are the ones who care the most. "Better is open rebuke than hidden love. Wounds from a friend can be trusted, but an enemy multiplies kisses" (Prov. 27:5–6 NIV). You need someone to watch your back to let you know when something you've done is making a mess of things. To knock you down when you need knocked down or lift you up when you need help getting back up.

You will always know who your friends are by one simple test. A true friend may need to knock you down sometimes, but they will always be right there, helping you get back up. A friend wants you to succeed where others want you to fail. "Two are better than one, because they have a good return for their work; If one falls down his friend can help him up. But pity the man who falls and had no one to help him up! Also, if two lie down together, they will keep warm. But how can one keep warm alone? Though one may be over powered, two can defend themselves. A cord of three strands is not quickly broken" (Eccles. 4:9–12 NIV). Larry had no idea that he had a streak up his back, nor did I, until I saw his and had him check mine. It is very easy to fall into the trap of thinking you can do everything on your own, to be the lone ranger of sorts, but it usually leads to nothing but hard times. In order to have friends, there is a very high probability that you will have to be a friend to them first. That means that there may be times when you will be hurt because you will invest in someone's life and they still will not be a friend to you. But when you find that friend or friends who will love you no matter what happens, treasure them and thank God for the blessing of friendship. "A man of many companions may come to ruin, but there is a friend who sticks closer than a brother" (Prov. 18:24 NIV).

Love,
Dad

The Last Dragon

I was riding in the car with Yvette when she was still in high school, listening to the radio, and she said, "Listen to this song. It's a really good song." As the song played, she said, "Well, I guess the lyrics aren't the best. I guess I never thought about it before." It reminded me of a similar time in my life. We had seen a movie called *The Last Dragon*, and I thought it was a good show. One night, my parents were coming over for one of your birthday parties, so I rented a couple of movies, one of which was *The Last Dragon*. I suddenly became painfully aware of how often the language was very vulgar, and began wincing every time certain words were uttered and apologized for the show. It was painfully embarrassing. Funny thing is, I'm sure my father had heard and seen worse before; it was just that his standards were set much higher than that. He never condemned the show or said anything about it. He didn't have to, because I grew up in my father's house, and I knew my father's standards. I thought about all the men I had seen swear and carry on until they found out my dad was a pastor, then suddenly they were apologizing for the way they were talking. My father never said anything; they just assumed that if he was a pastor, it wasn't acceptable to talk that way. Yet the one he represented was there all the time, hearing everything, everywhere they went, yet they didn't think about that at all.

As an adult, it was amazing how much more sensitive I was to the things around me when my father was present, knowing the standard I had been taught, just like Yvette was with me. Unfortunately, we don't recognize God's presence as often as we say we do, or we would be more sensitive to what we take in or do. Just as I was with my parents and Yvette was with me. I also think the closer we walk to God, the more aware we will be of things the Father finds offensive. What we allow many times taints the way we view God. Now, I'm not talking about holding others to the standards God has given us; I am talking about holding ourselves accountable for what God has impressed on us. Do we truly wince in shame when something is said or done in our presence that is offensive to our heavenly Father? Do we ask forgiveness for those around us and ourselves for falling short of His standards? He doesn't demand we do this or else; He just lets us know as we grow in His Word what His standards are and waits for us to wince when we finally see how short we all have fallen. How we react to our own sin and the sin around us before the Father is an indication of how close we are to the truth of who He is.

I think we say we seek the truth of God, yet we taint it with what we want the truth to be, and every generation seems to change the way they view God's Word. "Jesus answered, 'I am the way and the truth and the life. No one comes to the Father except through me. If you really knew me, you would know my Father as well. From now on, you do know him and have seem him'" (John 14:6 NIV). I sometimes think we get so caught up in being right that we miss the principle of what God is trying to teach us. We hold to trivial truths and miss the very character of God. Now, the reason I was uncomfortable when my father was there, hearing that movie, if I go deeper, is not a truth of what was right or wrong; it was a perception of right and wrong taught to me by my father. And everyone has those perceptions taught to them at some point in their lives. The truth in all that situation that God wanted to reinforce was not that I was uncomfortable about what was said because it was so wrong but because I loved and respected my father enough to want to please him and not offend him.

We should want to do things and not because God will be upset if we do them and punish us but because we love and respect Him and we want to be pleasing in His sight. People talk about truth and use those truths to separate themselves from others who call Christ Lord. God's truth will lead to love, forgiveness, and unity. In Romans chapter 14, Paul speaks to how truth can so quickly become a lie. Truth is no longer truth when we lose the heart and the character of God in it. You can follow the letter of the law and totally miss the intent of the law. I think if we try to learn the truth of God's Word without learning about the character, the heart, and the passion of God, then every truth we find in His Word will become a lie. A perfect example of this is the separation of church and state in our Constitution. Our Founding Fathers put that amendment in the Constitution because they had fled state-sponsored religions and they wanted to see that government was given no control over the religious ideals of the people. They never intended it as a way to take God out of the schools and out of government. They knew that the only way to take God out of government would be to take the people who believe in God out of government, and then it would not be a government by the people, for the people; it would be a government by some of the people, for all the people. That is what people today have deemed the amendment to say, and they are using a law meant to protect religious liberty to remove the very thing put in place to protect that liberty. All this is done by interpreting the truth of the law in absence of the intent of the law.

We Christians do the same thing. We use God's Word without knowing His heart, and because we do this, we go around spewing lies. Our lives should not be about being right but about truth, and if Christ is the way and the truth, then Christ's way is the only way to truth. "For God did not send his son into the world to condemn the world, but to save the world through him" (John 3:17 NIV). Christ came to love the world so the world, through Him, could be saved. There is nothing pretentious in that, only the heart of God. The truth of the law can't save us; only the heart of a loving Father. Kids, we can't honor and respect a loving God by being right or pretending to know the truth of God's law. That can only happen when we desire His heart and His character so intensely that we are willing to wrestle with ourselves and Him for it, like Jacob did in Genesis 32:24–28: "So Jacob was left alone, and a man wrestled with him till daybreak. When the man saw that he could not overpower him, he touched the socket of Jacob's hip so that his hip was wrenched as he wrestled with the man. Then the man said, 'Let me go, for it is daybreak.' But Jacob replied, 'I will not let you go unless you bless me.' The man asked him, 'What is your name?' 'Jacob,' he answered. Then the man said, 'Your name will no longer be Jacob, but Israel, because you have struggled with God and with men and have overcome'" (NIV).

How often do we care so much about what God cares about that we struggle, like Jacob, and won't let go until we see God's glory manifested in our lives and the lives of those around us? Contend for your faith. If you do, you will find that instead of your life being filled with the gifts of the

Spirit, your life will actually be filled with the fruits of the Spirit. "But the fruits of the Spirit is love, joy, peace, patience, kindness, goodness, faithfulness, gentleness and self-control. Against such things there is no law. Those who belong to Christ Jesus have crucified the sinful nature with its passions and desires. Since we live by the Spirit, let us keep in step with the Spirit" (Gal. 5:22–25 NIV). I know very few people who consistently demonstrate these fruits so it is something that you constantly have to struggle to do. I think for me I have always come closer to achieving that goal when I put Philippians 4:8–9 into practice. "Finally, brothers, whatever is true, whatever is noble, whatever is right, whatever is pure, whatever is lovely, whatever is admirable—if anything is excellent or praise-worthy—think about such things. Whatever you have learned or received or heard from me, or seen in me—put it into practice. And the God of peace will be with you" (NIV). Whether you are wrestling with God for the answers or walking with God, the important thing to remember is, through it all, God is with you.

Love,
Dad

Modern Medicine

I remember my dad talking about his time in the service and how the GI Bill was the way God supplied the tuition money for him to get through Bible college. Now, that may not seem like that big of a deal normally, but for my father, it was pretty amazing. My father never was able to be too active in sports because he had really bad asthma and he said a brother had tried to join the service and was denied for medical reasons, yet he was drafted and run right through. He told me how he made it through basic training and was about to be shipped over to Korea and he broke his leg in a training exercise and had to wait, and by the time it had healed, the war was over. When he was being checked out for his discharge, the doctor had asked him when he had gotten asthma, and my dad had told him he had had it his whole life. He said the doctor had then asked him how he had ever gotten in the service and, more importantly, how he had ever survived basic training. My dad told me God gave him what he needed to do what he needed to do. He said that there was always a reason for what happened to us, and there was always strength to get through those things that were put in front of us. He always would tell me not to worry about what was ahead, that God would take care of it. That whenever he didn't have insurance, we rarely needed it, and when we had insurance, that was usually when we needed it. He never came out and said it, but I think he was trying show me that it is not medicine that actually heals—it is God. It's not insurance that provides a way for us to be healthy, it is God, and sometimes God uses those things to accomplish His will.

It became evident how easy it is to fall into the trap of trusting or believing in the things God uses instead of God a year or two after their accident. We were in church, talking to some of the older people in the church, and one of the older men had just been released from the hospital and was recovering from a heart attack. I had made a statement saying that it was amazing how God had healed him, and he immediately said it wasn't God that healed him; it was the doctors. I had said that God had used His miracle of modern medicine to heal him, and once again, he said it was not God, it was the doctors and modern medicine, that had healed him, and he almost seemed to be getting upset. So I just dropped it. But I wondered how a Christian could think that way, having experienced the power of God. It was later that I was reading John, and I read John 3:14–15. "Just as Moses lifted up the snake in the desert, so the Son of Man must be lifted, that everyone who believes in him may have eternal life" (NIV). Now, I had heard the stories of the serpent in the wilderness as a kid, and I had seen the medical symbol of a snake wrapped around a post, and I knew that was what it represented. So I decided to look at it all from a different perspective, so I grabbed a concordance and read all the references to the serpent in the wilderness, and what I found kind of shocked me.

The account of it in Numbers 21:6–9: "Then the Lord sent venomous snakes among them; they bit the people and many Israelites died. The people came to Moses and said, 'We sinned when we spoke against the Lord and against you.

Pray that the Lord will take the snakes away from us.' So Moses prayed for the people. The Lord said to Moses, 'Make a snake and put it up on a pole; anyone who is bitten can look at it and live.' So Moses made a bronze snake and put it up on a pole. Then when anyone was bitten by a snake and looked at the bronze snake, he lived" (NIV). Now, something new struck me in the story. That the people had asked Moses to pray to God and have Him take away the snakes and God did not take away the snakes; He made a way for them to live through it. No wonder He points to it as a representation of Him. God didn't take away our sickness; He provided us a way to live through it. Christ died for our soul, but still, we live in a sinful world. God also gave us medicine to help us to live through our physical sicknesses, and the early pioneers of medicine recognized that. Thus the symbol that they chose to represent modern medicine.

But that is not the end. There was another reference that I had never heard of before. The second book of Kings 18:3–4 said this of Hezekiah, "He did what was right in the eyes of the Lord, just as his father David had done. He removed the high places, smashed the sacred stones and cut down the Asherah poles. He broke into pieces the bronze snake Moses had made, for up to that time the Israelites had been burning incense to it. (It was called Nehushtan)" (NIV). It is talking about Hezekiah destroying idols and the places they were worshipped, and the bronze serpent that Moses had made was one of the things he destroyed—they were worshiping it. The thing they were to look to that represented God's healing and deliverance should have reminded them of the great things God had done for them, and of His mercy. Only it became the very thing they worshipped and trusted in. It's alarming how little credit we give God for modern medicine and how much we worship and trust our medicine today. It's not just medicine; God can use vitamins, diet, chiropractic, acupuncture, and any number of other types of health alternatives, but ultimately, it is God that heals us or keeps us healthy. And it is important that we don't forget that and give God His proper place in all these situations.

I know a lot of people who believe God has nothing to do with it and that if He really cared we wouldn't need medicine because there would be no need for it. Bad things wouldn't happen, and people wouldn't suffer. Yet the evil we endure is the product of sin in the world, just like the snakes in the wilderness were sent to cause them to repent and look back to God as their deliverer. Sickness many times does the same thing; it causes us to turn to God, and the things God gives us to deliver us are the things we start to turn to instead of turning to God. Now, just because you are sick does not mean you are being punished; it just means that you are living in a world with sin and, therefore, sickness as well. So God, in His grace, has provided ways for us to receive healing. "Every good and perfect gift is from above, coming down from the Father of the heavenly lights, who does not change like shifting shadows" (James 1:17 NIV).

We have a tendency to serve all the things God has given; even our traditions, our churches, and our church programs many times become more important than God. Many of these things were started for all the right reasons, yet in the end they become more important than the God they were meant to serve and honor. Many times, we do them just because they seem like the thing to do and not out of a pure desire to honor God. We worship God, yet our focus is on how we worship or where we worship instead of who we worship, and we focus on what we give, not why we give it. I don't want to sound like all churches are bad, because there are many good people and good churches in the world and in this country. I guess all that I am saying is, there seems to be an alarming trend toward us losing our focus on what God is doing and a tendency to refocus on what we are doing. We need to always remember that it is not what we do, it is what God does with what we do, and the only thing that oftentimes determines what God does with what we do is the heart with which we do it. So keep your heart pure and pursue God with all your heart.

Love,
Dad

3D Pictures

"Blessed is the man who does not walk in the counsel of the wicked or stand in the way of sinners or sit in the seat of mockers. But his delight is in the law of the Lord, and on his law he meditates day and night. He is like a tree planted by streams of water, which yields its fruit in season and whose leaf does not wither. Whatever he does prospers" (Ps. 1:1–3 NIV). I think we all want to be the person that whatever we do prospers, and I think most parents want that for their children. But I don't think we even have a very good understanding of what it means to meditate on God's Word. I think, for most people, meditation conjures up visions of monks in some monastery chanting and sitting cross-legged in some corner for their entire life and fail to see the prosperity of that. I grew up thinking I just needed to read my Bible more. So I would read and, half the time, not remember a thing that I read a few minutes later. It wasn't until after you guys were a little older that I realized that meditation is not about how much you read but how much of what you read is applied to your life. The stuff you put into practice, that affects the way you think and what you do.

It is kind of like those 3D pictures that looked like a page of patterns and shapes that at a glance looked more like abstract wallpaper than a picture. But if you relaxed your eyes and stared a certain way, you would see the 3D picture. I remember going to art shops, and you kids would go up, and in just a few minutes you both would say, "This one is a picture of whatever it is" and move on to the next one. I would have to stand there twenty minutes, and finally I would see it, and because it took so long to see it, I wanted to see everything in the picture, for fear of losing it and having to start over. Later, I would ask one of you if you had seen this or that in the picture, and you wouldn't remember it or had not lingered long enough to even see it. I believe meditation is like those pictures. God's Word has so much hidden below the surface, and if we look at it in a hurried kind of way, we either only see wallpaper that makes no sense at all or we only see part of the picture. I have found that I only dig deep and mull over God's Word when I am asking a question and am serious about finding the answer. Then when I read certain passages, I don't quit thinking about them when I am finished reading. I think about it for days, trying to figure out what God's answers are to the questions I am asking, and it usually ends in an aha moment. That "Oh, I get it. That was so simple. Why am I so stupid? Why did it take me so long to get it?" Jesus was talking about prayer, and He said in Luke 11:9–10, "So I say to you: Ask and it will be given you; seek and you will find; knock and the door will be opened to you. For everyone who asks receives; he who seeks will finds; and to him who knocks, the door will be opened" (NIV). If you're not looking for something, you won't find anything, so why do we open our Bibles without wanting to find something? It's kind of pointless, I think, and a waste of time. The God of all creation said, if we seek we will find, and we enter a time with Him or pick up our Bibles and don't have any questions we want answered, or we don't want to know badly enough to spend the time and thought necessary to get the answers we seek.

There are some questions that we need to constantly keep asking ourselves, not because we haven't thought about them before, but because these questions should affect every aspect of our life. How we answer these questions determines how we treat ourselves, our friends, our family, and even our enemies. So as our experiences change the way we view life, they may, without us being aware of it, be changing the way we view or answer these questions. Even cause us to lose our focus on what the answers to these questions really mean and how they affect, or should affect, our attitudes and actions in life. It is my hope that you will answer these questions just off the top of your head first, then later go back and see what God's Word tells you the answers are and really think deeply on what God wants you to believe at this time in your life. Answering these questions should affect your relationships and every other aspect of your life.

Life Questions

- What makes you a Christian? Why?
- How can you be sure? What makes this truth?
- What are you basing your truths on?
- What makes you right? What makes you wrong? How can you be certain in either case?
- As a Christian, what is your main objective?
- How do others know you follow Christ? Are you sure that is the way that honors God?

- What things in your Christian walk exalt God? What actually exalt yourself?
- What sets you apart from other Christians? What do you have in common?
- What makes someone godly, righteous, holy, or spiritual?
- What makes someone ungodly, unrighteous, unholy, or not spiritual?
- What is God looking for in you?
- What are you looking for in yourself?
- What are you wanting from God? What do you think you deserve?
- What is grace? What is mercy? What is free will?
- What makes you angry? Why? How do you justify your anger?
- What hurts are you feeling? Why? Do you allow yourself to feel like a victim? Do you live in self-pity?
- What do you fear? How do you let your fears control who you are and what you do with your life?
- What is love? What does it mean to love someone? What tells you someone loves you?
- Who are you supposed to love? Why?
- Who do you love? How do you know you love them? How do they know you love them?

- What conditions do you put on your love?
- What makes you feel loved? What makes you feel unloved?
- What makes you better than someone else? What makes them better than you?
- What makes you a winner? What makes you a loser?
- What truths are you believing? How do you know they are truth?
- What lies are you believing? How do you know they are lies?
- If you know they are lies, why do you continue to let them control you as if they were truth?
- How do you know the difference between what God is telling you to do and what you want to do?
- What is faith? Where does faith take over and fact leave off? Is that point where it should be?

You may not have the answers to these questions ever. Some may elude you and yet be right in front of you. Sort of the can't-see-the-forest-because-of-all-the-trees type of thing. Yet we have to continue to look. Wisdom doesn't come in knowing; it comes in the search for truth, and the adventure is in the journey, not the destination. If you find truth, you are sure to find Christ and His love. "Jesus answered, 'I am the way and the truth and the life. No one comes to the Father except through me'" (John 14:6 NIV). "As the Father has loved me, so I have loved you. Now remain in my love. If you obey my commands, you will remain in my love, just as I have obeyed my Father's commands and remain in his love. I have told you this so that my joy may be in you and that your joy may be complete. My command is this: Love each other as I have loved you" (John 15:9–12 NIV). If we want to prosper with God, then we must meditate. "Be strong and courageous, because you will lead these people to inherit the land I swore to their forefathers to give them. Be strong and courageous. Be careful to obey all the law my servant Moses gave you; do not turn from it to the right or to the left, that you may be successful wherever you go. Do not let this Book of the Law depart from your mouth; meditate on it day and night, so that you may be prosperous and successful" (Josh. 1:6–8 NIV). There is one more question you may need to ask yourselves: What actually is a prosperous and successful life? Kids, if you're not asking questions, then you won't be looking for answers, and if you're not looking for answers, you probably won't be finding any of the answers that make your life prosperous and successful.

Love,
Dad

The Letter

I am sure I have probably told you before how my dad had been the pastor of small churches over the years of his life and how they had just built a new church and the first service in the completed building was their funeral. I am sure I have also told you over and over how, when we pulled in the grave site for the burial service, we could see cars coming with their lights on for miles. It is amazing how many lives two people can touch and how many people over the years have shared with me what my parents meant to them. So I want to share three of the stories of how my parents had an impact on those around them yet probably never realized it.

One day, when we were in the church where Dad had preached for years in Shelton, we had a guest speaker from Gideon Bibles. Local Christian businessmen would go around, speaking and asking for donations for Gideon Bibles to buy and distribute Bibles free of charge to students, motels, and hospitals. After the service, I introduced myself and thanked Floyd for the work that he was doing, and he immediately asked me if I was related to Sam Lehman. I told him he was my father, and he proceeded to tell me how indebted he was to my father. He said that his father had never been a believer and hated Christians, and especially pastors, but when his father got sick and went into the hospital, he had asked my father if he would visit him, and my father had agreed. He said, when he went to see his dad the next day, his dad told him he hated pastors but he liked that Sam guy; he was okay. He said my dad had visited his dad two or three times a week every week, and they talked about farming and business and any number of things that his father liked to talk about and he looked forward to seeing my dad. He said, "My dad loved your dad," and then he said, "Two days before my dad died, your dad shared the plan of salvation with him and led him to the Lord. My father is in heaven today because of your dad."

Marge lived just down the street from us when we lived in the Shelton. You kids probably don't remember her. She was one of the older women in the church when I was a kid, and her husband had died when I was sixteen. I would go over and visit her every so often to see how she was doing and just talk. One night, she said how much she had appreciated my parents and that she was never able to tell my parents how much they had meant to her, especially my mother. She said when her husband died, my mom stayed, even though her mother was in the hospital and didn't look like she was going to make it, and sang at her husband's funeral, then flew out that night to be with her mom. I remembered my mom had gotten to see my grandmother right before she died, but I had no idea that she had waited a day so she could be there for Marge. My mother had never mentioned it, and I don't think she ever realized how much what she did meant to Marge.

The last one I am going to share with you is a letter that we received about a year after the accident. Your mother got a call one day, asking if we were any relation to Sam and Marilynn Lehman, and when your mom said I was their son, she said she hadn't heard about the accident until much later and wanted the family to know how much my parents had meant to her. So she had left a letter in a candleholder at the grave site and hoped that we would be able to go and get it. We went out and got it, and I have kept that letter all these years. And I would like to share it with you. It was addressed thus: "To: The family of Sam and Marilynn Lehman, with much love."

Dear family of Sam and Marilynn Lehman,

Please allow me to introduce myself. My name is Nancy ———, and I would like to share with you the impact that Sam and Marilynn had on my life many years ago. Because of their willingness to serve the Lord, I am a life that was changed.

I first met them when I was about 11 years old. I was a camper at Camp Joy Bible Camp, Alma, NE, and Sam was the minister and speaker. Sam and Marilynn would bring their camper and park it under the trees at Camp Joy. I remember sneaking out of the camp dorms late at night and going to their camper and playing cards. They always welcomed me with open arms and put up with the silly antics of an 11-year-old. I always called Sam Uncle Sam. The camp director was called Uncle Pete, and it seemed only right to call Sam Uncle Sam. He never seemed to mind.

I had asked Christ into my heart at the age of 8. When I was around 12, I was asked to be a counselor's helper at Camp Joy. I readily accepted the challenge because it would get me away from a home in which love was rarely shown. I had no idea how unprepared I was to be a counselor's helper. The first night of camp, a young child came to me and wanted to ask Christ into their heart. I had no idea what to do or say. I was able to find a senior counselor, and they were able to lead this child to Christ.

It was late that night, and Sam and Marilynn were very tired, yet when I knocked on their door and asked them if they could teach me how to share the plan of salvation, Sam grabbed a couple of pops and bibles and said, let's go! Sam and I went to the camp kitchen, and for hours, he took the time to instruct me in "the Romans Road," teaching me how to share what those verses meant and how to help someone say the sinner's prayer. Marilynn stayed in the camper and prayed for us the whole time.

Because of their willingness to do this, I have had the blessed honor of leading others to Christ and have been with them as they accepted Christ as their personal Savior.

Through the next several years, I grew up and experienced many things that were emotionally and mentally hurtful, and I allowed those experiences to scar my heart and soul. I am not an attractive person, and by the age of 17, I felt I had absolutely no value to my life. No one knew that, as I had become an expert at keeping the truth hidden, and all people could see was a very confident, cool, and hardworking teenager who loved the Lord.

I still went to camp, and at the age of 17, God helped Sam and Marilynn see right to my heart and soul. I had been counseling for several weeks, and one day the staff was given a two-hour break to go swimming at the lake. When it was time to get out of the water and go back to camp, I looked at all the people on the beach watching me and had what I call a panic attack of the soul. I could not get out of the water and have these people see how ugly and valueless I was. I was able to keep up all appearances and was able to make everyone believe I was going to swim some more and catch up with them later. Sam and Marilynn knew exactly what was going on with me. In front of all these people, Sam came to me, kissed me right on the lips, and walked with me out of the water, just like I was the most beautiful person in the world. Marilynn met us at the shore and hugged me and said, "I love you." I had not been given a loving touch or had those words said to me in many years.

Because of them, I knew that I was loveable and had value in this world. Now, I have been able to reach out to others who are hurting inside and give them a touch of love also. I was living in KS and did not learn of their death until months later. I believe the time has come for me to share how their lives touched mine in the simple things they did. If God is willing and the fine family of Sam and Marilynn find this, please know how valuable their lives were. This candle holder is given as a reminder of that.

Nancy ——

I don't think my parents ever realized the far-reaching effects of the little they did. "But whoever lives by the truth comes into the light, so that it may be seen plainly that what he has done has been done through God" (John 3:21 NIV).

Love,
Dad

To Fear God

Lately, I have thought a lot about what it means to fear God and what that looks like in the Christian's life. I don't think we reverence God the way we should anymore, and I think it shows up in how we serve Him and what we do with Him in our lives. I was thinking back to when you kids were younger and began to realize that it is similar to electricity. When my dad was helping me tear out the north upstairs window to put in a bigger one, he was outside on a ladder, and I was upstairs on the inside. We had torn out the existing window and were tearing loose the siding and boards to make room to frame in the new window when I found two single conductor wires, wires with only one copper wire, in the old-style insulation just stuck in the wall about six inches apart from each other. Now, Dad figured that they were just abandoned wires with no power to them, because who would be dumb enough to leave energized wire just stuck in a wall somewhere? So he pulled them out, and they were hanging along the wall next to the aluminum extension ladder he was on. It was making me really nervous and afraid that he would get electrocuted, so I asked Dad if we shouldn't check the wires. My dad said, "Surely, they wouldn't have left power on them," but he agreed and grabbed the wires one in each hand by the insulation and held them out away from the ladder and brushed the ends together. And sparks flew everywhere. It scared the crap out of me, but it didn't even faze my dad—he just muttered something about having a hard time believing anyone could be so stupid. Then he said, "I guess we'll just have to put an outlet under the window," and told me to go shut off the fuse box. After I began to work with electricity more, I realized he was not afraid to touch the wire because, along with him only touching the insulation, he also had on leather gloves, which act as a form of insulator, too, and as long as they didn't touch the ladder, he would be okay. He didn't fear electricity because he understood it better than I did and understood what he needed to do to be safe.

Later, after I had been working with electricity for years, I was wiring up something at work and a guy I was working with said, "I don't know anything about electricity and I don't want to. I just stay away from it because it scares me." And I had told him, "You don't have to be afraid of it, but if you don't respect it, it will kill you." Looking back, I realize he was right to fear it because he recognized the power that was there and didn't understand what he needed to do to work with it and be safe, but he also allowed his fear to keep him from learning any more about electricity. Then, I have seen others who have gotten hurt because they didn't respect the power that electricity possesses and were complacent in how they worked with electricity. If you are not diligent to learn everything about the nature of electricity and vigilant to be aware of your surroundings, what you are doing or touching, and how it affects your safety, you could lose your life very quickly.

I think God is very much like electricity. If you don't know anything about the nature of God, then you should fear Him, and if you don't fear Him, then you either have denied or know nothing of the power of God. Today many people flip a switch to turn on a light and never consider the great power that is there and how it can help or hurt them. But people do the same thing with God; they see creation yet don't fully consider the power He has to give and to take away. Job recognized it, and that is why, after losing everything, he could respond the way he did in Job 1:20–21: "At this, Job got up and tore his robe and shaved his head. Then he fell to the ground in worship and said: 'Naked I came from my mother's womb, and naked I will depart. The Lord gave and the Lord has taken away; may the name of the Lord be praised'" (NIV). Even in Christian circles, we minimize God's power. I have heard so often, "It is disturbing." God created the things in Genesis 1 in a day, but that day could have been a thousand years. Let's just forget the fact that He created the light and the dark and that was the first day, and through all of recorded time, it has never changed. You can set your watch to it. Oh, maybe that's already been done. But of greater significance is the fact that you have just minimized the power of an awesome, infinitely powerful God and made His power easier to comprehend. How foolish we are! We enter His presence not in fear and trembling but in an almost lackadaisical fashion.

Yes, He loves us and gave His Son to deliver us from ourselves, but that hasn't changed His power and righteousness. I hear people talk of knowing God as if we can figure Him out or meeting with God face-to-face like Moses did in Exodus 33:10–11: "Whenever the people saw the pillar of cloud standing at the entrance to the tent, they all stood and worshiped, each at the entrance to his tent. The Lord would speak to Moses face to face, as a man speaks with his friend. Then Moses would return to the camp, but his young aide Joshua son of Nun did not leave the tent" (NIV). Now, I don't how that was accomplished, whether there was a veil or it was the Spirit of God, but Moses never saw God in the fullness of His glory because of what is said in chapter 33 verses 17–23: "And the Lord said to Moses, 'I will do the very thing you have asked, because I am pleased with you and I know you by name.' Then Moses said, 'Now show me your glory.' And the Lord said, 'I will cause my goodness to pass in front of you, and I will proclaim my name, the Lord, in your presence. I will have mercy on whom I will have mercy, and I will have compassion on whom I will have compassion.' 'But,' he said, 'you cannot see my face, for no one may see me and live.' Then the Lord said, 'There is a place near me where you may stand on a rock. When my glory passes by, I will put you in a cleft in the rock and cover you with my hand until I have passed by. Then I will remove my hand and you will see my back; but my face must not be seen'" (NIV). "Then the Lord came down in the cloud and stood there with him and proclaimed his name, the Lord. And he passed in front of Moses, proclaiming, 'The Lord, the Lord, the compassionate and gracious God, Slow to anger, abounding in love and faithfulness, maintaining love to thousands, and forgiving wickedness, rebellion and sin. Yet he does not leave the guilty unpunished; he punishes the children and their children for the sin of the fathers to the third and fourth generation'" (Exod. 34:5–7 NIV). The result of Moses just looking at the back of God is recorded in Exodus 34:29–35: "When Moses came down from Mount Sinai with the two tables of the Testimony in his hands, he was not aware that his face was radiant because he had spoken with the Lord. When Aaron and all the Israelites saw Moses, his face was radiant, and they were afraid to come near him. But Moses called to them; so Aaron and all the leaders of the community came back to him, and he spoke to them. Afterward all the Israelites came near him, and he gave them all the commands the Lord had given him on Mount Sinai. When Moses finished speaking to them, he put a veil over his face. But whenever he entered the Lord's presence to speak with him, he removed the veil until he came out. And when he came out and told the Israelites what he had been commanded, they saw that his face was radiant. Then Moses would put the veil back over his face until he went in to speak with the Lord" (NIV).

To look at Moses after he saw just the back of God in His glory was like looking straight into a spotlight, and it doesn't sound like it went away. It sounds like he wore a veil the rest of his life. No wonder it was Moses who wrote in Deuteronomy 4:9–10, "Only be careful, and watch your-selves closely so that you do not forget the things your eyes have seen or let them slip from your heart as long as you live. Teach them to your children and to their children after them. Remember the day you stood before the Lord your God at Horeb, when he said to me, 'Assemble the people before me to hear my words so that they may learn to revere me as long as they live in the land and may teach them to their children'" (NIV). Well, this was the place in the Bible I started on this venture. Funny how I made a full circle. Moses also wrote in Deuteronomy 4:24, "For the Lord is a consuming fire, a jealous God" (NIV). Who better to make that statement than the only man to ever witness it firsthand?

I hope I established God's power and that He should be feared, but He is also a God of compassion and mercy, and He established that with the sacrifice of His Son. "Because those who are led by the Spirit of God are sons of God. For you did not receive a spirit that makes you a slave again to fear, but you received the Spirit of sonship. And by him we cry, 'Abba, Father.' The Spirit himself testifies with our spirit that we are God's children. Now if we are children, then we are heirs—heirs of God and co-heirs with Christ, if indeed we share in his sufferings in order that we may also share in his glory" (Rom. 8:14–17 NIV). Now this says we are the sons of God and we don't have to be afraid of Him, so it means like understanding electricity means: we don't fear it but respect it. Becoming the children of God means we no longer have to fear God but we have to respect Him. "Endure hardship as discipline; God is treating you as sons. For what son is not disciplined by his father? If you are not disciplined (and everyone undergoes discipline), then you are illegitimate children and not true sons. Moreover, we have all had human fathers who disciplined us and we respected them for it. How much more should we submit to the Father of our spirits and live! Our fathers disciplined us for a little while as they thought best; but God disciplines us for our good, that we may share in his holiness" (Heb. 12:7–10 NIV). *Respect* and *submit* seemed almost interchangeable in that passage, and we learn how to respect and submit to God from how we respect and submit to our parents. Something I wasn't good at.

When you spend a lot of time in the Bible, you learn all the verses to justify your rebellion, like "Don't provoke your children to anger," or when you get a little older, there is the excuse that you're no longer a child. But the other day, I was listening to a sermon on Jesus turning water into wine, and something struck me. Even though the sermon didn't cover this point, and to be honest, I have never heard it talked about this way, I want to tell you what I found after I researched it a little more. Jesus as a boy in the temple, talking with the teachers and leaders, and when Mary and Joseph found him, in Luke 2:48–52 it says, "When his parents saw him, they were astonished. His mother said to him, 'Son, why have you treated us like this? Your father and I have been anxiously searching for you.' 'Why were you searching for me?' he asked. 'Didn't you know I had to be in my Father's house?' But they did not understand what he was saying to them. Then he went down to Nazareth with them and was obedient to them" (NIV). Jesus was the perfect Son of God and knew all things, so He knew far more than His imperfect parents, yet He was obedient to them. How many times must He have known what they were doing was wrong and what they were telling Him to do was wrong, yet He was obedient to them anyway? Doesn't leave much room for rebelling against my parents just because I didn't like what they were telling me to do or because I thought they were wrong.

But it gets even deeper in John 2, when Jesus and His disciples were at a wedding with his mother. "On the third day a wedding took place at Cana in Galilee, Jesus' mother was there, and Jesus and his disciples had also been invited to the wedding. When the wine was gone, Jesus' mother said to him, 'They have no more wine.' 'Dear woman, why do you involve me?' Jesus replied. 'My time has not yet come.' His mother said to the servants, 'Do whatever he tells you.' Nearby stood six stone jars, the kind used by the Jews for ceremonial washing, each holding from twenty to thirty gallons. Jesus said to the servants, 'Fill the jars with water'; so they filled them to the brim. Then he told them, 'Now draw some out and take it to the master of the banquet.' They did so, and the master of the banquet tasted the water that had been turned into wine. He did not realize where it had come from, though the servants who had drawn the water knew. Then he called the bridegroom aside and said, 'Everyone brings out the choice wine first and then the cheaper wine after the guests have had too much to drink; but you have saved the best till now.' This, the first of his miraculous signs, Jesus performed at Cana in Galilee. He thus revealed his glory, and his disciples put their faith in him" (John 2:1–11 NIV). Now, I've heard a lot of different angles on this miracle and what was said and done, but I have never heard anyone look at it this way. This whole miracle was not to show His power or His glory, although that was a result. The whole purpose of this miracle was to demonstrate His submission to His mother, the parent God, His Father, put in authority over Him. She was wrong, because He made it clear it was not His time yet; still, He did it anyway. And because He had always been obedient and subject to her, when He told her it wasn't His time, she never wavered, because she knew He would do it, because He had always done what she asked before. He was in his thirties and had followers of His own; still, He submitted to the authority that was placed over Him, which tells me that is the way God truly designed it. That is why Jesus could pray in Luke 22:42, "Father, if you are willing, take this cup from me; yet not my will, but yours be done" (NIV).

Now, I have heard others say that He really didn't mean that it was not his time, which makes Jesus a liar, or that it was translated wrong, so if you look in John 7, it kind of puts that to rest as well. "Jesus' brothers said to him, 'You ought to leave here and go to Judea, so that your disciples may see the miracles you do. No one who wants to become a public figure acts in secret. Since you are doing these things, show yourself to the world.' For even his own brothers did not believe in him. Therefore Jesus told them, 'The right time for me has not yet come; for you any time is right. The world cannot hate you, but it hates me because I testify that what it does is evil. You go to the Feast. I am not yet going to this Feast, because for me the right time has not yet come." Having said this, he stayed in Galilee' (John 7:3–9 NIV). When He told His brothers it wasn't time yet, He didn't do it because He was not subject to them. There are so many ways I rejected my parents' authority when I was younger, and most of it I recognized after I became a parent myself. Most were justified by my parents not understanding me or loving me enough and that they made mistakes and that was the reason I had problems. Once I had you kids and realized how much my parents loved me and how hard they tried to teach me what was right, it also made me aware of how big the responsibility is, how easy it is to fail, and how selfish I had been.

So everything's good now, right? Wrong. Lately, I have become aware of hidden things that I'm just now finding I have passed on to you, and it is affecting how you fear and serve God. The first is, as a kid, I always hated that when I was told to do something, and I would ask, "Why?" My father never gave me an explanation; his reason was always "Because I said so." I determined that children's ability to understand was underestimated by my father and that this statement was just a way to make me do things for which Dad didn't have a good reason, and I would never say that. I would always explain why anytime I asked you to do something. Lately, I have talked about certain things I had required you to do and had explained why, and I thought when they came up in conversation, you would now appreciate it. Instead, all I sensed was bitterness and anger, and it was then that I began to realize that no matter how sound the judgment was in my mind, or still is, if you have a different perspective, then you will still feel it's wrong and that I have wronged you or failed you somehow. That was the attitude I had when my father had told me to do it because he told me to. Even though I had explained everything, I got the same response, only amplified. It was only then that I realized God tells me to do things that I don't understand and I need to do them just because He says to do it, not because it makes sense to me. My father was teaching me that when he said, "You do it because I said to." In my rebellion against my father, I learned the lesson for myself without even knowing it, but I didn't teach it to you, and I believe you both have struggled with that aspect of your faith. I guess I wasn't alone, because I see it everywhere and I hear that mentality rehearsed over and over. I guess, as a child, I ignored Proverbs 22:15, "Folly is bound up in the heart of a child, but the rod of discipline will drive it far from him" (NIV).

The problem is, I taught you that if you don't understand it or like it, it must be wrong and not that you should do what I say because I said so and that I said so because I love you and I am trying to protect you and teach you how to follow God. The second is, I always thought that I should have gotten to do like the other kids and play more. I always had to work in part to make money for myself, but also, we kids worked with Dad on things that we never got paid for. We worked in the garden, cutting down trees and tearing down buildings, just to make ends meet. So as parents, your mom and I determined that we weren't going to work like that. Yes, I made you work, but that was the money you spent on what you wanted, and other than that, you didn't have to do much of anything. I guess the underlying feeling was that I felt I was having to serve my father and mother, and if my father and mother were really doing what they should as Christians, they would have been examples and served us kids. So that was what we did, to some degree. The only problem is, God has designed that the children serve the parents, and what I have found is that when you serve a child, they don't learn to serve; they learn to expect their parents to wait on them and to be served. Most kids today sit and let someone else wait on them. Now, I think you kids have done remarkably well in spite of your parents' foolishness in this matter, but I still see the effects. Now, I have always read Philippians 2:5–11: "Your attitude should be the same as that of Christ Jesus: Who, being in very nature God, did not consider equality with God something to be grasped, but made himself nothing, taking the very nature of a servant, being made in human likeness. And being found in appearance as a man, he humbled himself and became obedient to death—even death on a cross! Therefore God exalted him to the highest place and gave him the name that is above every name, that at the name of Jesus every knee should bow, in heaven and on earth, and every tongue confess that Jesus Christ is Lord, to the glory of God the Father" (NIV). I have always read this from the perspective of a Christian serving others, but it is actually about Jesus serving His Father. Just like the children are part of the parent and therefore could be consider equal to them, only in submitting and serving the parents can the child ever be exalted.

I taught you kids to work for rewards. Not for the joy of serving. This mentality also teaches us that God should serve us, do things our way, and give us what we want, not that we should serve Him without regard for ourselves and our own comfort. If we quit on God when we don't understand why things have happened the way they have or we treat God like the great vending machine in the sky, can we say we fear Him, respect Him, or love and serve Him? In our serving, joy does not come from what is received; the joy comes in the service and what is accomplished in the service. I know I have taught you out of a heart that was resisting or rebelling against my parents, and I know you may not want to hear or accept what has been said here. I can only hope that you hear and don't perpetuate the same things I have done. We cannot serve, submit, and respect God the way we should if we fail to practice it on our parents. As the prodigal son, I keep finding the ways that I have screwed up, and every time I think

I'm back home, where I belong and am living in submission, I find something else and the journey begins all over. I am so thankful God is a consuming fire, just and holy. But I am even more thankful that He is merciful, compassionate, and patient.

Love,
Dad

Shepherds or Sheepherders

You kids might remember us going out to the farm of some friends of ours, but you were pretty young when we would go up to Joe and Becky's farm, so I don't know how much you remember. Joe and Becky raised sheep and cattle, and one time, when we were there, as it got to be later in the evening, Joe had said it was time to bring the sheep in, so I went with him fully expecting to go out to the pasture next to the house and bring them in. Instead, we went to the fence and he whistled and hollered something to the border collie that was out with the sheep. The dog jumped into action, barking and herding them toward the barn. Running back and forth, making sure none of the sheep went anyway but to the barn. Joe and I just watched while the dog did all the work. I was impressed, so I asked him how he trained the dog to do what it did. He said that they would take the dog when it was a puppy and put it in with the lambs, so it grew up with the sheep. It slept with them, ate with them, and played with them. The dog was viewed by the sheep as one of them, and the dog felt he was one of the sheep. Joe had said the only difference between the dog and the sheep was that he could train the dog to take the sheep where he wanted them to go and he would protect the sheep from the coyotes that would kill the sheep, and was willing to die for them as if he were one of them. I never thought much about it after that, until recently.

I have noticed that many pastors, Christians, and business leaders have taken on the mentality of the sheep owner of today. Just like to Joe the sheep represented an investment or income, employees or people going to a pastor's church, maybe even people in general to Christians, many times become viewed as objects that are a means to an end. They become the way to a big, successful business, a thriving church, or even a way to find favor with God. The dog was the real shepherd. His whole life was the sheep. They knew him, he was a part of them, and he looked out for them and protected them. Business owners and CEOs, for the most part, don't care about or protect and provide for their employees the way they used to. Pastors and Christians in general, likewise, have gotten too busy to be a part of the lives of the people around them. We generally watch from the fence while we send someone else and hope that they get the job done. No wonder many of American businesses and churches are in the state they are in. Jesus left us an example of how we are to lead people by telling us how He cared and looked out for us in the gospel of John. "'I tell you the truth, the man who does not enter the sheep pen by the gate, but climbs in by some other way, is a thief and a robber. The man who enters by the gate is the shepherd of his sheep. The watchman opens the gate for him, and the sheep listen to his voice. He calls his own sheep by name and leads them out. When he has brought out all his own, he goes ahead of them, and his sheep follow him because they know his voice. But they will never follow a stranger; in fact, they will run away from him because they do not recognize a stranger's voice.' Jesus used this figure of speech, but they did not understand what he was telling them. Therefore Jesus said again, 'I tell you the truth, I am the gate for the sheep. All who ever came before me were thieves and robbers, but the sheep did not listen to them. I am the gate; whoever enters through me will be saved. He will come in and out, and find pasture. The thief comes only to steal and kill and destroy; I have come that they may have life, and have it to the full. I am the good shepherd. The good shepherd lays down his life for the sheep. The hired hand is not the shepherd who owns the sheep. So when he sees the wolf coming, he abandons the sheep and runs away. Then the wolf attacks the flock and scatters it. The man runs away because he is a hired hand and cares nothing for the sheep. I am the good shepherd; I know my sheep and my sheep know me—just as the Father knows me and I know the Father—and I lay down my life for the sheep. I have other sheep that are not of this sheep pen. I must bring them also. They will listen to my voice, and there shall be one flock and one shepherd. The reason my Father loves me is that I lay down my life—only to take it up again. No one takes it from me, but I lay it down of my own accord. I have the authority to lay it down and authority to take it up again. This command I received from my Father'" (John 10:1–18 NIV). Jesus also told the parable of the lost sheep, how the shepherd left the ninety-nine sheep to search for and find the one lost. In all this, He never said "I watch from the fence and wait for the dog to herd them in," or have a hired hand bring them in; He was personally invested in each one of His sheep. They knew Him, and He knew them, and He was prepared to and did lay His life down for them.

How personally invested in others' lives are we? Leaders are not smooth talkers, people who can convince people their way is best. They are not sheepherders that compel people to do and operate certain ways by threat or bribery. True leaders have people follow them because they have seen their example, experienced their protection, recognized their sacrifice, and trust and love them. David, of course, was one of the shepherds that became a great leader, and we can see in his life his passion and love for those around him. But I think the greatest example in the Bible of what it takes to be a leader is Moses. Think about it; he grew up in the pharaoh's house, was able to tell people what to do, and was educated by the best of the best. He grew up being what we call a leader, yet God sent him into the wilderness to be a hired hand for what was later his father-in-law. And what did he do to prepare him for leading the children of Israel out of Egypt? You guessed it—he was a shepherd. To be a good leader, he had to become a good follower, serve someone else, and be able to identify with those he would leading. "To the elders among you, I appeal as a fellow elder, a witness of Christ's sufferings and one who also will share in the glory to be revealed; Be shepherds of God's flock that is under your care, serving as overseers—not because you must, but because you are willing, as God wants you to be; not greedy for money, but eager to serve; not lording it over those entrusted to you, but being examples to the flock. And when the Chief Shepherd appears, you will receive the crown of glory that will never fade away" (1 Pet. 5:1–4 NIV).

I have heard over and over young people say that they were called to be leaders, that they have a gift of leadership, and usually I find that they mean they don't want to work and they want to tell people what to do. If you want to find the true leaders, that will be the ones serving everyone else. They will be the last person to put themselves in a leadership role and are not interested in telling people what to do. They just do what needs to be done, and the people who are paying attention will soon start to emulate them because they recognize that this person cares about them, not about being in charge. Being a shepherd instead of a sheepherder is not that complicated. I believe personally it is giving more than you take, investing recklessly in others' lives, leaving yourself vulnerable and leaving this world and the people around you better off than they would have been without you. I don't think it is complicated, but I know it's not easy. We have conditioned ourselves to believe we are leaders if we run a big business or have a large church, but running something and leading something are two very different things. We always hear the 23 Psalm read at funerals, and I understand why, but maybe we should look at it in a different light. We are called to be shepherds until Christ's return, so maybe we should use it as an indicator of where we are as far as being a leader is concerned. Do we make people feel just a small part of what the psalmist felt from God? If not, what are we doing to resolve the problem? So give your best to those around you without expecting anything in return, and someday you may turn around and find that there are people following you.

Love,
Dad

Who's in Charge?

My last real meaningful conversation with my father happened only about three weeks before Mom, Dad, and Randy died in the wreck, and I would say it was probably the last words of advice to me even though it didn't soak in for a while (always been a little slow), and I keep learning from my parents through things I remember. Anyway, I would like to share it with you since I'm nearing the end of this little venture. The church Dad was pastor of was nearing the completion of their new building, and I was going to hang some drywall in our house. My dad had said they had some leftover drywall that I could buy from the church at the contractor's cost. So I took our old black Chevy van and pulled out the back seat. I picked up Dad, and we drove to the church to get the Sheetrock. Dad was showing me around the new building, showing how they had done this or how they had decided to do that, and then his tone changed and he told me how God had taught him an important lesson through the building of that church.

He proceeded to tell me that the guy they had contracted to build the building was a good Christian man and that the project was bid really cheap because most of the people working on the project were volunteers from the church or friends. As the work went on, because Dad had plenty of experience with construction work and the people all knew him, they all started coming to him and asking him what to do, so he would tell them to do what he thought needed to be done. Finally, the contractor pulled my dad aside and told him that if he was going to be in charge, Dad needed to talk to him before he told people what to do, because they weren't on the same page and jobs were getting done either before they were ready for them or even done twice. My dad said he told him that there could only be one person in charge, and since he had been contracted to be the one in charge, my dad needed to let him do his job. Dad said that it was hard to hear and that it was a hard lesson to learn but that it was a lesson he needed to learn. After that, when people asked him what needed to be done, he would send them to the contractor, and things worked a lot smoother.

He said that once you have been in charge, it is almost second nature to just take charge, to take over and just do it your way even when it is not your place. As hard as it was, he said it taught him a lot about just being there to serve just as a servant would serve a master and how he needed to serve God. He never said it, but I think he saw in his children, and I'm sure probably more so in me, the capacity to take over and take charge of certain situations even when it wasn't our place to do so. Years after he was gone, I began to see that I was doing just that. I would just do something myself rather than letting someone else do it because I wanted it done a certain way and I wanted everything done my way because my way was better, even if I wasn't the one in charge. That was when God reminded me of what my father had told me. It was difficult, but I started making a practice of every so often stepping back and letting someone else be in charge. Just doing what I was told and helping out where I could was hard, but it was something that I had to practice to be what God wants us to model to the world.

Submission is not something that comes natural to most, and the ones who are always submissive probably need to learn to take a stand every now and then. For most people, submission is a trait that has to be learned, and it is never easy to learn. Paul writes over and over in the New Testament for the young to submit to the old, the children to submit to their parents, and the wives to submit to their husbands, but I think he sums it all up in Ephesians 5:21, "Submit to one another out of reverence to God" (NIV). I believe, until we learn to submit to those around us, it is highly unlikely that we will submit to God, and if we want to be near to God, then we must submit to Him. "But he gives us more grace. That is why the Scripture says: 'God opposes the proud but gives grace to the humble.' Submit yourselves, then to God. Resist the devil, and he will flee from you. Come near to God and he will come near to you. Wash your hands, you sinners, and purify your hearts, you double minded. Grieve, mourn and wail. Change your laughter to mourning and your joy to gloom. Humble yourselves before the Lord, and he will lift you up" (James 4:6–10 NIV).

I think Dad was saying that God was teaching him to deal with a measure of pride and He wants to keep us humble. It's kind of shameful, but when we begin to think we need to be in charge, we many times begin to tell God what He should do and how He should be instead of listening and following Him. God can't come near to us when we are operating with pride in our hearts, because He opposes the proud. Kids draw near to God so He can be near to you. That only comes by way of a humble heart.

Love,
Dad

Add White

My senior year of high school, I only had one class I needed to graduate, so I took all the more difficult classes in the morning. For the three classes in the afternoon, I had art, study hall, and was a student aid in art for the last class of the day. My art teacher was also the English teacher, and her husband was an art professor at the college in Kearney. She liked me, and most days, she would give me a pass so I could skip study hall and just spend all afternoon in the art room, either helping her or painting. I wasn't the world's greatest painter, but I did all right. Early on, I would have problems mixing the color I wanted, and so I would ask her what color I needed to get the color I wanted, and almost every time she would say "Add white" and walk off. Almost every time I would add white, and it was exactly what I needed, so I got to where if I was having a problem getting the right color, I would automatically add white. Funny thing is, it was so simple, but it almost always worked. When I was working as a student aid and younger students would ask what they needed to get the right color, I found myself telling them the same thing, "Add white." It is strange how something so basic can be overlooked. You don't see white in the different colors until you have it pointed out to you and start looking at it from that perspective. Once you begin to look at the different colors that way, you usually can see the minute you need to add white, but until you become accustomed to it, somehow it escapes you and you will try almost every color there is, trying to get it to look right.

Life is a lot like painting, and many times we try all kinds of different things to give our lives the right color, to make them look right and feel right. And most of us have the tendency to overlook the basic color or aspect of life that makes our lives work the way they are supposed to. Jesus. Now, the first response of Christians is to say, "Duh, that's a no-brainer," but if that is true and we believe it, then why are our lives in such turmoil all the time and the color is all wrong? Jesus is the white we need to add to our lives, yet we don't spend very much time listening to what He has to say or learning what He did. You hear about the red letters in sermons and songs referring to the words of Christ in the red-letter editions of the Bible, and there was that movement for a while where everyone was wearing necklaces and brace-lets with WWJD, "What would Jesus do," on them. I understand that people need to remind themselves to try to conduct themselves the way that Christ did, yet you will find it difficult to do if you have no idea what He said and did. We all need to take the time to look deeply at the life of Christ and the words He spoke and add them to our lives.

You kids are old enough now that if something is lacking in your life, I won't be able to help you much. You will have to go to the Source, add white, add Jesus, and apply to your life the wisdom that only He can offer. This is the last parable of this prodigal son, at least for now. I have given you one for every year I have been alive, and I don't really know how much longer I will be around. Looking back, I realize I probably didn't do the best job of passing on my parents' legacy to you. Now I am the same age as my mother when she died in the accident and only two years younger than my father was. You kids are now older than I was when my parents died, and older than my father when his father died, and I feel like I have given you less of a legacy than they left me. So as I bring this whole adventure to a close, I just want to share what I saw in my parents that best describes what I think they stood for. My father was kind but loved people enough to tell them the truth, even the truth they didn't want to hear. My mother was also kind but tempered my father's tough love with a great measure of compassion. Together they loved God deeply, served people without reservation, and sacrificed their time, talent, and money to have an impact on the world around them for God. Like I said, I am not sure I demonstrated that to you kids adequately, but all I can say is, if your life is not as colorful as you desire, add white. "I have come that they may have life, and have it to the full" (John 10:10 NIV).

Love,
Dad

PS: I guess I am still here, so you're going to get a few more of my parables.

What Would I Say To Me?

Kids, this is a perspective on being a parent that I thought you might benefit from. As a father, if I could go back and give myself advice when I was just starting out, what would I say to myself? First of all, I have to look back and, in hindsight, grade myself honestly, evaluating what I think I did right and what I failed at. Not easy, because half the time I'm not sure where I succeeded and where I failed. So to start, I'd give myself a C-, an average, because I loved my kids to the best of my ability and I desired the very best for them. After that, if I am honest with myself, my kids turned out as good as they did in spite of me, not because of me, and therein lies the grace and goodness of God. No matter how well-meaning we are as parents, there is only one thing that is certain, and that is, we are going to fail. That is when we have to rest in the fact that we serve a God who can and will take our foolish mistakes and make them into something good. If Joseph can say this about those who intended to harm him: "Don't be afraid. Am I in the place of God? You intended to harm me, but God intended it for good to accomplish what is now being done, the saving of many lives" (Gen. 50:19–20

NIV), then I think it is safe to say that God can do the same with the mistakes I made while intending to help.

I never lacked the desire or commitment to do what was right when it came to raising my kids. I think only a parent can understand the love and overwhelming responsibility that you feel when you realize that God has charged you with training this child to serve Him and the humanity around him or her. I was constantly reading books and the Bible, trying to figure out how to be that perfect parent, and I failed to be that perfect parent even with all the information available to me. My mom once told me she and Dad had none of the help books available to them, and after reading and hearing some of the speakers on the subject, they were sorry that they didn't know better and wished they had had better information to go by when they were raising us. I believe a good parent's number one goal is to equip their child to face the world on their own, and it starts from the very first day they are born. I believe that starts with letting them know that they are loved by their parents and by God and that, in reality, they never have to face anything truly alone. Many of the aspects of parenting that I once believed had to be one certain way or another have softened over the years, and I find that every child is different and requires or responds to different things and that some things, in the light of eternity, are just not that important.

On discipline, the younger you teach your child that you are in charge and you are responsible for how things happen, the better it is. Complacency and pride have no place in parenthood. Never give anything but your best. If you believe God has shown you the way to raise your child, don't be lazy and settle for second best or what is easy. Sacrifice whatever you have to make it happen and give nothing less than everything to what God has given you to do through your children. But with that said, don't be proud and think that what God has given you is the only way and that there is no room for improvement through the advice of others. Consider everything carefully without taking anything for granted, because sometimes God can give you direction hidden in what is actually bad advice. I determined when my kids were young that I wouldn't do anything I didn't want them to do, and I did that in most things, but I find that my vision of that was shortsighted and probably my biggest failure. It stems from the verse in Proverbs 22:15, "Foolishness is bound in the heart of a child, But the rod of correction shall drive it far from him" (NIV). I always focused on the discipline part. What I have seen over and over in parents and their children is that they miss the first part of that verse. Foolishness is bound in the heart of a child.

My mom and dad wanted forgiveness for the mistakes they made as parents, and now that my kids are older, I want forgiveness for the mistakes I've made, yet when I became a parent, my attitude was not forgiveness; it was that I can do better than my parents. Now, every parent should try to improve on what their parents did and learn from their parents' mistakes, but that can only happen by seeking advice from your parents. If you make decisions on how to raise your child by the mistakes you thought your parents made when you were a child, your perception of those mistakes is made as a child, and foolishness is bound in the heart of that child, not wisdom. I can go into all the things I decided to do as a parent based on the perceptions of a foolish child. Some came out okay, and others I see deep and lasting effects in my kids that I am ashamed to think they carry because I used the input of a foolish child to determine how to mold the lives of my greatest responsibility and joy. I want them to forgive me for being an imperfect parent, but I modeled and molded something completely different. If you want your child to forgive, respect, and honor you as a parent, even when you're older, you have to do the same for your parents when your children are young.

The problem is, if in arrogance you don't think you're going to make mistakes, you'll blunder in and it will be too late when you finally realize what has happened. I see, in society today, parents who hated having to work and do chores even though they have a great work ethic, and because of it, they have raised their kids never working and giving them everything they wanted. That results in their children not having a clue how to work, not being able or willing to hold down a job, and hating their parents for messing them up. Then there are parents thinking that their parents were far too strict when it came to dating, so they raise their kids with really relaxed morals and guidelines on dating and their children wind up pregnant or caught up in all kinds of illicit activities and hate their parents anyway. I think I now understand, that if I want my children to make wise decisions based on adult perspectives, not from the perspective of a foolish child, it has to start with me honoring and respecting my parents enough to forgive them for the mistakes they made and the mistakes I thought they made as a foolish child. Training your child to forgive and honor his parents starts with you forgiving and honoring yours and you laying the groundwork twenty years before it happens. My advice to me is to go get and base my adult decisions of how to raise my children on adult perspectives and learn to discern the difference between a wise adult perspective and the foolishness of a child's.

Love,
Dad

Hypocrisy and Who's Selling It

One day in the lunchroom at one of my places of employment, I got into a discussion with our safety coordinator about sex education in the schools. She proceeded to say all Christians were hypocrites and that they had been against it because they were trying to force their beliefs on everyone else. I told her, because she was much younger and had not even been alive when it was all happening, that Christians had been against it because they didn't believe it was the government's place to teach their children something they didn't believe in and that it was something that was the responsibility of the children's parents to teach their own children. That this was, in fact, just the opposite—the government was forcing its views on the children of Christians. She wasn't quite sure how to respond to this statement, so she proceeded to say that most kids were not being taught about sex at home, so the government needed to step in because of all the teenage pregnancies. My response was that teaching children all about sex and how to do it safely doesn't work because they are children and not responsible enough to handle the responsibility that it requires and, furthermore, since sex education began, teenage pregnancies and abortions had increased. Telling a child how to be safe in a passion-fused moment is like telling a dog not to wag his tail when he is happy. Telling children it is okay to do it and then expecting them to think rationally in that heated moment is absurd. I said most adults don't even think rationally in that moment. I said a kid is more apt to take unnecessary risks than an adult, and they should be encouraged to avoid it until they are older.

She disagreed and said once again that I was out of touch with reality and all Christians were hypocrites. We left it at that, and nothing more was said. About a week later, we had a safety meeting where she was talking about unsafe acts. She proceeded to tell us that young people were more apt to get hurt at work because they were more apt to take unnecessary risks and that if we thought there was any way that we could get hurt, we shouldn't do it. She looked up and saw the look on my face, which I'm sure said what I was thinking, which was, *And you called me a hypocrite.* She would not look at me the rest of the meeting. My point in this is, I constantly hear people saying Christians are hypocrites, and you know what? They are right—we are. But the very ones pointing out our hypocrisies are also peddling their own. So I just want to point out all the hypocrisies I see on both sides because it seems like in this country, truth is something that no one values anymore. Everyone is busy spinning a version that best suits them, and it seems to be at the root of our country's decline. By the time I'm done, I may not have any friends left and everybody may hate me, but here goes anyway.

I will start with Christians and the church. Christians are called Christians because they are supposed to follow Christ, and if Christ is our leader, then we should strive to emulate Him. Most Christians can tell you, "Christ died for my sins," yet after that, they haven't got a clue what He did.

I am going to keep it simple because He did five things that stand out to me: (1) He submitted to the authority over Him, His heavenly Father and his earthly parents. (2) He pointed out the hypocrisy of the religious leaders of His time. (3) He befriended and visited regularly the down-and-out riffraff of that day. (4) He fed the hungry. (5) He healed the sick.

If we, the church, are to be Christ's apprentices and we are striving to be like Him, why do we have churches like stadiums that sit empty 80 percent of the time just so we don't have to be bothered with doing anything on Sunday morning? We have the ability, through medicine and Christ's healing power, to heal the sick. If the paid personnel of the church took less money so most of the staff could be doctors, nurses, dentists, chiropractors, and optometrists, if the buildings were designed to be more like hospitals and clinics during the week, offering free health care while, at the same time, praying with those going though these hard times, we could be the gospel, not just preach the gospel. If the church offered free day care, how many children would the church and Christians have the ability to influence? Or free Christian school where any child could get an education and even help with the health care or maybe even aid in the care of the elderly. If Christian businessmen were willing to make a little less in order to offer more jobs and the church offered job training and help finding jobs, the complexion of the church would completely change. Just by adding these few things, our churches would be busier during the week than on Sunday. But it would require us to put more money into what Christ did and less into ourselves. Would we be willing to give more and get less to do what Jesus did? I am tired of the WWJD (what would Jesus do) movement that is going around. Mostly, what I see is us Christians doing what Judas did. Judas betrayed Jesus because he could not wait for a greater reward in the next life and he sold it for immediate gratification in this life. With what I see today, most of us should be called Judasians, not Christians. If the church did what Jesus did, there would be no need for government health care, welfare, or social security. Imagine a country where we actually trust God for the things we need instead of the government. None of these changes are without cost. If we want to make a difference in this country and our world, it will cost us.

Now, let's talk about the hypocrisies of this world, and we will start with our government. The Supreme Court says a woman has the right over her own body, so she has the right to abort her unborn child if she wants to. Let's leave out the moral implications, because I don't believe you should legislate morality—even God allows us a free choice. Let's leave out the fact that there is a chance that the baby is another person or at least the potential for life exists and should be protected at least as strictly as we protect an eagle's egg. If a woman has the right over her own body to terminate what can potentially be life, how can this same government force us to wear a seat belt in a car that is safer than a bicycle and motorcycle on the road and where the only person you are hurting is yourself? How can they also force us to have health insurance where, once again, the only one you would hurt is yourself? The Supreme Court has not defended my right to choose.

Let's make more people mad. The Supreme Court now seems to be involved telling us that we have to accept the gay lifestyle as normal and natural. Yet they don't force zoos to put two male cats or two female cats together to get kittens. Now, if people are making the choice to be gay, then that is their business. Once again, I don't believe in legislating morality. But I believe the Bible is where marriage is derived from and that it is only spoken of as between a man and a woman. Furthermore, if God had meant for people to be gay, He would have designed us to be able to procreate man on man and woman on woman. Sex involves sexual reproductive organs, and those organs don't work to reproduce in the gay lifestyle. But let's say you don't believe in God and you believe in evolution. Evolution speaks against the gay lifestyle as well. Evolution is the survival of the fittest, and without medical intervention, if everyone were gay, the entire race would disappear off the face of the earth, as would any other species. For our government to say that we have to approve the lifestyle and teach that it is normal and natural instead of the foolishness that it is is total hypocrisy. So until someone can come up with another form of creation, it is a choice in lifestyle that others should be allowed the right to disagree with or even call foolish. But no one should be allowed to physically harm someone who is gay. It is their right in this country to live without the fear of being harmed for their beliefs. We, as Christians, should never condone what is not in God's will for us, but we should also defend the gay person and their right to choose. Christ said, with the measure you give, it will be given to you. We need a lot of mercy, so therefore we should also extend that mercy to those that don't agree with God's laws. Remember that He loved us while we were still sinners. So it is our responsibility as both Christians and Americans to defend their right to choose what they believe while not condoning the act that we believe is wrong.

This leads us right into the next hypocrisy, which is part of the last one. For this I am quoting the US Bill of Rights. "Amendment 1. Congress shall make no law respecting an establishment of religion, or prohibiting the free exercise thereof; or abridging the freedom of speech, or of the press; or the right of the people peaceably to assemble, and to petition the government for a redress of grievances." Let me be clear on this. In this country, no one should be able to harm anyone for their beliefs or damage their property. But this amendment allows for anyone to say anything they want about anything or anybody they want in whatever forum they choose. We now have hate speech laws and terrorist speech laws. People have the right under this amendment to hate anyone and say so. The only thing they cannot do is harm them or their property. It's time to tell ourselves and teach our children that what is said about us has very little to do with our character and everything to do with theirs. There are a lot of ignorant people out there who hate others, but as I said, it is not the government's job to legislate morality; it is the job of the government and fellow Americans to keep a person from harming another person or his property. But it is amazing to me how a Christian can say, "I love the gay people, but I don't believe that the lifestyle is correct," and the masses scream hate speech and a gay person can say, "I hate those Christians, they all should be killed," and that somehow is not hate speech. By the first amendment, they both have the right to say what they said; that is why the hate speech law is wrong. Because when you start dictating what is right speech and what is wrong speech, it gives the government the right to start imposing their beliefs, and thus their religion, on everyone. They have already done this by changing the way it is stated, separation of church and state. Nowhere in this amendment does it say "Separation of church and state"; it states that no laws shall be passed in respect to establishing a religion. So when they try to remove all historical Christian symbols and references of God out of the government, they are in fact instituting the religion of atheism, which is, in fact, a religion. People's beliefs and religion make them who they are, and because one person states his beliefs in a government setting does not mean he is instituting a religion or establishing a religion, it only means that this is where their values come from, and historically, our forefathers held to Christian values and founded the Constitution on the freedom that they believed they found there and were deprived of in England. To force political entities to avoid any religious references is to impose a belief that the amendment does not speak to; it does not impose the absence of religion but says no law will be made to establish a religion. Every person has the right to share not only his opinion but also his religion with anyone who will listen. It is covered under the "Free exercise thereof" written in the amendment and is also covered under the freedom of speech. This includes a government setting as well as in church.

This country also has made a big deal about racism, yet racism is a prejudice, and somehow the only prejudice recognized is white on black; it's not black on white, atheist on Christian, poor on rich, rich on poor, skinny on fat, gay on straight, straight on gay, Republican on Democrat, Democrat on Republican, etc. Prejudice is any time you prejudge someone on something other than their actions. But because our country has turned prejudice into a white-on-black thing, certain people have used it to capitalize on everyone's fear of being called racist. Police officers can't do their jobs without fear of repercussion if a minority is involved. Certain people have whipped up such hatred for law enforcement that people are going around, trying to force them into compromising situations. Even targeting them and killing them. These people form mobs, beat up innocent civilians, and burn their stores, all in the name of someone's possible racism. They are there because they hate and hate because of the color of someone's skin or their position. What this speaks to is not racism but a lack of character. There is a difference between peaceful protest, guaranteed in the Constitution, and mob violence. Many of the same types of people of all races looted and stole during Katrina, and I don't believe Katrina was racist. Instead of our government punishing the people responsible, they get a pass because they are "so oppressed." Their leaders stir up these people into a frenzy and cause riots and then collect money from companies to help it all go away. The only words that come to mind are *extortion* and *terrorism*. They are trying to force what they think on others—that is, terrorism—and profiting by destroying one business or livelihood—that is, extortion. There were some mob families who used to beat up store owners and bust up their shops if they didn't pay for protection from themselves. Many of them have been thrown in jail for extortion. Today we champion the same types of people as civil rights advocates. The Constitution allows people the right to be prejudiced, or you would have to throw everyone in jail, because we all have the tendency to be prejudiced in one way or another. It's a human condition that infects us all. But the government and fellow Americans should protect the right of all peoples to believe what they want without fear of being harmed. The reason I say "fellow Americans" is that it is every American's responsibility to protect the rights of those around them.

The greatest example of this is when a church (sad day) was holding protests at young military servicemen's funerals. I personally thought it was disgraceful, but they had the right to peaceful protest. But the motorcycle groups placed themselves and their bikes along the road and revved their engines as the procession went by so the people in the procession could not see or hear the protest. When mob violence breaks out, it should not only be shop owners standing to defend their shops but the entire community. Now, for those of you who would say I'm racist, I have to say I am married to someone of another race, and in my extended family, there is every race imaginable. Which brings me to the last point on this subject. If you are a citizen of this country, you are an American. Not African American, Mexican American, German American, Italian American, and so on and so forth, just American. The government, though, has created racism on every job application that one will fill out. The only pertinent question that an employer needs to know is, Are you a citizen? Yet they ask all these different questions about ethnicity and race. My wife has to answer Hispanic if it asks for ethnicity, and white if it asks for race. My nephew, when he gets older, will have to answer African American, but he is of Haitian descent. For our government to assume that because you are black you come from Africa is racism. Although I prefer to call it what it really is, prejudice.

One more to go before I finish with what I call scratching the surface of the lies we tell ourselves and the lies of others. This is the Second Amendment, which states, "A well-regulated Militia, being necessary to the security of a free state, the right of the people to keep and bear arms, shall not be infringed on." Now, there are people who say that because of all the shootings, we should ban firearms, but I say that it is proof the amendment was right. The majority of the shootings have taken place where the government went against the Second Amendment. The majority of the shootings—we will call terrorist actions—happened where firearms were banned. Even at the Fort Hood military base, where all the personnel were trained in the use of firearms, the terrorist went to the one place on base where they were banned from carrying firearms. Every adult citizen of this country should be able to carry a firearm anywhere in public, with the only restriction being private businesses and properties, which the owners have the right to decide if they want to allow firearms on their property. The amendment is to ensure all citizens have those rights. No records should be kept on who has firearms, and the only requirement to purchase a firearm is a background check to see if you committed a felony with a firearm, which revokes your right to possess one. This background check should be done when you get your driver's license, and if you pass your background check, a picture of a gun or some other emblem should be printed on the license, just like the heart for organ donors. Then everyone selling a gun would be required to check ID, just like someone buying alcohol. Just a side note: if someone commits a crime under the influence, they should lose their right to drink, just like those who commit crimes with guns. But the government should not know who has weapons, how many, and whether you have weapons at all. The Supreme Court has not upheld our right to bear arms. And the hypocrisy of it all is, they seek to impose more restrictions when the main places we have been attacked are where they have not upheld our rights to bear arms. We have presidents and politicians who have worked to infringe on our constitutional right to bear arms and other constitutional rights and ran on campaigns to do so, yet they take an oath to uphold the constitution. Are we okay with a bunch of liars in office? How can we trust anything else that they say? In the upcoming election, we have people running for office on the premise that they will ignore the Constitution and restrict guns even more, knowing that they will take an oath to uphold the Constitution. This means they are hypocrites and liars, and anyone who votes for them is either a fool or a hypocrite themselves. This is why I say this: Your right to vote was bought and protected with the blood of men and women who believed in this country and the ideals set forth by our forefathers and protected by the Constitution. If you believe in and vote for people who want to take away your freedoms guaranteed in that same Constitution and you exercise the right to vote yet vote against what protects the right of the people to govern, you are a hypocrite. You are against the very thing that guarantees you that right.

I could go on with both sides, but the point is, there is enough to go around, and until we, the body of Christ, quit allowing hypocrisy to run rampant in our midst, nothing will change in our country either. This will require great sacrifice on both fronts. If we continue to take the easy way out in the matter of our country, we will fall. If we continue to be more like Judas than Jesus, our world will fall. If we value our freedom and our country, we must be more like Jacob and less like Esau. "Once when Jacob was cooking some stew, Esau came in from the open country, famished. He said to Jacob, 'Quick, let me have some of that red stew! I'm famished!' (That is why he was also called Edom.) Jacob replied, 'First sell me your birthright.' 'Look, I am about to die,' Esau said. 'What good is the birthright to me?' But Jacob said, 'Swear to me first.' So he swore and oath to him, selling his birthright to Jacob. Then Jacob gave Esau some bread and some lentil stew. He ate and drank, and then got up and left. So Esau despised his birthright" (Gen. 25:29–34 NIV). Esau sold his inheritance for a bowl of stew because he didn't value his inheritance and was only concerned about his present situation. He wanted what was easy, and he wanted it now, and even though he was extremely hungry, it wouldn't have killed to wait or cook something himself. He sold his inheritance for a bowl of stew because he was not willing to make the sacrifices, the hard choices necessary to keep his inheritance.

We are at the same crossroads in our country. Many people are selling their freedom for a bowl of stew. That bowl of stew comes in the form of not voting or selling your vote to get something for nothing, welfare, government health care, and even social security. Now you may say, "I paid into social security, so I'm owed it," but we lost that money when we allowed someone else to manage our retirement. We let crooked people concerned only with power and control take control of our future because we were too lazy, or maybe we wanted more for less or were just too busy with our own lives to bother or care. Now we are nearly twenty trillion dollars in debt. The money we paid in is *gone*! Whatever the reason, we have sold our freedoms for nothing more than a bowl of stew. Now, Jacob, on the other hand, struggled for the blessing in Genesis 32:24–32. "So Jacob was left alone, and a man wrestled with him till daybreak. When the man saw that he could not overpower him, he touched the socket of Jacob's hip so that his hip was wrenched as he wrestled with the man. Then the man said, 'Let me go, for it is day-break.' But Jacob replied, 'I will not let you go unless you bless me.' The man asked him, 'What is your name?' 'Jacob,' he answered. Then the man said, 'Your name will no longer be Jacob, but Israel, because you have struggled with God and with men and have overcome.' Jacob said, 'Please tell me your name.' But he replied, 'Why do you ask my name?' Then he blessed him there. So Jacob called the place Peniel, saying, 'It is because I saw God face to face, and yet my life was spared.' The sun rose above him as he passed Peniel, and he was limping because of his hip" (NIV). Jacob put it all on the line to receive his blessing, and he had to live with a phys-ical disability for the rest of his life in order to get it. Esau did not value what was given to him, yet Jacob fought for what he desired. Hebrews 12:16–17 states, "See that no one is sexually immoral, or is Godless like Esau, who for a single meal sold his inheritance rights as the oldest son. Afterwards, as you know, when he wanted to inherit this blessing, he was rejected. He could bring about no change of mind, though he sought the blessing with tears" (NIV). If we sell our freedom and despise our birthright for the comforts of today, we will never get it back.

Love,
Dad

Should We Kneel?

There are two football players from the NFL whose careers were much shorter than I believe they should have been. I was a fan of both when they first started playing, but I am only a fan of one now. They both claimed to be Christians publicly, which takes some courage, and I admire the courage it takes to put yourself out there like that. They are Tim Tebow and Colin Kaepernick. Both invoke a great deal of controversy. But the reason I am still a fan of one and not the other is what they stood for and what they knelt for. Tim Tebow won over 70 percent of his games as a starting quarterback and won a playoff game yet was traded and never given another chance to start in an NFL football game. To my knowledge, no other quarterback has been treated as such. (A little perspective, he has lost fewer games and playoff games than Tom Brady and Peyton Manning.) He was never given the chance to fail on the field, and I believe he was pushed out and not given the chance because of a prejudice. People didn't like that he knelt to pray while everyone else was standing and cheering a great play; they thought he was too open with his faith. He was honoring and respecting the God he believed made it all possible. Kind of funny how baseball is giving him more of a chance to succeed than football. The last I knew, the Heisman wasn't given to best college baseball player. But what I respect the most about this young man is what he did off the field. He would take his own money and purchase tickets to the games for children with special needs and then spend time with them after the games. He is still helping and spending his time and money loving on these kids that have probably experienced more prejudice than most Americans could ever image and are helpless to respond. He is loved by them because instead of talking about or protesting it, he just went to them and loved them. He put his money where his mouth is. I am still a fan.

So that leaves Colin Kaepernick, which obviously means I am not a fan. Now, for those who say it is because he is black and I'm racist, let me say when I first saw him, I thought he was Hispanic, and I am married to one, so my opinion of him didn't change when I found out he was black. He, like Tim, is a great athlete, given even more opportunity and a bigger audience for a longer period. But unlike Tim when he saw a prejudice, he, instead of using some of his eleven-million-a-year salary to help create an atmosphere of reconciliation and love for young fellow Americans, made it personal. He made the statement he was an oppressed black man. Now, when a guy who makes more in one year than I will make my whole life makes a statement like that, well, let's just say the guy needs a reality check. That's not oppression. Has he experienced prejudice in his life? Undoubtedly! Everyone has experienced prejudice of some sort. I was made fun of by some because I was poor, a preacher's kid, for my faith, later for the length of my hair. I was taught that prejudice has nothing to do with me and everything to do with their character. It only has something to do with my character if I let it change who I am or what I think of others and myself. It is time we start teaching that to our children again. Judge people on merit only. Now, Colin had more of a stage and more money to have an impact on those around him than most people will ever have. Yet instead of kneeling after every touchdown and telling the news media he was praying for racial reconciliation and equality in the country and using his money to create programs to promote this, he chose to kneel when everyone was standing to honor our country, our veterans, and those who gave their lives defending it and the freedom that he was able to exercise.

Now, some would say that his career was floundering and he just wanted to get the spotlight back. I'm not going to judge his motives. His cause may be just, but you cannot drive out disrespect, contempt, animosity, prejudice, violence, hatred, and selfishness with more of the same. Just like darkness cannot coexist with light, hatred cannot coexist with love. Christ said, "Love your enemies, not hate those who hate you." It is the only thing that can bring about any form of unity, equality, and reconciliation. If Colin were to say his motives were right but say his methods were wrong and encourage everyone to use their resources and position to find positive ways of changing the climate of hatred instead of disrespecting others and our country, I would be a fan again. The last two presidents have done more to promote a climate of intolerance than any other presidents since I was born. It's time for us to just be Americans and leave our race and position out of it. Even though I disagree with both of them on much of what they have said and done, I find it just as offensive when people openly call our current president a bum and a cracker as I did when people openly called our previous president an idiot and a n———r. People are entitled to their opinion, right or wrong, but to disrespect the office publicly does no one any good (disagree on policy, fine), and it only creates more dissention. While I'm on the subject, there may be some bad cops out there, but there are many good cops out there, and I think it is wrong for protesters to march around with signs saying "F—— the cops," even if it is their right.

We have the right in America for white people to hate black people and black people to hate white people, and it is my right to disagree with them. It is not a right to injure others and their property out of hatred. It is also the right of employers to fire people for their beliefs. It is my right as a consumer to not support the institutions I disagree with. Our Constitution guarantees those rights to all. Even the right to be prejudiced. Just because something is our right doesn't mean it is right. Basically, prejudice says all cops are the same, all white people are privileged and racist, all black people are oppressed and victims, rich people are selfish, poor people are lazy, fat people are unhealthy, skinny people are healthy, mentally handicapped people are of no value to society, and the list goes on and on. The only thing that can defeat prejudice is love, and it has happened before in this country. The movie *Woodlawn* is the true story of Tony Nathan, a running back in Birmingham, Alabama, in the seventies during a time of racial unrest, and how love conquered hatred. I think everyone who has an opinion on this should watch this movie and see how love unified a city and began to drive out hatred. It is the only way our country will ever experience true unity and equality. Our country has never been perfect, nor will it ever be, but it is only as good as we, the people, make it. Hatred only creates more hatred, and only love can drive it out. Who better to start a new trend than those who claim the name of Christ? We should all be kneeling in prayer for our country, just not during the national anthem.

Love,
Dad

The Ocean Of Life

Kids, you're adults now, but I have made a few observations over the past several years, and I hope you will hear what I have to say with an open mind. Life is like an ocean, with people floating around in it, trying to survive. I went to the movie *Dunkirk* with your mother Friday night, which is where God brought this analogy to fruition. God has planted a rock in the middle of the ocean within reach of all that is Christ Jesus, but the ocean of life is formidable. Some people have learned to float through life with very little effort until life eventually wins and they finally are lost to this life. Others struggle against the currents, and no matter how strong they are, they fail because there are too many enemies working against them, trying to destroy them. Some drift by the rock and crawl on and are saved, while some leave the rock and try to bring others back to safety. Now, some don't want to be saved because they think they are fine where they are. You can't save someone who doesn't want to be saved. Others want to be saved, but on their terms, so they will fight the very one trying to save them. In most of these cases, both the one being saved and the one saving them will perish.

What I have found is, once on the rock, it requires constant vigilance, sacrifice, and discipline to stay on the rock or be anchored to it. The storms and enemies in life are sure to knock you off the rock if you are not perfectly anchored to it. Since no one is perfectly anchored to the rock, it is a given that no matter how hard we cling to it, we will get knocked off from time to time. It is what we do when we get knocked off that matters. Do we swim back to the rock no matter how hard it is, do we swim away from the rock angry because it's the rock's fault we fell off, or do we get lazy and just learn to float through life like a lot of other people are doing? But we have to remember that if we are not actively moving toward the rock, the currents of life will carry us farther away from it. Therefore, if we are not intentionally moving toward the rock, we will be moving away from it. Now, once on the rock, I have seen people so afraid of getting knocked off the rock that when someone comes close and needs their help getting on the rock, they retract and let the person drown; some even go as far as pushing others off the rock or hindering them from getting on the rock for fear they will cause them to fall. I have seen others with a desire to help others trying to help someone and getting knocked off the rock and others who dive right in, swim out away from the rock, to try to save someone. Most fail because they underestimate the currents of life, they overestimate their own strength, and they don't take into account whether the person even wants to be saved. In short, they were unprepared.

Once on the ocean of life, we have no footing. If we venture out into the ocean of life, we have to have built a lifeline that is strong and unbreakable to someone who can pull us back to the rock, and protection from the enemies trying to kill us. That someone is the Holy Spirit, and if we have not carefully prepared, those we try to bring to safety will destroy us, as well as those with us. A wise person will not trust how strong the lifeline is that he has crafted; he will find multiple friends and family anchored on the rock and craft lifelines to them as well. Then, if one line fails, he has other lines that can help pull him back. He has to know that all those holding his backup lifelines are not all jumping into the water at the same time because no one will have the footing to pull him back to the rock. How we anchor ourselves to the rock is the key in our walk with Christ. When we venture out to bring someone to safety, it is not us who saves that person, but Christ using us, because without Him drawing us back in, all would be lost. Nothing can save us but Him, for we can do nothing without Him. "Therefore everyone who hears these words of mine and puts them into practice is like a wise man who built his house on the rock. The rain came down, the streams rose, and winds blew and beat against that house; yet it did not fall, because it had its foundation on the rock" (Matt. 7:24–25 NIV). Be wise, kids!

Love,
Dad

The Goose with the Purple Head

I had a dream the other night, and the fact that I even remembered it and that I remembered it so vividly made me wonder if there was something to it. We had some Mormons come by, wanting to share their faith, and I wanted to hear firsthand what they believed and why. Before they left, they gave me a Book of Mormon, so I set about researching the faith and how it compared to the Bible, because they said they believed the Bible and that their book was just an extension of the Bible. In the research, I determined to stay away from Christian commentaries and just use the Bible, their own book, and the commentaries not written to prove Christianity right and the Book of Mormon wrong. It was while I was in the middle of this that I had this dream. This was my dream: Doreen and I were out driving somewhere, looking for wildlife for her to take pictures of, when we saw a place to pull off the road that overlooked a field, where several people were standing and looking at something. So we pulled over and Doreen got her camera, and we went over to see what they were looking at.

At first glance, when I saw them, I thought they were pigeons, because they were gray and white and one of them had a purple head, but as I was about to walk off, I looked

311

a little closer and realized that they were geese, and the one goose had a purple head, just like the marking of a pigeon. So naturally, Doreen wanted to take some pictures. After taking a few shots, she decided to try to get closer, so she walked down the hill and slowly started across the field with her camera and tripod, stopping every so often to set up and take pictures. Everyone was engrossed in watching the geese and Doreen, as was I, when suddenly, out of the corner of my eye, I saw something move. Everyone was still watching Doreen and the geese, but just in the trees, about five hundred feet away, something was moving. As I watched, all of sudden, I realized there were a half a dozen adult bison and a calf moving through the trees on the edge of the field. Then another movement caught my eye a little ways behind the bison. A lone wolf was moving behind the bison. The bison seemed unaware or unconcerned about the wolf. Maybe it was why the calf was toward the center of the herd, and maybe they figured a lone wolf was no threat to an adult bison.

As I watched the bison skirt the field in the trees, all of a sudden, I realized that the wolf wasn't following them anymore and he was moving through the grass in the field, headed toward the geese, so I looked over to the geese, and Doreen was only about ten yards from the geese. And they still had not flown; they seemed totally oblivious to her or the wolf. When I looked back at the wolf, it was apparent that he wasn't targeting the geese—he was headed straight toward Doreen, who had no clue of the danger behind her. So I started to yell and tell her to watch out, that there was a wolf behind her, but she was too busy and seemed to be ignoring me. I became frantic and tried to scare the geese. They didn't fly; they just waddled around, oblivious to everything that was going on. It was like they were deaf and blind. Finally, Doreen looked back at me, obviously annoyed, and yelled, "What?" I said, "There is a wolf behind you!" and she turned to face the wolf. The wolf stopped and, seeing me coming down the hill and Doreen now facing him, turned and resumed following the bison. Through all that commotion, the geese still didn't fly away. When I looked over to see where the bison and the wolf went, I saw a hiker and her dog walking right into the path of the bison. I yelled, but it was too late—the bison trampled her and her dog ran away. As she lay injured, I could see that the wolf was heading for her and that he was going to get there before we could.

Then I woke up with this totally helpless feeling and started to pray, asking what it all meant, because it was all so vivid and because it was so strange. It might have just been a weird dream, but it seemed more like a parable from God. I don't know. But I do know that as I thought about the dream that day, some of the things in that dream can also be very symbolic of different facets of our society today. Let me explain. The goose with the purple head is the religion that takes God's Word or variations of it to deceive, confuse, or even just make themselves feel okay with where they are at in life. It can be any religion that confuses the truth of the gospel, and you will only be able to see a counterfeit if you know the original well. "For the time will come when men will not put up with sound doctrine. Instead, to suit their own desires, they will gather around them a great number of teachers to say what their itching ears want to hear. They will turn their ears away from the truth and turn aside to myths. But you, keep your head in all situations, endure hardship, do the work of an evangelist, discharge all the duties of your ministry" (2 Tim. 4:3–5 NIV). The other geese are those who find their place with the purple-headed goose. They feel safe because the wolf does not attack them. Because they will always be there in their ignorance, they are already easy prey. He can have them anytime he wants. The wolf is obviously Satan and false prophets. "Watch out for false prophets. They come to you in sheep's clothing, but inwardly they are ferocious wolves" (Matt. 7:15 NIV). "Be self-controlled and alert. Your enemy the devil prowls around like a roaring lion looking for someone to devour. Resist him, standing firm in the faith, because you know that your brothers throughout the world are under-going the same kind of suffering" (1 Pet. 5:8–9 NIV). I was that Christian that sees what is happening but hasn't put themselves in a position to make a difference. "Be imitators of God, therefore, as dearly loved children and live a life of love, just as Christ loved us and gave himself up for us as a fragrant offering and sacrifice to God. Be very careful, then, how you live—not as unwise but as wise, making the most of every opportunity, because the days are evil. Therefore do not be foolish, but understand what the Lord's is" (Eph. 5:1–2, 15–17 NIV). Doreen was that Christian who gets distracted from the big picture by becoming focused on one small thing. For example, being so consumed with knowledge, whether it be proving other religions false or yourself right. Maybe it is trying to defend yourself from being wrongly accused or just being consumed with all the everyday stuff that distracts you from doing what you were meant to do. This leaves you vulnerable to wolf attacks. "Not that I have already obtained all this, or have already been made perfect, but I press on to take hold of that for which Christ Jesus took hold of me. Brothers, I do not consider myself yet to have taken hold of it. But one thing I do: Forgetting what is behind and straining toward what is ahead, I press toward the goal to win the prize for which God has called me heavenward in Christ Jesus. All of us who are mature should take such a view of things. And if on some point you think differently, that too God will make clear to you. Only let us live up to what we have already attained" (Phil. 3:12–16 NIV). The bison were Christians in general. We have a tendency to not worry very much about our security from the devil. The adult bison were not in danger of being taken down by a lone wolf, but their focus was on protecting the calf, which the wolf could destroy. Christians know that once they belong to Christ and follow Him, Satan has no power over them, but all their energy and emphasis are placed on protecting their children from Satan. We should protect and train our children in such a manner as to show them the way to Christ and bring them to spiritual maturity. But we have a tendency to have ingrown eyes when it comes to the church's purpose here on earth. We were not called to defend our own. We were called to love one another. "If you love me, you will obey what I command" (John 14:15 NIV). "This is my command that you love each other" (John 15:17 NIV). But Jesus gave us another mission when He left. "Therefore go and make disciples of all nations, baptizing them in the name of the Father and the Son and the Holy Spirit, and teaching them to obey everything I have commanded you. And surely I am with you always, to the very end of the age" (Matt. 28:19–20 NIV). Our mission here is not to take care of ourselves. This is how we show God we love Him, by loving others and making it our mission to show those who don't know Him that He loves them. Which brings us to the last character in my dream. The hiker is that person who doesn't know Christ that many times gets trampled by well-meaning or maybe not-so-well-meaning Christians who, whether out of fear or selfishness or a host of other reasons, leave a path of injured, disillusioned people who fall prey to Satan because they equate us with God, and because of our representation of Him, they choose to deny Him.

Love,
Dad

A New Christmas Perspective

I guess as you get older, your perspectives on things are bound to change. Like when I was young, I wasn't happy unless I was reaching for the stars. Now, I'm happy if I can reach my toes. I thought happiness was at the destination, and now I find that the joy is in the journey. I also thought that the more Christmases I went through without my parents and Randy, the less I would miss them. This year marks thirty Christmases without my parents and little brother, and thirty-one years since our last Christmas with them. And I think I miss them more now than I did thirty years ago. How proud they would be of my children and how much they would have enjoyed my grandchildren! There is always a day or two when it is more intense, and one day, as I was sitting, looking at our tree, it hit me really hard how much I missed them. I thought about all the Christmases we had together and began to reflect on what those Christmases were like. It dawned on me that there's only one time I can remember getting what I had wanted. In fact, by the time I was ten, I don't ever remember asking for anything for Christmas. We never had much, yet every year Dad and Mom made sure we got something for Christmas. In fact, most of what we got was what we needed, and the things we didn't need were not necessarily what we wanted.

Looking back, I find that I enjoyed them just as much, maybe more, than I would have if I had gotten what I thought I wanted. But as I reflected on all the Christmases with Mom and Dad, I began to realize that it wasn't just at Christmas. My parents never had the means to give us what we wanted, but we always had what we needed. But then I realized that it wasn't just us; it was all year around and everyone who came in contact with them. If you were hot and thirsty, they were a big glass of ice tea. If you were hungry, they were a hot meal. If you needed a place to stay, they were a warm bed. If something was broken, they would fix it. If you needed a friend, they were a big hug and a listening ear. The list goes on and on. I realize now the greatest gift God gave to the world was His Son; He didn't give the world what it wanted. He gave it what it needed. But He also gave other gifts to the world around my parents. It was them. My parents were God's gift to the world around them, and they gave the world around them what it needed. It is easy to get caught up in trying to give people what they want and forget what they actually need.

But then I realized that if my parents were God's gift to the world around them, then that means I am God's gift to the world around me. That is humbling and a bit terrifying. I can't help thinking the world around me got the short end of the stick. It took me over fifty years to figure this out. Not the brightest bulb on the string, but I guess it is better late than never. I am thankful that God can use broken gifts. I have determined that if I am God's gift to the world around me, I need to be a better gift. I can't help but wonder what our world would be like if all of God's gifts to the world, all those who claim the name of Christ, spent less time trying to give the world around them what they want and spent more time being what they need. So this Christmas, it is my prayer that God richly blesses all his gifts and to all those God has given to us as gifts, we want to wish you a merry Christmas and a very happy New Year.

Love,
Dad

The Surgery

When people say a loving God would not send anyone to hell, or a loving God would accept everyone no matter what, or even when Christians say, "I prayed the prayer, that's good enough, and I don't have to change a thing," I find it very hypocritical. First of all, why would you ever pray the prayer if you think you're okay where you're at? Second, a loving God made a way for you to avoid hell by sacrificing His Son; it's your choice to take it or leave it, so you chose hell. Third, I have never heard anyone claim that they are perfect. If they make a mistake, they will say, "Oh well, nobody's perfect," yet they think God, who is perfect, should let them into a perfect place without being perfect. This means heaven would no longer be perfect. Perfection, by definition, means there are no flaws—everything in that place or person is perfect. If something imperfect is allowed in, it is no longer perfect. You will find that the most intolerant people are the people who truly believe they are always right. Now you need to believe what you believe or it's not a belief. But these people are unable to tolerate any point of view that differs from theirs, because they believe that their ideas are perfect. Yet these same people completely understand when surgeons don't just let everyone into a surgery room, just like they are.

This year, I just had hip replacement surgery, and I, for one, am glad the surgeon didn't have a janitor plunging a toilet in the corner or a lawyer at a desk in the corner doing paperwork in their work clothes. I was out, so I don't know if they were there or not. But I hope the surgeon would not allow it. Because of the risk of infection, the surgeon won't allow anyone in the surgery room who is not properly cleaned and wearing the proper clothing. The lawyer may appear cleaner than the janitor, but he may be carrying a far more deadly infection, carrying bacteria, so without the proper cleansing process and the proper clothing, he can make a purified room impure in a matter of seconds. The surgeon had me take antibiotics and scrub my body with an antibacterial scrub for a week before the surgery. As much as possible, he wanted me to be clean. The room and everything in it had to be sterilized so no bacteria was introduced into the room. Because the surgeon and everyone that is needed in the room cannot completely get rid of all the bacteria on their body, they clean themselves as best as they can, and then they wear clothing that is not alive and can be heated and washed to a temperature to kill all bacteria. And they cover themselves with this clothing from head to foot so none of the imperfections left on their bodies can contaminate the perfect room. Now, I am glad they take these precautions, and I don't think I know of one person, even the ones saying everyone should be allowed into heaven, that think that these standards are unreasonable.

Now, let us make the parallel between heaven and the surgery room. If heaven and God are perfect and you can't come into God's presence unless you are perfect and the surgery room, although not perfect, is as close as we can get and we can't enter without following certain procedures, don't you think we should have to follow a purification process for heaven as well? Nobody's perfect, and most will agree; some are just closer than others—just kidding. But the minute people hear the word *sin*, they say, "I'm not a sinner." Yet *sin* is a Greek archery term that means to miss the mark. If you don't hit what you're aiming at every time, then you sin. I miss what I'm aiming at every day. If I don't fix a machine correctly the first time I try, then I have sinned. In Romans 3:23, it says, "For all have sinned and fall short of the glory of God" (NIV). This means nobody's perfect, and God is. In Romans 3:24–25, He gives the solution: "And all are justified freely by his grace through the redemption that came by Christ Jesus. God presented Christ as a sacrifice of atonement, through the shedding of his blood—to be received by faith" (NIV). He made a way for us to get into His presence. "Jesus answered, 'I am the way and the truth and the life. No one comes to the Father except through me'" (John 14:6 NIV).

Just like the only way to get into the surgery room is to put on purified clothing so as not to contaminate the room, the only way to enter God's presence and not contaminate the perfection is for our imperfections to be covered by something that can be perfect. Our covering comes when we put our faith in Christ as our covering. "Rather, clothe yourselves with the Lord Jesus Christ, and do not think about how to gratify the desires of the flesh" (Rom. 13:14 NIV). Faith in Christ covers up our imperfections until we leave this world and are made perfect. Just like no one in the surgery room can be perfectly clean so they have to put on sterilized clothes, as long as we live in this world and are not perfect, the only way to come into God's presence is to be clothed in Christ by faith in Him. Now you may say, "Why would I even want to be in God's presence?" Romans 6:23 says, "For the wages of sin is death, but the gift of God is eternal life in Christ Jesus our Lord" (NIV). You may say, "I'm doing fine. Eternal life or eternal death—what's the difference?"

Eternal death is to be separated from God for eternity, and *eternal life* is to be in God's presence for eternity. Now, the Bible teaches that eternal death is a place of torment. I believe it is physical, but I also believe the greatest part of the torment will be remorse and regret. Every day for eternity rehearsing in your mind, "If only I had done this" or "If I only hadn't done that." An eternity of regret and remorse or an eternity of peace and joy. Which one sounds better to you? Now, what does that have to do with here and now? You have probably heard the expression "You haven't lived until you have done this or that." Whatever that person did that gave them an experience that either made them feel more satisfied or more fulfilled or more excited or more secure than ever before, they experienced life in a way they never thought possible.

My life over the last eight to ten years had slowly gotten more painful. I dealt with it, but it just kept getting worse. I went from being the guy people called to help lift things to the guy who could barely carry himself. It was all I could do to get my socks on in the morning, and tying my shoes would wear me out. I hurt all the time. Now, I could go on living that way, but it really is not life the way it could be. So when I finally got my hip replaced, I woke up from the surgery and could immediately tell the difference. No pain, not even surgical pain. From day 1, I could put weight on that leg, and it didn't hurt or pop or grind. But now the other hip that I didn't really feel before is hurting. Because the pain from the other leg was masking the pain from the hip I haven't had done yet. But now I can't wait to have the other hip done. I am looking forward to it. Being able to walk without pain is kind of like living again. I am more than happy to do what is necessary to be able to walk normal again.

Life with Christ is the same way. When life gets bad, you can muddle through, thinking you're all right. Struggle with the simple things in life, or should I say death, until one day you decide that there has to be a better way. Those who put on Christ and enter the presence of a holy God find life unlike anything ever experienced before. Are we still imperfect? Yes, we are. At least until we leave this world. But we get to experience a life in the presence of God, right here, right now. A life where my faith and trust are placed in someone that is perfect and loves me perfectly. A life where pain is only temporary, and one day, when I leave this world, it will be taken away forever. That's eternal life, and I would take that any day over eternal death. Even if my life is not perfectly aligned with God's will in this world, it doesn't mean I should be satisfied with the way I am. A good surgeon is not satisfied with just putting on the sterilized clothes. He scrubs himself and does everything in his power to make sure the bacteria on him does not somehow infect the patient he is trying to heal. Even though we cannot perfectly align ourselves with God's will all the time, we should never quit striving for that perfect alignment with His will. No one who has ever succeeded at a profession has ever been satisfied with failure. Everyone misses the mark, but those who believe in what they are doing and are successful at what they do get back up and try again.

If you call yourself a Christian, meaning you claim Christ as your Lord and are trying to emulate Him, and you are okay with where you are at in your life, I would seriously doubt that you are, and at the very least you are a hindrance to the faith and not an asset. If you truly recognize all that God did for you, you can never be satisfied with a less-than-perfect effort. Good athletes all recognize that they will make mistakes, but I always hear the good coaches and players say, "We expect a perfect effort every play." What that means is, you don't belong on the team if you are satisfied with okay. I don't believe you should call yourself a Christian if you are satisfied with less than a perfect effort. "Do you not know that in a race all the runners run, but only one gets the prize. Everyone who competes in the games goes into strict training. They do it to get a crown that will not last, but we do it to get a crown that will last forever. Therefore I do not run like someone running aimlessly; I do not fight like a boxer beating the air. No, I strike a blow to my body and make it my slave so that after I have preached to others, I myself will not be disqualified for the prize" (1 Cor. 9:24–27 NIV). "Not that I have already obtained all this, or have already arrived at my goal, but I press on to take hold of that which Christ Jesus took hold of me. Brothers and sisters, I do not consider myself yet to have taken hold of it. But one thing I do; Forgetting what is behind and straining towards what is ahead, I press on toward the goal to win the prize for which God has called me heavenward in Christ Jesus" (Phil. 3:12–14 NIV). Like Paul, let's make a perfect effort on every play, every day.

Love,
Dad

A Matter of Submission

I feel the need to share these thoughts on all the controversy still swirling around the NFL and our nation. Brandon, you and Lorene have been fostering teenagers for the last several years, and I believe I now see the root of our problem, not just the symptoms. You have had both boys and girls, black and white, in your home. With most of them you have talked of adoption, and each one of them acted as if they wanted to be adopted. They liked the security of the home and all the privileges that come with being a part of a family, until they had to follow the rules of the home. They didn't want to do anything that they didn't want to or wanted to do what they wanted to do when they were not allowed to. So in one way or another, each walked away from you, the very people trying to help them. But the underlying problem is not that these children were not granted the opportunity to belong to a family that loved them and wanted what was best for them, because we still pray for them all the time. It is that they didn't want to submit to any type of authority in their life. They wanted the privileges of a family without following any of the rules created to keep the family from total chaos.

This is what I see happening on a larger scale in our nation. This generation has been taught that you should have the rights of a citizen of this country but that you don't have to be subject to the laws of this country, and they bought it. Anyone living in this country should be subject to the laws of the country, and most certainly the citizens, for without law there is chaos. Every employer requires that their employees adhere to policies put in place by the employer to avoid negatively affecting the business or its other employees. If these policies are not adhered to, they have the right to terminate their employment. If I am to enjoy the privileges of working for my employer, I must adhere to the rules set down by my employer, whether I agree with them or not. If I cannot work within those guidelines, then it is up to me to quit and find an employer I can. The overwhelming problem when it comes to conflict with the police or in the workplace is not racism, although it happens; it is rebellion and the unwillingness to submit to anyone in authority over them. I would say that we who claim Christ as Lord should be working to change this growing trend, but I find that most of us are just as guilty of this type of behavior. I myself and most of the people I know want all the privileges of being a child of God, yet we want to pick and choose how we will follow Him. We want to be called his children, but we don't want to be subject to his authority in our lives.

I began to realize this as I was praying for our country. As I prayed, I really began to get discouraged and started asking God if there was any hope for this country or this world. This week, even though it was a little late for the fall colors trip we take every year, we decided to take the trip anyway. It is always beautiful here in the mountains, and I just needed to remind myself how big our God really is. When we left, we prayed for safety and all the things we normally pray for, but this time I also asked God to show us what He wanted us to see. Toward the top of one of the passes, something caught my eye, and I decided to turn around and go back to see what it was. There, tucked up behind some trees and brush, was a memorial set up for an eighteen-year-old young man. There was a small statue of a soldier, a flag, a sprocket from a bicycle, flowers, what looked like a dog collar, and engraved on the sprocket the name, date of birth, and death. As Doreen started to take pictures of this, I could do nothing but cry, even though I knew nothing about him or if, in fact, this person even was a man and not a woman. This person is truly an unknown soldier to me, but because the statue was that of a man and the name sounded like a man's name, I will refer to this person as such. This young man was loved by his family, who went to great lengths to honor him in a place that he undoubtedly loved. He had left what he loved and fought for this country and had paid for my freedom with his life. Not only had he sacrificed, but his family and friends will also live with the pain of his loss every day for the rest of their lives. I believe their sacrifice is greater even than his, for they live with the loss.

I believe not standing for the flag is disrespectful, but if I don't make my freedom and my relationship with the ones who have sacrificed for it personal, I also disrespect them and the flag they died for. I also disrespect the sacrifice of the fathers and mothers who laid their sons and daughters on the altar of freedom. I will never look at a flag or hear the national anthem the same. I will always remember that site, that young soldier, and his family when the anthem is played and our flag displayed. These men and women and their mothers and fathers are the hope for our country. But they only mirror the sacrifice made by God the Father and His Son, and I don't believe I will ever look at the cross the same either. For Jesus Christ is our hope for this world. I think it would be good to remember the words Abraham Lincoln penned when he wrote his Gettysburg Address:

> *Four score and seven years ago our fathers brought forth on this continent, a new nation, conceived in Liberty, and dedicated to the proposition that all men are created equal. Now we are engaged in a great civil war, testing whether that nation, or any nation so conceived and so dedicated, can long endure. We are met on a great battle-field of that war. We have come to dedicate a portion of that field, as a final resting place for those who here gave their lives that that nation might live. It is altogether fitting and proper that we should do this.*
>
> *But, in a larger sense, we cannot dedicate, we cannot consecrate, we cannot hallow, this ground. The brave men, living and dead, who struggled here, have consecrated it, far above our poor power to add or detract. The world will little note, nor long remember what we say here, but it can never forget what they did here. It is for us the living, rather, to be dedicated here to the unfinished work which they who fought here have thus far so nobly advanced. It is rather for us to be here dedicated to the great task remaining before us, that from these honored dead we take increased devotion to that cause for which they gave the last full measure of devotion, that we here highly resolve that these dead shall not have*

died in vain, that this nation, under God,
shall have a new birth of freedom, and that
government of the people, by the people, for
the people, shall not perish from the earth.

Abraham Lincoln
November 19, 1863

Just a little more food for thought. Kneeling is an act of submission. We stand to honor our country and those who died for it because our forefathers came from a country that made them bow to the king as if he were God. I believe that we stand and not kneel because the only one we should kneel before in this country is our God. "In your relationships with one another, have the same mindset as Christ Jesus: Who, being in the very nature of God, did not consider equality with God something to be used to his own advantage; rather, he made himself nothing by taking the very nature of a servant, being made in human likeness. And being found in appearance as a man, he humbled himself by becoming obedient to death—even death on a cross! Therefore God exalted him to the highest place and gave him a name that is above every name, that at the name of Jesus every knee should bow, in heaven and on earth and under the earth, and every tongue acknowledge that Jesus Christ is Lord, to the glory of God the Father" (Phil. 2:5–11 NIV). We are now turning an act of submission into an act of rebellion. In reality, these people are saying the government is God with their actions and somehow think it is an act of rebellion. They are very shortsighted and foolish even in their rebellion. But we, as followers of Christ, are not much wiser. Rather than explain, I will type in almost all of Isaiah 58, which describes the church of today better than I could and gives the way to fix it.

"For day after day they seek me out; they seem eager to know my ways, as if they were a nation that does what is right and has not forsaken the commands of its God. They ask me for just decisions and seem eager for God to come near them. 'Why have we fasted,' they say, 'and you have not seen it? Why have we humbled ourselves, and you have not noticed?' Yet on the day of your fasting, you do as you please and exploit all your workers. Your fasting ends in quarrels and strife, and in striking each other with wicked fists. You cannot fast as you do today and expect your voice to be heard on high. Is this the kind of fast I have chosen, only a day for people to humble themselves? Is it only for bowing one's head like a reed and for lying in sackcloth and ashes? Is that what you call a fast, a day acceptable to the Lord? Is not this the kind of fasting I have chosen: to loose the chains of injustice and untie the cords of the yoke, to set the oppressed free and break every yoke? Is it not to share your food with the hungry and to provide the poor wanderer with shelter—when you see the naked, to clothe them, and not turn away from your own flesh and blood? Then your light will break forth like the dawn, and your healing will quickly appear; then your righteousness will go before you, and the glory of the Lord will be your rear guard. Then you will call and the Lord will answer; you will cry for help, and he will say: Here am I. If you do away with the yoke of oppression, with the pointing finger and malicious talk, and if you spend yourselves in behalf of the hungry and satisfy the needs of the oppressed, then your light will rise in the darkness, and your night will become like the noonday. The Lord will guide you always; he will satisfy your needs in a sun-scorched land and will strengthen you frame. You will be like a well watered garden, like a spring whose waters never fail. Your people will rebuild the ancient ruins and will raise up the age old foundations; You will be called Repairers of Broken Walls, Restorers of Streets with Dwellings. 'If you keep your feet from breaking the Sabbath and from doing as you please on my holy day, if you call the Sabbath a delight and the Lord's holy day honorable, and if you honor it by not going your own way and not doing as you please or speaking idle words, then you will find your joy in the Lord, and I will cause you to ride in triumph on the heights of the land and to feast on the inheritance of your father Jacob.' For the mouth of the Lord has spoken" (Isa. 58:2–14 NIV).

People want us to become like them. They want to impose their standards on us and be just as miserable as them. For the most part, we seem to be doing a better job of conforming to the world's standards than conforming to God's standards. I want to find my joy in the Lord. I want to be called the repairer of broken walls, a restorer of streets with dwelling, or maybe even just a man who loved God enough to make a difference in the world around him. I hope you kids will find your joy in the Lord and will be remembered as people who built up the people around them.

Love,
Dad

A Split Personality

When I initially gave you the parables, I gave you fifty-one because that was how old I was. One for every year I was alive. My dad was younger than thirty when his dad died. I was younger than thirty when my parents died, and you were both around thirty years old when I gave you the letters. I guess I wasn't sure how much longer I was going to be around, screwing up your lives. Just kidding. Or not. I wish I had done as good of a job preparing you for life as my parents did for me. Maybe it is God's grace. He is giving me extra time to try to get it right before He takes me home, or maybe He is just testing you. Either way, I'm still here, and so I figured I needed to update the letters, so you have one for each year I have been here. Some of these letters written for each year after fifty-one were things I posted or letters to you that were not included in the first one I gave you. I have now outlived both of my parents by six years, and since I am only fifty-nine, I should have stopped at fifty-nine, but you get a bonus one if I don't make it to sixty. I am concerned for you and my grandchildren growing up in country that has lost its identity and has begun to remind me of the character Gollum, torn apart by the fight between good and evil that was going on inside him as he let the desire for that one thing he wanted so desperately consume him, stealing his true identity.

I believe it is because we don't understand or even know anymore the true definition of grace and repentance. I know this is probably a confusing statement, so hang with me as I explain. I will start with what it is defined as today, and even though they are actually what they mean, I think there is a much deeper aspect of them that we are missing. When we talk of grace, I think the Newsboys said it best on their album *Going Public* in the song "Real Good Thing." The song lyrics say, "When we don't get what we deserve, it's a real good thing" (this is mercy). "When we get what we don't deserve, it's a real good thing" (this is grace). When we talk of repentance, I hear people say it's just rethinking your situation or its remorse. It is all about being sorry for where you are at or what you have done and going a different direction. These definitions are correct, but I believe in the context of our faith, they fall way short and leave us confused and incomplete.

I have heard Christians say, when someone is doing something wrong, "I just offer grace." I believe that there are very few instances where we can offer grace in the context of what grace from God truly is, and furthermore, grace cannot come without repentance. We can forgive people for what they have done to us, we can offer mercy, but we can't offer grace. Let me explain. Christ was asked where His authority came from, and this is the exchange. "Jesus entered the temple courts, and while he was teaching, the chief priests and the elders of the people came to him. 'By what authority are you doing these things?' they asked. 'And who gave you this authority?' Jesus replied, 'I will also ask you one question. If you answer me, I will tell by what authority I am doing these things. John's baptism—where did it come from?

Was it from heaven, or of human origin?' They discussed it among themselves and said, 'If we say from heaven, he will ask "Then why didn't you believe him?" But if we say, of human origin, we are afraid of the people, for they all hold that John was a prophet.' So they answered, 'We don't know.' Then he said, 'Neither will I tell you by what authority I am doing these things'" (Matt. 21:27 NIV). John came preaching repentance, and Christ came full of truth and grace. Luke 3:2–20 talks of John's ministry and says he was "preaching a baptism of repentance," while John 1:1–34 talks of Jesus and says, "Grace and truth came through Jesus Christ."

Jesus knew that if the priests and elders did not believe John's call for repentance, then they would not receive his truth or grace. You have to believe you are wrong before you can receive grace. But just saying you're wrong or that you don't know is not enough either. You can exchange one lie for another and be just as lost as you were before. Grace doesn't work without acknowledging the truth of who God is and what He has done for us through Christ. When you recognize that truth, it has to be an all-in type of an attitude as well. A halfway attitude is an "I believe it could be the truth, but I don't want to put all my eggs in one basket" kind of an attitude. Grace is God giving us citizenship in His kingdom, but you are not a citizen until you choose to be a citizen. I believe the closest we can come to offering grace is when we choose to adopt a child. "According as he hath chosen us in him before the foundation of the world, that we should be holy and without blame before him in love: Having predestinated us unto the adoption of children by Jesus Christ to himself, according to the good pleasure of his will" (Eph. 1:4–5 NIV).

One thing that I have learned over the years about adoption, though, is that you can choose to adopt a child but that child must choose you to be their parents and submit to them as their parents, or the adoption is never complete. I believe God has chosen all of us, but only the ones who are willing to choose Him and submit to His authority in their lives become true heirs and children of God. "Those who live according to the flesh have their minds set on what the flesh desires; but the those who live in accordance with the Spirit have their minds set on what the Spirit desires. The mind governed by the flesh is hostile to God; it does not submit to Gods law, nor can it do so. Those who are in the realm of the flesh cannot please God. You, however, are not in the realm of the flesh but are in the realm of the Spirit, if indeed the Spirit of God lives in you. And if anyone does not have the Spirit of Christ, they do not belong to Christ. But if Christ is in you, then even though your body is subject to death because of sin, the Spirit gives life because of righteousness. And if the Spirit of him who raised Jesus from the dead is living in you, he who raised Christ from the dead will also give life to your mortal bodies because of his Spirit who lives in you. Therefore, brothers and sisters, we have an obligation— but it is not to the flesh, to live according to it. For if you live according to the flesh, you will die; but if by the Spirit you put to death the misdeeds of the body, you will live. For those who are led by the Spirit of God are the children of God. The Spirit you received does not make you slaves, so that you live in fear again; rather, the Spirit you received brought about your adoption to sonship. And by him we cry, 'Abba, Father.' The Spirit himself testifies with our spirit that we are God's children. Now if we are children, then we are heirs—heirs of God and co-heirs with Christ, if indeed we share in his sufferings in that we may also share in his glory" (Rom. 8:5–17 NIV). Christ himself said in Matthew 6:24, "No one can serve two masters. Either you will hate the one and love the other, or you will be devoted to the one and despise the other. You cannot serve both God and money" (NIV). No one can have two sets of parents that we pledge our allegiance to. We have to choose whether we submit to God as our father or the world and Satan as our father. Satan and this world are our birth father, for we are born in sin. God, through Christ, has offered us adoption papers, but the only way the adoption is complete is when we reject our birth father and cling to our adoptive father.

Christians today try to hang on to God and the world, and it tears them apart; they wind up with a Gollum kind of life that only brings destruction. One time a while back, this was made real to me when your mom and I were going to one of her coworkers' son's wedding, and we picked up another one of her coworkers on the way. Your mom had told me that she had been adopted and that her adoptive parents had recently died. As we were all chatting on the way to the wedding, she mentioned that she had found and met her birth mother and that she was amazed at how similar they were. I asked if she called her birth mother Mom, to which she responded very quickly, "No, she's not my mom. My mom and dad are dead." I then asked if she knew where her birth father was, and she said yes. I asked if she ever wanted to meet him, to which she responded no. "We would have been a family if he had wanted us." That conversation has stuck with me for a long time. This woman was all in for her adoptive parents. They were her heritage, and she was theirs. They were the ones she was determined to emulate.

I have started to notice that divorce is doing the same Gollum thing to our children in this country. Children don't know who to pledge their allegiance to. Their devotion is being torn apart because they are having to choose and don't want to. I am not saying that you cannot love more than one set of parents, but you can only pledge yourself to one life-style or master that guides you through life, and generally, a child learns about life and how to effectively navigate it from his parents. I also think that is why adoptive children who dwell on the belief "They are not my real parents" never get a real sense of belonging even if they find and connect with their birth parents. This is because they are just taking the security and what they like about the adoptive parents with the attitude of "I need something that you can provide, so I'll take it until I can find my real parents and become like them." They begin to despise the very ones who are offering the closest thing to God's grace that we can offer to others. They also wind up with that Gollum type of split personality, or should I say a split allegiance, that leaves them consumed with themselves and torn apart. I believe this is because they don't realize grace and adoption are not about replacing what you already have; it is about providing what you need and the sense of belonging you don't have or deserve. We cannot serve two masters, so we have to choose. Choose between what we already have and what we truly need.

To choose, you must repent of what is wrong or the lies you serve in your life and pledge your allegiance to the truth and the author of truth. Being sorry you got caught or regretting your actions is not enough. Moving in another direction is not enough. Judas is a good example of this. Judas was chosen by Christ to be His follower, and I don't know what his thought process was when he betrayed Christ, but in Matthew it says what his response was after the fact. "When Judas, who had betrayed him, saw that Jesus was condemned, he was seized with remorse and returned the thirty pieces of silver to the chief priests and the elders. 'I have sinned,' he said, 'for I have betrayed innocent blood.' 'What is that to us?' they replied. 'That's your responsibility.' So Judas threw the money into the temple and left. Then he went away and hanged himself" (Matt. 27:3–5 NIV). Judas died as lost as the chief priest and elders even though he was sorry and they were not. What is the difference between Judas and the thief on the cross in Luke 22:39–43? "One of the criminals who hung there hurled insults at him: 'Aren't you the Messiah? Save yourself and us!' But the other criminal rebuked him. 'Don't you fear God,' he said, 'since you are under the same sentence? We are punished justly, for we are getting what our deeds deserve. But this man has done nothing wrong.' Then he said, 'Jesus, remember me when you come into your kingdom.' Jesus answered him, 'Truly I tell you, today you will be with me in paradise'" (NIV). The one who went to heaven redeemed was just as guilty as Judas, but he actually recognized the truth of who Christ was and how much he needed Him.

Many of the people who claim to be Christians are more like the other criminal who had the attitude of "If you are who you say you are, then get me out of my mess." They pray the prayer, but it is nothing more than fire insurance just in case, but they plan on living their life for something else besides Him. I think this mindset has taken over our country as well. Nobody requires that you pledge your allegiance to this country anymore. We say it, but most don't mean it. The thing with God is, He knows our hearts and if we are truly pledging our allegiance to Him. We cannot tell who is a true citizen and who is lying. All we can go by is their fruits.

A young woman joined ISIS, helping those who oppose the USA and their ideals, and then when things got bad, she wanted to come back and claim her citizenship. She pledged her allegiance to something that hates America, and now she claims she's a citizen. She made her choice, and we can forgive her for it, but I don't believe you can ever let her back in the country, because she made her choice. I believe she is like those who Christ spoke of in Matthew 7:21–23. "Not everyone who says to me, 'Lord, Lord,' will enter the kingdom of heaven, but only the one who does the will of my Father who is in heaven. Many will say to me on that day, 'Lord, Lord, did we not prophesy in your name and in your name drive out demons and in your name perform many miracles?' Then I will tell them plainly, 'I never knew you. Away from me, you evildoers!'" (NIV). As a country, we are not able to know the heart of a person, so we have to go by the outward manifestation of their actions. We have politicians who advocate things contrary to the Constitution in one area and then want to leave out the things they don't like. We have a Muslim who fled her country because of the oppression of those in her religion, is elected and experiencing freedom she would have never received in those countries, granted to her in a country founded on the liberty and freedom found in Christ Jesus, and at the same time extols the virtues of oppressive Muslim regimes. She supports those who directly want to work against the nation that has given her these freedoms. But we have others who vote to let people who are in our country illegally participate in our election without being a citizen and want to allow anyone into our country without going through proper channels.

They also claim it is unchristian to try to stop them. This is false. Christ pointed out what our borders should look like in John 10:1–15. "'Very truly I tell you Pharisees, anyone who does not enter the sheep pen by the gate, but climbs in by some other way, is a thief and a robber. The one who enters by the gate is the shepherd of the sheep. The gate-keeper opens the gate for him, and the sheep listen to his voice. He calls his own sheep by name and leads them out. When he has brought out all of his own, he goes on ahead of them, and his sheep follow him because they know his voice. But they will never follow a stranger; in fact, they will run away from him because they do not recognize a stranger's voice.' Jesus used this figure of speech, but the Pharisees did not understand what he was telling them. Therefore Jesus said again, 'Very truly I tell you, I am the gate for the sheep. All who have come before me are thieves and robbers, but the sheep have not listened to them. I am the gate; whoever enters through me will be saved. They will come in and go out, and find pasture. The thief comes only to steal and kill and destroy; I have come that they may have life, and have it to the full. I am the good shepherd. The good shepherd lays down his life for the sheep. The hired hand is not the shepherd and does not own the sheep. So when he sees the wolf coming, he abandons the sheep and runs away. Then the wolf attacks the flock and scatters it. The man runs away because he is a hired hand and cares nothing for the sheep. I am the good shepherd; I know my sheep and my sheep know me—just as the Father knows me and I know the Father— and I lay down my life for the sheep'" (NIV). We have a lot of politicians who don't care about this country or defending the Constitution and are more than happy to let people climb over the fence and harm the citizens of this great country. They are hired hands who only care about power and getting paid. They are also helping to create the Gollum effect in our country.

We have people all over this country who want the freedoms granted them by the Constitution that was based on the liberties our forefathers found in their faith in Christ. The only problem is, we no longer pledge allegiance to those values and this country. We embrace values contrary to those values and wonder why we are being torn apart as a nation and a people. We have a split personality as a nation; we want both God's grace and liberty without repentance and leaving what the world has to offer. We are in a Gollum state in America, chasing after a golden ring that only has the power to destroy and enslave us, yet we want the freedom and liberty that only can come by pledging allegiance to God and country. Kids, we can only have one master and remain whole. Our country cannot stand if we, the people, have not pledged our allegiance to this country and if we don't vote people into office that have pledged their allegiance to it as well. This is the Pledge of Allegiance: "I pledge allegiance to the flag of the United States of America and to the Republic for which it stands, one nation under God, indivisible, with liberty and justice for all." We cannot have a split personality as a nation, and we dare not have a split personality when it comes to our faith. I pray that God will reveal His truth to you and that you will cling to it, rejecting the lies of the world. Pledge your allegiance to the Father of truth and life. He is the only good Father.

Love,
Dad

Conclusion

I hope you have enjoyed these letters and, more importantly, they gave you something that you can use to make your life a little better. At the very least, I hope they gave you some food for thought. It is ultimately my hope that this inspires you and others to begin writing down the things you have learned, whether you have children or not. If I can do it, anyone can. A friend of mine read the letters and determined to write one a day. That is way too ambitious for me. I am still just leaving one a year. My point is, whether it is one a day, one a week, one a month, or one a year, leave what you have learned. It doesn't matter where or who you are, whether you're a banker or in prison; share the knowledge and wisdom you have gained. Write it down for those who follow us, and maybe we can change the world, our country, our communities, and our family's future. We can only return to the greatness of the past when we begin to value the wisdom of the past and use it to create a future that values all that we have learned in our past and expands on it. We can never go further than those in our past until we build on what they have already learned to be true. So share what you have learned.

Now, you may say I am not a writer and I have no clue how to write things down. I remember a time when a man was talking to my dad and he said he didn't know how to pray. My dad just told him, since he was talking to him, he was able to pray, because praying is just talking to God, and if he could talk to him, he could talk to God. If you have thoughts and ideas, you can write, and if you can't write, then record your thoughts. I once went to a worship conference at a church, and one of the classes was on writing songs. The instructor said that a lot of good worship songs came to people when they began writing down their prayers and then reading them later. I also had heard that others journaled and that the thoughts that they wrote down many times led to songs. So I decided to try it. All I can say is, they must have been much more spiritual than I, because when I read back a week of my prayers, all I saw was "I need." It felt like I was watching the movie *What About Bob*, in the scene where Bob (Bill Murray) finds Dr. Marvin and he starts begging. This is a rough paraphrase: "I'm not a slacker, I'm doing the work, I'm stepping, give me, give me, I need, I need." I never got a song out of writing down my prayers, but it did make me aware of some tendencies and caused me to change the way I pray. My point is, write down what you want to share with others, then go back a week or two later and read it to see if it says what you wanted to say. God will open your heart and mind to be able to say what needs to be said and passed on. Of that I have no doubt. It is what He has called us all to do. Share what He has done for you. No one can refute what God has done for you and in your life.